k

ONTOLOGICAL CATEGORIES

Ontological Categories

Their Nature and Significance

JAN WESTERHOFF

CLARENDON PRESS · OXFORD

OXFORD
UNIVERSITY PRESS

Great Clarendon Street, Oxford OX2 6DP

Oxford University Press is a department of the University of Oxford.
It furthers the University's objective of excellence in research, scholarship,
and education by publishing worldwide in

Oxford New York

Auckland Cape Town Dar es Salaam Hong Kong Karachi
Kuala Lumpur Madrid Melbourne Mexico City Nairobi
New Delhi Shanghai Taipei Toronto

With offices in

Argentina Austria Brazil Chile Czech Republic France Greece
Guatemala Hungary Italy Japan Poland Portugal Singapore
South Korea Switzerland Thailand Turkey Ukraine Vietnam

Oxford is a registered trade mark of Oxford University Press
in the UK and in certain other countries

Published in the United States
by Oxford University Press Inc., New York

© Jan Westerhoff, 2005

British Library Cataloguing in Publication Data

Westerhoff, Jan.
Ontological categories : their nature and significance / Jan Westerhoff.
p. cm.
Includes bibliographical references.
1. Ontology. 2. Categories (Philosophy) I. Title.
BD311 W47 2005   111–dc22   2005019955

Library of Congress Cataloging in Publication Data

Data available

Typeset by SPI Publishers Services, Pondicherry, India
Printed in Great Britain
on acid-free paper by
Biddles Ltd., King's Lynn, Norfolk

ISBN 0–19–928504–7   978–0–19–928504–4

1 3 5 7 9 10 8 6 4 2

Parentibus optimis

Acknowledgements

Many people helped me to write this book. I am particularly indebted to my parents, Herbert and Annette Westerhoff, without whose constant intellectual, practical, financial, and emotional support it would not have been written. I would also like to thank my grandmother Paula Buschkötter for her continuous help during the past seven years.

Michael Potter read innumerable versions of this book with indefatigable patience and meticulous care, supplied me with many new ideas and helped to eliminate a variety of errors, pertaining both to punctuation and philosophy. Others who have read all or part of the manuscript, often more than once and were most generous with their time, suggestions, and criticism include: Arif Ahmed, Nicholas Denyer, Jörg Fischer, Georg von Hippel, Arnold Koslow, Jonathan Lowe, Hugh Mellor, and Peter Simons. Tim Stadelmann and Margrit Edwards kindly supplied computational and administrative help.

I also have to thank the audiences at Cambridge, Cologne, Vienna, the MIT, Harvard, Dresden, York, Helsinki, Berlin, Lund, Leeds, Bonn, Belfast, and Istanbul for various comments on earlier versions of the material, as well as Trinity College, Cambridge and the *Studienstiftung des deutschen Volkes* for their generous financial support.

I am obliged to Oxford University Press and Springer Publications for allowing me to use material which has appeared in *Erkenntnis* and the *Australasian Journal of Philosophy*.

The referees for Oxford University Press provided detailed comments and criticisms of various parts of the manuscript. I am indebted to them for their suggestions which made the following pages much less unclear than they would otherwise have been.

J. C. W.

Summary Contents

Detailed Contents

Introduction

This book is an investigation of the notion of an ontological category. 'Ontological category' is a technical concept present in philosophical discussion at least since the time of Aristotle. Nevertheless, antiquity does not necessarily entail theoretical interest. Why should we want to analyse a piece of philosophical jargon like 'ontological category'? Categorizing is a fundamental human activity. Indeed,

there is nothing more basic than categorization to our thought, perception, action, and speech. Every time we see something as *kind* of thing, for example, a tree, we are categorizing. Whenever we reason about *kinds* of things—chairs, nations, illnesses, emotions, any kind of thing at all—we employ categories. [. . .] An understanding of how we categorize is central to any understanding of how we think and how we function, and therefore central to an understanding of what makes us human.[1]

The development of cognitive science during the last decades has led to a renewed interest in categorizations and seen the construction of new theoretical frameworks for explaining categorization.[2] The concept of an ontological category is philosophy's unique contribution to the study of categorizing. Not all categories human beings come up with are ontological categories. Only very general and fundamental categories are accorded this title. These categories are assumed to be of central importance in metaphysics, since they represent a fundamental inventory of the world, a list of the most basic kinds of things, a veritable alphabet of being. Even a cursory acquaintance with philosophical questions makes it evident that the answers to many depend on a clear account of ontological categories.

First of all there is the question whether some particular entity belongs to this or that ontological category, for example when we ask whether

---

[1] Lakoff (1987: 5–6).

[2] Rosch's prototype theory (1981) is particularly noteworthy in this respect. For a good summary of various other approaches see Lakoff (1987: 13–57).

causes are facts or events, or whether properties are sets or mereological sums. To understand what it means to decide such questions we need to know quite a bit about ontological categories. For example we will want to know when two ontological categories are identical, how ontological categories differ from other categories, whether a thing can belong to two categories at once, or whether belonging to some ontological category is an essential property of a thing, or rather a convenient classificatory decision on our part.

Secondly, ontologists often talk about reducing one ontological category to another (such as reducing numbers to sets, or physical objects to bundles of tropes). What is meant by this again heavily depends on what exactly ontological categories are. Is giving a coextensional class sufficient for such a reduction, or do we need something more? Is reduction essentially asymmetric, or is it possible that category A is reducible to B and B is also reducible to A? Is ontological reduction just a theoretical simplification, or is it somehow grounded in the nature of things?

Finally it is clear that ontological categories constitute a recipe for slicing up the world in a very fundamental way. Does this imply that there is at most one 'right' way of doing this, or are we invariably faced with a multiplicity of different, perhaps incommensurable, systems of ontological categories, with different conceptual schemes between which translation is not possible? Is it possible to give some procedure for picking out the 'best' of these various systems? Is there some set of constraints one could expect any sensible system of ontological categories to obey?

All of these are central philosophical questions the answers to which depend crucially on the account of ontological categories we give. Yet we find that in the philosophical debates of the recent past questions about the nature of these categories are hardly ever formulated, let alone answered.

The aim of this book is to give a precise account of ontological categories which provides a solid basis for addressing these questions. My investigation has two main conclusions. The first is that it is possible to give a coherent account of ontological categories which incorporates many of the features philosophers have traditionally ascribed to them: that they are the most general kinds of things, that they are organized in a non-overlapping hierarchy, and that certain categories are too special to be ontological categories. The second conclusion is that the conception of ontological category which emerges from this specification cannot justify the fundamental status it is usually assumed to have.

The importance of ontological categories in metaphysics and in philosophy more generally is usually argued for by claiming that they constitute a unique set of the most fundamental kinds of things under which everything can be subsumed, and that they provide us with a characterization of objects based on their necessary features: while objects can change the *ordinary* categories they belong to (what is a seed now might be a tree in ten years, time) their membership in *ontological* categories marks one of their necessary features (no matter what happens to the seed, it will always remain a concrete individual object).

Both these claims, the absolutism of a unique system of ontological categories and the essentialist view of membership in ontological categories as necessary features are denied in the present account. I argue that when constructing a precise conception of ontological categories which incorporates the core features usually ascribed to them these two claims simply do not follow. It is therefore important to reassess the importance we accord to the construction of systems of ontological categories in metaphysics, and in philosophy more generally. I will argue that they are important tools for systematizing very fundamental features of the world, but that they do not carry any special philosophical weight. As will become clearer in the course of this discussion I regard the theoretical status of ontological categories as similar to that of axioms of formalized theories. Though the notion of an axiom is theoretically important, we do not attach any special epistemological significance to them as 'self-evident truths' any more. In the same way we should give up the idea that ontological categories, the axioms of things, have the philosophical significance usually ascribed to them.

Our inquiry can be divided into three main sections. The first, consisting of chapters I and II, is mainly *critical*: it looks at various ways of defining the notion of an ontological category and discusses their various defects. The second section, consisting of chapters III and IV, is *constructive*: it contains my own account of what an ontological category is and tries to show how this account escapes the problems encountered by the previous attempts at defining them. The final section (chapters V and VI) discusses the *implications* of this new account of ontological categories for different categorial distinctions and examines its place in a wider philosophical context.

Let us now survey the argument set out in the following six chapters in greater detail. As explained above, the main aim of our inquiry is to give a satisfactory account of the notion of an ontological category. It is therefore necessary first to get a clear idea of what it is we are going to define here. In § 1 we look at different examples of systems of ontological categories from the history of ontology, beginning with Aristotle and ending with a recent system employed in Artificial Intelligence. The following § 2 then isolates different common features, both regarding the *content* of the systems, i.e. the categories they employ, as well as regarding their *structure*, the way in which these categories are organized. These common features will serve as a yardstick for measuring the adequacy of different proposed definitions of ontological categories we are going to discuss in the following pages.

Chapter II examines different definitions of ontological categories which have been proposed. Two positions, one declaring the problem to be inherently unsolvable (§ 3) and one taking recourse to lists of categories (§ 4) can be dismissed relatively quickly. The more successful approaches are grouped into three main kinds, relative to the intuitions about ontological categories they exploit. The first intuition is that ontological categories are *more general* than other categories (§§ 6–13), the second that objects belonging to the same ontological category can be *intersubstituted* in certain contexts (§§ 14–24), and the third finally that objects of the same category have the same *identity criteria* (§§ 25–7).

We discuss four major accounts based on the notion of generality. The first, due to Bryan Norton, tries to identify ontological categories with maximal elements in an ordering of categories by generality (§§ 6–8). The second, which forms part of Jerrold Katz's general semantic theory, identifies them with special, 'redundant' semantic markers (§§ 9–12). A third, closely related one, links the notion of an ontological category to that of an 'essentially arising question' (§ 12). All three are vexed by a common problem, called the *cut-off point* problem. They manage to identify ontological categories as categories sufficiently high up in a particular ordering, but cannot tell a story about how far down we are allowed to go before the categories become too special to qualify as ontological categories. The final account based on generality, due to Joshua Hoffman and Gary Rosenkrantz (§ 13), manages to address that problem but unfortunately fails in a number of other respects.

The concept of intersubstitutability seems to be more promising in delivering a satisfactory definition of ontological category. We must note, however, that there are two distinct notions of intersubstitutability in place, intersubstitutability preserving *grammaticality* and intersubstitutability preserving *meaningfulness*. In order to get a clear conception of how these differ we first look at the way intersubstitutability criteria are employed in current grammatical theory for sorting expressions into different grammatical types and also discuss their place in Husserl's theory of categories (§§ 15–17). We then turn to the most prominent version of applying the notion of substitution in ontology, namely that of using intersubstitutability preserving meaningfulness to define ontological categories. As a philosophical account this has most notably been defended by Gilbert Ryle and has later been developed in a much more detailed fashion by Fred Sommers by introducing a primitive 'predication' operator for indicating that the combination of two predicates is not nonsensical (§ 19). Unfortunately both versions suffer from what might be called the problem of *too specific categories* (§ 20). They identify categories which are clearly too special to serve as ontological categories (such as 'building' or 'furniture'). The Ryle–Sommers account therefore seems to be able to pick out some sort of categories, but this set will at best contain the set of ontological categories as a proper subset.

One of the most interesting attempts at getting around this problem is based on Carnap's work on categories and employs the idea that there are 'universal predicates' applicable only to objects in a given category. This will indeed allow us to filter out the unwanted and too specific categories generated by the Ryle–Sommers account (§ 21). Unfortunately it then implies that in the system of ontological categories generated no two categories can contain one another (§§ 22–3). But the existence of such a containment structure on systems of ontological categories seems to be implied by the examples we discussed in chapter I. The Carnapian account therefore imposes structural demands on potential systems of ontological categories that are too heavy for it to be satisfactory. We then argue that although Carnap's constraint is too restrictive there is another, more convincing one called *Sommers' law*, which demands that ontological categories cannot overlap (§ 24). As opposed to Carnap's, this constraint is in harmony with the examples of systems of ontological categories discussed and might also possess some psychological plausibility.

The final family of proposed definitions we look at is based on the idea that objects belonging to the same category have the same criteria of identity. This view was first explicitly endorsed by Gottlob Frege in the *Grundlagen* and was later systematized by Michael Dummett (§ 25).

Dummett employs a set of sortal identity relations obeying certain conditions which can then be used to define the required categories. While this provides us with a very elegant way of tackling the problem it has the unwanted consequence that objects in the resulting categories cannot share properties. This is closely related to the difficulty Carnap's account faces and is moreover rather unintuitive: we sort objects into different ontological categories because there are *particular* important qualities on which they differ, not because they differ regarding *all* qualities.

After these initial critical arguments in chapters I and II the following two constructive chapters attempt to construct a positive account of ontological categories which escapes the problems encountered by other proposed definitions. As we have seen above, such a successful account should have a way of dealing with the cut-off point problem and the problem of too specific categories, it should not imply that systems of ontological categories are exclusive, and it should obey Sommers' law.

Chapter III prepares the ground for such a account. It focuses on the notion of a state of affairs as a fundamental primitive which will serve as a basis for the following discussion of ontological categories. §§ 28–9 argue for the centrality of states of affairs both from an epistemological and a semantic perspective. States of affairs constitute our first point of cognitive contact with the world and also play an important rôle in semantical theories. They therefore constitute a suitable starting-point for philosophical investigations.

In the second part of this chapter §§ 30–5 examine the relationship between states of affairs and their constituents. It becomes evident that my arguments for the centrality of states of affairs entail that states of affairs should be conceived of as prior to their constituents at least in the order of cognition. We get to know a state of affairs as a whole first and only afterwards analyse it into the different items it is made up of. This priority of states of affairs has important implications for the account of ontological categories I develop. Most importantly, I am *not* going to assume from the beginning that states of affairs can be analysed in the familiar way into individuals, properties, and relations, as is usually done.

Chapter IV contains the details of my account of ontological categories. It relies on two basic notions, that of a form-set and that of a base-set (§§ 36–42). The fundamental idea is that form-sets are sets of constituents of states of affairs which have the same form: they are intersubstitutable in states of affairs. Base-sets, on the other hand, are a particular kind of form-set, namely those form-sets which can be used to construct other form-sets. I identify ontological categories with base-sets. The idea is thus that collections of form-sets usually contain some redundancy, some sets which, were they deleted, could immediately be reinstated by constructing them from other form-sets. Only those form-sets which are employed in such a construction constitute the actual core of the collection of form-sets.

The discussion of form-sets (§§ 43–8) introduces a basic mereological concept applicable to states of affairs: that of two states of affairs sharing a constituent. This allows us to adapt Carnap's method of quasi-analysis to accomplish the division of states of affairs into their constituents, based on a primitive similarity-relation between states of affairs. It is thus possible to have sets of states of affairs going proxy for their constituents, which can then in turn be sorted into different form-sets and ordered in a hierarchical manner.

The core of my account of ontological categories lies in the distinction between form-sets and base-sets (§§ 49–55). Base-sets are those form-sets we use to construct other form-sets, in the same way in which axioms are those sentences of a theory we use to derive other sentences. The main emphasis of this section lies on giving a clear conception of what it means to 'construct' one set of form-sets from another one. In particular I need to give some account of when something is an adequate construct of something else. The notion of extensional identity does not provide us with a good criterion. I argue that adequacy depends on the construct's sharing its essential properties with the object it is supposed to replace (§§ 51–2). This part also considers two important relativistic implications of our notion of base-sets. The first is that there is not necessarily one unique right answer to the question what the ontological categories (i.e. the base-sets) relative to some set of states of affairs are, but that there can be several equally adequate sets of onto-logical categories. This is called *local relativism* (§ 50). The second is that no category is *essentially* an ontological category. Whether it is or not depends crucially on what *other* kinds of things are around. This is called *global relativism* (§ 54). It therefore becomes clear that our the-ory in terms of base-sets forces us to adopt a relativist, rather than an absolutist view of ontological categories (§ 55).

I conclude this chapter by summing up how our account solves the problems faced by the other definitions proposed so far (§§ 56–8). The distinction between form-sets and base-sets solves the cut-off point problem and the problem of too specific categories (§ 56). The existence of a containment-hierarchy on the set of form-sets is shown to explain the tree structure of systems of ontological categories (§ 57). A final section (§ 59) examines the modularity of the account of ontological categories given. I describe how it could be used outside the framework of a theory of states of affairs in which it is presented here. It is not tied to the notion of a state of affairs and is compatible with a variety of different metaphysical frameworks.

The following chapter V focuses on a particularly important set of philosophical implications of our account of ontological categories. This account is fundamentally *structuralist*: it tries to get at information about the different constituents of states of affairs not by any direct information about them but by considering specific *relations* between them, that is in particular information about which of them can go together to form states of affairs. It is now interesting to note that a certain distinction between constituents of states of affairs which we would normally regard as clearly structural (namely that between individuals and properties of different orders and adicities) cannot in fact be structural at all, given that they cannot be distinguished by the above structuralist account of ontological categories. Chapter V will be concerned with showing why this is so and what wider philosophical implications it has.

Information about which objects can go together with which other objects in states of affairs will be considered as our ontological data. A division of these objects into different types according to that information will constitute a typing, and thus a theoretical systematization of the ontological data (§§ 60–1). We then show how such typings can be represented by graphs, and how we can transform such graphs in ways which result in graphs which are still in accordance with the data, but which change the way in which the objects are assigned to different types (§§ 62–70). We prove a *flexibility result* which basically says that for each object we can put this object into any type we want and still get out an adequate typing (§ 64). This implies in particular that we cannot distinguish in a purely structural way between individuals and properties.

The reader may remember that Frege's distinction between saturated and unsaturated entities was supposed to do just this. We devote several sections to describing how he set out to do this and why it did not work (§§ 71–6). As was realized *inter alia* by Ramsey, Frege had to deviate from the complex principle at a crucial point in order to distinguish individuals and properties. Such a deviation, however, is not acceptable if we want to give a purely structural distinction between individuals and properties.

We continue our discussion by asking whether perhaps the combinatorial information about which objects can go together with which others in states of affairs is not the only *structural* information we can bring to bear on the problem of distinguishing individuals and properties. Perhaps it is possible to distinguish the two once we take *logical* relations into account as well.

We consider an account which argues that individuals and properties should be distinguished by the fact that the logics quantifying over them have different metatheoretical properties (§ 78). However, this difference is only due to the fact that we construct individuals and properties in different ways at the level of semantics. The metatheoretical properties are thus only a *result* of a distinction already drawn elsewhere, rather than an *indicator* of such a distinction. To stress this point I show how we can formulate a system of logic which has the same expressive power as classical first order predicate calculus, but which does not distinguish between individuals and properties at the semantic level (§§ 79–80). The chapter concludes by giving an overview of the distinctions which can be drawn on the basis of a purely structural account of ontological categories (§ 83). Many of these are quite unlike the traditional ontological distinctions, while some traditional distinctions (such as that between individuals and properties of different adicities and orders) cannot be made without further non-structural assumptions.

The final chapter VI consists of three parts. It begins by giving a survey of the main assumptions underlying the account of ontological categories presented (§§ 84–5). The second section (§§ 86–9) is devoted to a discussion of the philosophical consequences of our account.

The three main conclusions we describe are a *relativistic conception* of ontological categories which considers them to be not primarily categories of being but categories of systematization (§ 86), a *holistic* and anti-essentialist view of them, which entails that it is not an intrinsic feature of an object to belong to a particular category (§ 87), and a conception of the distinction between individuals and properties which denies them the status of a fundamental ontological distinction (§ 88). These three entail that the status of ontological categories within the philosophical discussion has to be reassessed: they cannot fulfil the important rôle which is usually ascribed to them (§ 89).

The last section (§§ 90–95) contains a number of comparisons of my account with philosophical projects which might be considered as closely related. Amongst other topics I consider the study of structuralist logic, the theory of tropes, and situation semantics. The first is a very general logical theory which provides the best attempt up to now to escape the syntax-dependence of most standard logical theories and constitutes the natural account of logic to complement our conception of ontology (§ 91). Trope theory, as a theory of 'particularized properties' has been prominent in the metaphysical discussion of the recent past. One variety, which considers so-called propositional tropes, has especially close connections with my account of states of affairs (§ 94). Situation semantics finally is a semantical theory developed as an alternative to traditional model theory in the 1980s for which the primitive notion of a 'situation' is similarly important as the notion of a state of affairs is for our account of ontology (§ 95).

Our quest for a workable definition of ontological categories will thus lead us on a philosophical Grand Tour across many parts of the discipline, touching on several of its borders with other fields of learning as we go along. We shall address questions from philosophy of language and the theory of meaning, consider problems of generality and dependence, and think about sortals and essential properties, about ontological reduction, the theory of quantification, saturated and unsaturated concepts, about structuralism, relativism, the distinction between individuals and properties, analysis and quasi-analysis. On the way we shall address concerns arising in linguistics and the theory of grammar, in type theory, problems of categorization, of semantics, as well as issues from second order logic and structuralist logic. This multitude of aspects demonstrates the central place of ontology within philosophy as a whole. Many central philosophical questions hinge on it and our general ontological outlook will influence the very shape of our large-scale philosophical theory. Within ontology, the problem of the nature of ontological categories is particularly fascinating. Few attempts have been made at giving a clear account of it, and the resulting vague and imprecise conception has been ascribed a philosophical importance which is not justified. Ontological categories cannot occupy the central philosophical place usually ascribed to them; their significance has therefore to be reassessed. The present inquiry constitutes a first attempt at doing so.

I

Sample cases: systems of ontological categories

§1 Some examples

Ontology does not deal with what there is. This would make ontology some kind of science of everything, which it manifestly is not. Ontology deals with certain kinds of things, namely the *most fundamental* kinds of things there are. It inquires which objects belong to which of these kinds (also called *ontological categories*). It also studies how these categories are related to one another: whether they contain or exclude one another, whether some of them can be reduced to others and so forth.

Every ontological theory will incorporate a system of ontological categories at its core. The history of ontology provides us with numerous examples of such systems. In this section we sketch a few of these, mainly to give the reader an intuitive and approximate understanding of what ontological categories are, but also to set out some data which can serve as the basis of the metaontological discussion of the following chapters.

We begin with the most venerable and famous system of ontological categories, due to Aristotle (Figure I.1). This scheme, which is presented in the *Categories*, is not the only one to be found in Aristotle's works—there are others with four, five, six, or eight members—but the first three categories (substance, quantity, and quality) constitute the 'hard core' of all of them.[1] Nevertheless, the list of ten categories proved to be the most influential during the later history of ontology and of philosophy in general. The Aristotelian categories as depicted in Figure I.1 are not hierarchically related by inclusion. They do not contain one another, nor is there one 'supercategory' which contains them all.[2] Nevertheless

---

[1] Smith (1995: 57).   [2] Smith (1995: 56).

Substance	Quantity	Quality	Relation	Place
Time	Being-in-a-position	Having	Doing	Being affected

Fig. I.1 ARISTOTLE

this does not mean that they cannot be hierarchically ordered.[3] One such ordering could be phrased in terms of *dependence*. Aristotle argues that other categories depend on the category of substance. It cannot be the case that something is green (has a quality) without there being something which is the bearer of that quality, i.e. some substance being green. Substances are existentially prior to qualities which are in turn prior to relations, since relations depend on qualities. Aristotle sometimes spells out this chain of dependence in terms of epistemological priority. Knowing *what* something is ('a cat') tells you more about it than knowing a quality ('it is brown') which again tells you more about it than knowing a relation in which it stands to other objects ('it is owned by me').[4]

An example of a system of categories which exhibits its hierarchical structure more explicitly is given in Figure I.2. This diagram is described by Roderick Chisholm on the first page of his *A Realist Theory of Categories*.[5] We note that there is one 'supercategory' ('Entia') which contains all other categories. The whole system has the form of a tree in which all nodes (with one exception) have two branches, if they have any branches at all. There is some overlap with ARISTOTLE—'substance', 'attributes' (roughly corresponding to qualities)—but there are also new categories CHISHOLM introduces, as well as others which he leaves out.

A similar, though rather more baroque system can be found in the works of Jonathan Lowe (Figure I.3). This scheme was first presented in Lowe (1997: 35) and has also reappeared in his (2001: 181). Lowe explicitly considers the system to be incomplete, 'allowing room for

[3] For examples of such orderings which introduce further categories (*accident, inherence* etc.) picked more or less at random from two 19th-century textbooks see Clarke (1889: 189) and Stöckl (1892: II: V: §24).

[4] It should be noted that different very general varieties of substance, such as primary and secondary substance (which are not mentioned as separate categories by Aristotle in the *Categories*), *are* supposed to be ordered by inclusion.

[5] Chisholm (1996: 3).

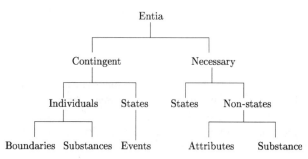

Fig. I.2 CHISHOLM

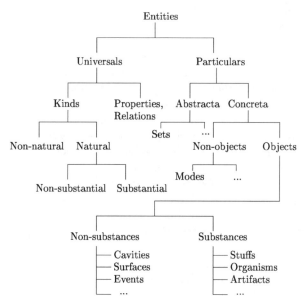

Fig. I.3 LOWE

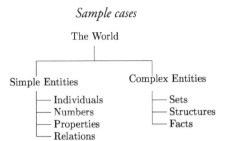

Fig. I.4 GROSSMANN

expansion at various points',[6] and also believes that the particular hierarchical structure exemplified by the system is more or less conventional.

> What the highest division of this category [of entities] should be is a matter of some dispute, however, as is the question whether a categorial scheme should permit a certain amount of cross-classification (my own view being that this is inevitable). [. . .] It is very probable that this choice [of the highest division of the category of entities] is not at all that important, rather as one can have different axiom-sets for the same logical system or system of geometry.[7]

A similarly flexible view about the relation between the ontological categories is held by Reinhardt Grossmann. He gives several patterns of arrangements of categories; the one given in Figure I.4 may serve as a representative example.[8]

Although he assumes that there is a fixed number of ontological categories,[9] their hierarchical arrangement is settled by pragmatic considerations; it 'depends on what distinction one wishes to emphasize'.[10] Nor does Grossmann seem to demand that such an arrangement be complete. He gives several examples of hierarchical arrangements of ontological categories which, like the one above, do not contain all the ontological categories his theory employs.

A system of categories which plays a major rôle in Joshua Hoffman's and Gary Rosenkrantz's account of substance is shown in Figure I.5. This system, which shows a considerable overlap with the two preceding ones, made its first appearance in Rosenkrantz and Hoffman (1991:

---

[6] Lowe (2001: 180).

[7] Lowe (2001: 180).

[8] Grossmann (1992: 87).

[9] Namely individuals, properties, relations, structures, sets, quantifiers, and facts (1992: 46).

[10] Grossmann (1992: 86).

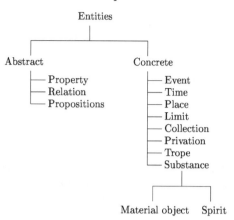

Fig. I.5 HOFFMAN/ROSENKRANTZ

839) and can be encountered again in Hoffman and Rosenkrantz (1994: 18) as well as in (1997: 48). It is introduced as part of an argument for the special rôle of substance among the ontological categories, as well as to provide a basis for an explication of the notion of an ontological category itself.[11]

The ontology discussed by Erwin Tegtmeier (Figure I.6) differs considerably from all of the above.[12] Two differences are most obvious. Firstly, unlike CHISHOLM, LOWE, GROSSMANN, or HOFFMAN/ROSENKRANTZ, TEGTMEIER does not incorporate a 'supercategory'. Instead, there are three maximal categories (things, states of affairs, and forms) but no greatest category. Secondly, there is a considerable difference in content. Many of the categories found in the other systems are absent here, whereas the finer subdivisions of universals and states of affairs accounted for here are missing in the other systems.

The final example of a system of ontological categories we shall consider does not come from mainstream philosophy but from research in Artificial Intelligence and Knowledge Engineering. These are the ontological categories of the computer program CYC. The motivation for the CYC project is to construct a program which is able to comprehend

---

[11] This will be discussed in more detail in § 13.
[12] Tegtmeier (1992: 52).

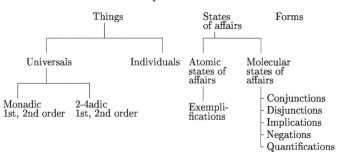

Fig. I.6 TEGTMEIER

texts in natural language such as those which may be found in a one-volume encyclopedia. To be able to do this, the program needs access to the basic knowledge which is *presupposed*, but not explicitly stated, in the text (i.e. knowledge of such statements as 'Only living things get diseases', 'Two objects cannot be at the same place at the same time', 'One cannot touch numbers', and so on). In order to organize this knowledge, which is supposed to be encoded manually, CYC needs a way of classifying items and of determining interrelations between classes, that is, it needs an ontology. Figure I.7 is an extremely simplified picture of what the top segment of the ontological categories of CYC looks like.[13]

It is evident that certain ontological categories which formed part of the systems we considered before (such as 'thing', 'individual', 'event', 'relation') are also present in the ontology of CYC. However, others are clearly examples of the internal architecture of the system (such as 'slot' and 'internal machine thing'). In fact there seem to be quite a few places in the setup of the CYC project where analytical rigour is replaced by purely pragmatic and philosophically rather unsatisfactory considerations (after all, the idea was to construct a system that works).[14] Thus although the ontology of CYC is a useful contrast to the more standard systems of ontological categories, it should nevertheless be approached with some caution.

---

[13] Lenat and Guha (1990: 171–2).
[14] Compare Copeland (1993: 107–20) for philosophical criticism of different parts of CYC's ontology.

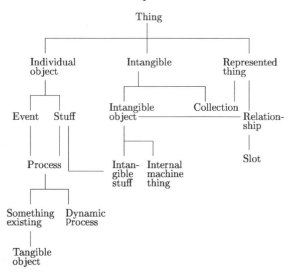

Fig. I.7 CYC

§2 Common features

The seven systems of ontological categories discussed above will have given the reader some impression of the diversity of accounts which have been advanced by ontologists. In spite of this diversity most of them have several features in common. These features can be divided into two groups: the *content* of the systems and their *structure*.

It is clear that there is no such thing as a set of ontological categories which all systems agree on. But there is a considerable degree of overlap. The category of properties and relations turns up in every system, individuals form a part of five, abstract objects, collections/sets and events are present in four and facts in two systems. Of course there are other more exotic kinds which are unique to particular systems ('privation', 'doing', 'cavities', 'conjunctions', 'structures'). Furthermore, at least two of the systems (LOWE and HOFFMAN/ROSENKRANTZ) explicitly claim not to be exhaustive: they agree that there could be perfectly acceptable ontological categories which are not included in their systems.[15]

There are three main aspects to be observed on the structural side. First of all, all the systems discussed so far take categories as *sets*, usually

---

[15] Lowe (2001: 180), Hoffman and Rosenkrantz (1994: 140).

as sets of objects.[16] This view of ontological categories is extremely widespread in philosophy and has been dominant in the more recent studies in analytic ontology. One notable exception to this position is Kant's view of categories; he introduces them in the *Critique of Pure Reason* as the most general forms of judgement and justifies their existence transcendentally by our ability to form judgements in the first place.[17] Although this is an extremely interesting idea, its divergence from the usual conception of ontological categories means that any treatment doing justice to it would presuppose a thorough discussion of Kantian philosophy and would therefore lead us too far away from the main topic of our inquiry. We therefore put the Kantian conception to one side and follow the philosophical mainstream by considering ontological categories to be sets.

The second structural feature to notice is that all systems including ARISTOTLE are *hierarchically organized* in some way or other. Ontological categories are not mutually disjoint: categories can contain other categories as subsets.[18] Furthermore, the categories are usually not just assumed to be ordered by containment, but also by generality.[19] In fact this is quite a substantial issue and will be discussed in greater detail in chapter II, part 2.

Finally, all of these systems apart from TEGTMEIER have a *greatest supercategory* ('entity', 'thing', 'the world') which contains all other categories. Equally, all systems agree that there are *minimal categories*, i.e. categories such that every category less general than them is not an ontological category (these are the categories where the diagrams end),[20] although CYC constitutes a possible exception since our account just presented the top part of its categorial structure cut off at an arbitrary point.

CYC also differs in another, final respect. All the other systems which possess a hierarchical organization have the form of a *tree* (or in the case

---

[16] In the case of ARISTOTLE this is at least one plausible interpretation of the system presented.

[17] Kant (1968: III: A80/B106).

[18] Meixner (2004: 19).

[19] See e.g. Hoffman and Rosenkrantz (1994: 16), Lowe (2001: 179–80).

[20] '[. . .] not all kinds divide up the world in ontologically important ways. Examples of kinds which are not ontological categories are: being a green thing, being a triangular thing, being a widow and (the disjunctive kind of) being a substance or an edge.' (Hoffman and Rosenkrantz 1997: 46–7). See also Meixner (2004: 18): 'A concept like human being, animal or living thing would be too special to function as an ontological category.'

of TEGTMEIER of a collection of trees, a forest). Thus categories which are separated at a higher node are never joined again at a lower node. This is not the case with CYC, which has the structure of a lattice. This means that here categories can properly overlap (such as 'intangible' and 'represented thing').

Taking these two groups of common features into account, two meta-ontological questions present themselves.

1. What kind of things are ontological categories? What makes the categories incorporated in the seven systems discussed *ontological* categories? Unfortunately this is far from obvious. Nevertheless it seems to be uncontroversial that an ontological theory deals with ontological categories. They do not make up the whole of the theory, but they are what it is about. It is therefore imperative to get a clear picture of what an ontological category is.

2. How can these ontological categories be related? As we shall see below, this is partially determined by the answer to 1. Certain definitions of ontological categories will imply particular accounts of the relations in which they can stand to one another.

These two questions will be addressed in the following pages. It is important, however, to distinguish these metaontological questions clearly from closely related object-level ontological questions which will not be discussed here:

1′. Which ontological categories should appear in an ontological theory?

2′. How are these categories in fact related, i.e. which are included in one another, which are coextensional etc.?

Our account will only cover questions 1 and 2, i.e. we will discuss what kind of things the ontologist talks about and will try to determine how answers to this question influence the structural relationships between ontological categories. It might be helpful to imagine the relation of metaontology to ontology as being similar to that of metaethics to ethics. An object-level ethical inquiry will try to find out whether some particular norm ought to be adopted as a moral norm or whether a specific action violates such a norm. Metaethics, on the other hand, asks what kind of norm a *moral* norm is (as opposed, for instance, to a legal, political, or religious norm) and then tries to identify some properties of such norms. In the same way metaontology is not concerned with questions such as whether the category of material objects can be reduced to that of events, or whether properties are abstract objects or not, but will rather ask why events and material objects are supposed to be ontological categories in the first place (while storms and tables are not) and whether it can be the case that ontological categories overlap or that things in different categories can share properties.

II

Attempted definitions of 'ontological category'

Having introduced the different kinds of categories featuring in ontological theories we now turn to the question of what *makes* all of them ontological categories. Why are *they* regarded as ontological categories rather than others? What makes the different categories hang together? Why are the systems of ontological categories structured in the way they are?

Answering these questions crucially depends on being able to give a satisfactory definition of the notion of an ontological category. There are two approaches for tackling this problem which might be considered attractive in some respects but which are nevertheless fundamentally deficient and can thus be dismissed relatively quickly.

1 UNSATISFYING ACCOUNTS

§3 Defeatism

When asked to provide a definition of 'ontological category', one response is to declare it to be an impossible enterprise:

Ontology [. . .] asks what the categories of the world are. What is a category? It is a kind or entity. What kind of kind? In answer to this question we can only give examples. It is a sort of kind, as we have seen, that distinguishes between individuals, on the one hand, and properties on the other. It is that sort of kind, as we have noted, which obeys a certain kind of law, namely, categorial laws. But this reply does not really help much either. We must therefore rest content, as on so many other occasions, with examples rather than definitions. In these most fundamental matters of metaphysics, definitions are impossible.[1]

The source for Grossmann's defeatism in matters ontological is not quite clear. He is not giving an argument why we should not be able to obtain

---

[1] Grossmann (1983: 5).

a definition of 'ontological category'. The only obvious argument I can think of is that the notion is inconsistent anyway, so that there is nothing to define. But we can hardly assume that this is the opinion of somebody who has just written a book called 'The Categorial Structure of the World'. In fact, ontology would appear in a rather strange light if we were not able to give a clear exposition of what the unifying element of its subject-matter is. Given that the study of ontology has been going on for more than two thousand years and has treated a relatively uniform collection of concepts—just compare it to what was regarded as logic at various times—I take it that there is some plausibility in assuming there to be a unifying bond which ties together what this discipline talks about. We only have to find out what this bond is.

I do not agree, however, that this is in any way obvious, as for example Nicolai Hartmann assumes in his four-volume study of ontology:

And if one inquires further what the [ontological] categories are, the answer is immediately obvious as soon as one considers some examples, such as unity and plurality, quantity and quality, measure and size, time and space, becoming and permanence, causality and necessity and so forth. One is immediately acquainted with such properties of being even without a detailed inquiry, we are used to them and come across them all the time.[2]

Given that the notion of an ontological category is a highly theoretical one, any claims regarding our 'immediate acquaintance' with it seem to be distinctly dubious. And even if we were acquainted with *examples* of ontological categories, this would not give us any knowledge of their *common features* which make them ontological categories.

§4 Laundry-lists

A second account, which is a bit more sophisticated than Hartmann's rather unsatisfying remarks, consists in giving not some particular examples of ontological categories, but an entire laundry-list of all of them. Of course it is useful to know what has been regarded as an ontological category in the history of philosophy or what a particular author regards as such, but, interesting as such a list might be in itself, it is certainly no substitute for a definition. It can only set the stage by indicating which kinds of things our definition should incorporate; it cannot enable us to

---

[2] Hartmann (1949: 2–3).

decide whether some particular object really is or is not an ontological category.

Again it is instructive to draw a parallel with logic. Even if we restrict ourselves to the development of modern logic in the twentieth century, we shall not find the list of notions which authors of this time considered logical to be particularly helpful in settling what the definition of 'being a logical notion' is. First of all there might be notions included which ought not be considered logical, or, conversely, there might be notions not included which are very similar to some which *are* included and which might thus have the same right to be considered logical notions as well. For example, quantifiers such as 'for most' or 'for at least five' are quite similar to the familiar quantifiers 'for all' and 'for some'. The last two but not the first two have traditionally been regarded as logical notions. But this is a purely historically contingent fact and nothing which gives us any structural reason for considering one sort of quantifiers rather than another as constituting a logical notion. For similar reasons it is clear that questions about the nature of ontological categories cannot be answered solely by reference to historically contingent laundry-lists.

§5 Possible bases for an account

Fortunately not all accounts which try to make the notion of an ontological category precise are as unsatisfactory as the two just discussed. Apart from these, which evade rather than answer the question, we can distinguish three kinds of accounts trying to deal with the matter in a systematic way. They can be grouped together according to the main kind of intuitions about ontological categories they exploit. It is usually assumed of ontological categories that

- they are the most *general* kinds of things;
- they can explain why certain *substitutions* in a statement (such as 'prime' for 'odd' in 'the number nine is odd') make the statement just false, while others make it meaningless (such as substituting 'sweet' for 'odd');
- they provide the *identity criteria* for classes of objects.

In the following pages we will discuss these intuitions and analyse some of the accounts which have been based on them. Given the diversity of the systems of ontological categories we discussed in § 1 it would be very unlikely that there should be some definition compatible with *every* one of these. And it is not clear whether this is actually desirable. We surely want our definition to incorporate the essential features of systems of ontological categories, rather than having a definition which is in harmony with even the most outlandish system one can come up with (in this case the definition presumably would not have much content in any case). After all, hard cases make bad law. We will therefore have to see in every case whether a discrepancy between our definition and the examples of systems of ontological categories presented here is a problem of the definition (which does not capture what it is supposed to capture) or a problem of the examples (i.e. that some of these are just wrong in calling themselves examples of systems of ontological theories). We will try to provide independent arguments in each case for assuming that some property of ontological systems is a key feature which a definition must satisfy, rather than a property which systems of ontological categories could equally do without.

2 ACCOUNTS IN TERMS OF GENERALITY

§6 Norton's account

The first promising definition of ontological category tries to utilize the concept of generality. It is relatively uncontroversial that the concepts ontology employs are distinguished from those of other sciences by their greater generality. Ontology considers such general notions as 'physical object', 'event', or 'property' but nothing as specific as 'pencil', 'explosion', or 'solubility', which are instances of such general notions. The difficulty consists in making the notion of generality precise enough to give a convincing way of picking out ontological categories. Bryan Norton has tried this in his paper 'On defining "ontology"'.[3]

A first idea might consist in saying that some class A is more general than a class B if A contains B. This explains why the class of mammals is more general than the class of cows, and why the class of numbers is more general than the class of complex numbers. This account works all right if we stick to fairly natural classes (such as mammals and cows,

---

[3] Norton (1976).

etc.). But as soon as we allow in *any* classes whatsoever it delivers strange results. The class of all material objects and the Versailles treaty properly includes the class of all material objects. But we would be reluctant to conclude that it is any more general than the latter.

Norton proposes the following way out:

a 'class' must be understood as a natural kind of entities, organized around an essential characteristic. It is a genus made up of sub-species including no objects which do not fit into one of the sub-species.[4]

This is all very well but brings with it a new set of problems. Not only are the notions of 'natural kind' and 'essential characteristic' notoriously unclear (the first is presumably *just as unclear* as that of an ontological category), it is also not evident that instances of the latter are what pick out the former.[5]

Fortunately, Norton himself does not use this analysis of generality. According to him, a class of objects A is more general than a class of objects B (which we will write as $A >_G B$) iff it follows from the fact that B has some members that A has some members, that is if A is empty, so is B.

He then argues that this gives rise to a hierarchical ordering of entities. He gives a toy example of a system of ontological categories with Entities on top, which are divided into Abstract Entities, Mental Entities, and Physical Entities, which are then in turn divided into Classes and Universals, Minds and Perceptions, and Solids and Gases. The idea is then to say that $(\exists x)(\Phi x)$ is a positive ontological assertion iff the denotation of Φ is one of the most general classes of entities.

Unfortunately, this does not make for a convincing account of generality. It is true that if there are bikes, there are wheels; if there are parties, there are guests; and if there are murders, there are murderers. But it is not the case that the class of wheels is more general than the class of bikes, the class of guests more general than the class of parties, or the class of murderers more general than the class of murders.

§7 A better account of generality

Thus we need a more satisfying definition of generality. Another attempt is made by Hoffman and Rosenkrantz in their account of substance.[6]

[4] Norton (1976: 107).   [5] See §27.   [6] (1994: 17).

For them a set A is more general than a set B if A subsumes B, where *subsumption* is defined as

Necessarily, B is a subset of A and it is possible that there is something which is in A but not in B.

Unfortunately, this encounters the same problem as the proposal discussed above. Clearly it is necessary that if something is a member of the set of ducks it is a member of the union-set of birds and British foxes (so the first conjunct is satisfied). But equally it is possible that this second set has a member which is not a duck (so the second conjunct is satisfied) and A, subsuming B, would counterintuitively have to be supposed to be more general than B.

What this shows is that in order to give a satisfactory definition of generality we need some way of keeping out strange gerrymandered classes like the union-set of birds and British foxes. One plausible way of doing this relies on the notion of *ontological dependence*. Norton seems to have been on the right track in realizing this. We can spell out this notion by saying that some property F depends on some property G if it could not be the case that the Gs did not exist, while the Fs did.[7] But this is a stronger claim than Norton's, since it incorporates a modal element: we do not just want to say that if there are no wheels there are *as a matter of fact* no bikes, but that the absence of wheels would make it *impossible* for there to be bikes. We can thus adopt the following definition:

F depends on G (which we will write as $F <_D G$) := *Necessarily, if there are no Gs, there are no Fs.*

A promising strategy for developing a satisfactory definition of generality might consist in using the notion of dependence just introduced and coupling it with the notion of containment. The two notions are generally independent. There can be containment without dependence (the books in Cambridge University Library contain an edition of the works of Shakespeare, but each could exist without the other existing). There can also be dependence without containment (cigars depend on tobacco plants, but the collection of all cigars does not contain that of all tobacco plants, or vice versa).[8]

---

[7] Simons (1987: ch. 8). For a more detailed discussion of the notion of ontological dependence see §§ 31–3.

[8] In the case of certain objects, however, there is a connection. Take sets: if the set S contains some object a, then S depends on a.

We could then define that a set A is more general than a set B ($A >_G B$) just in case

1. B is a proper subset of A,
2. B depends on A,
3. for no $a, a' \in A$, and no $b, b' \in B$ is it the case that $a <_D a'$ or $b <_D b'$.

Thus one set is more general than another if 1) it contains it, and 2) this other set could not exist if the first set did not exist. Condition 3, which says that no two elements from the same set can depend on one another, is just there to exclude certain counterexamples not covered by 1 and 2. For example, by 1 and 2, the set N^* containing the natural numbers and the singleton of the number two is more general than the set of natural numbers, which seems to be rather unintuitive. But since 2 and $\{2\}$ belong to N^* and $\{2\} >_D 2$, condition 3 excludes this case.[9]

On this account we can easily see why the set of vertebrates is more general than the set of humans, why the set of metal objects is more general than the set of golden rings, and why the set of natural numbers is more general than the set of prime numbers. It also shows us that the set consisting of all material objects and the Versailles treaty is *not* more general than the set of material objects: although the latter is contained in the former, the set of material objects could exist even if the set of material objects and the Versailles treaty did not exist (for example if there were no human beings and therefore no treaties).

§8 The persistence of the problem

Now that we have a satisfactory account of generality, does this solve our problem of finding a satisfactory definition of ontological category? The short answer is no. This is because ontological categories can *depend* on other ontological categories. For example, mathematical structures depend on the existence of abstract objects, events depend on the existence of time-instants, concrete properties depend on the existence of concrete objects. All of the examples of systems of ontological categories

[9] Of course the dependence of the unit set of 2 on its only member is only plausible if we can make any sense of mathematical objects like the number two not existing. I think we can, but unfortunately this footnote is too small to contain my argument for this. If we *cannot*, however, then the above counterexample is ruled out, as condition 2 ('necessarily, if N^* does not exist, N does not exist') would not hold, since it has an unintelligible antecedent.

we gave in chapter I agreed that the set of ontological categories is partially ordered by generality (in the case of ARISTOTLE we had an ordering by dependence). But then it is obvious that we cannot just define the set of ontological categories as that of $>_G$-maximal ('most general') sets. This will only pick out the most fundamental ontological categories (those depending on no other ontological categories).

This problem is clear even from Norton's own example. If this is anything to go by, the ontological categories cannot be just the most general notions, because clearly ontological categories (Entities, Abstract Entities, Universals) occur on all levels of generality he cites. Moreover, on his example we get two expressions on the same level of generality of which one ('universal') seems to be clearly an ontological category while the other ('gases') is clearly not. So even if we could assign to each category its level of generality, this would be of no help in dividing the ontological sheep from the non-ontological goats.

§9 Categories as semantically redundant: Katz's account

An interesting definition of ontological categories based on the notion of *redundancy* has been developed by Jerrold Katz as part of his general semantic theory.[10] This is closely related to the idea that ontological categories are the most general kinds of entities there are. If you imagine all kinds of entities to be brought together in one enormous taxonomic tree, we could give a description of any object belonging to some kind by starting at the top node or nodes and then working downwards from kind to kind until we have found the kind which directly contains the object which we want to describe. If we compared several such descriptions we would soon realize that many of them exhibit a great deal of redundancy. If a certain node (a name of a certain kind) is included in the description, it will always be the case that the nodes which can be reached by going upwards from this node will also be included in the description. So including these nodes is in fact redundant information. Katz now tries to get a definition of ontological category out of this.

One of the fundamental concepts Katz employs is that of a *semantic marker*. He claims that a word, phrase, clause, or sentence has one or

---

[10] Katz (1966: 224–39), (1972).

several meanings (he uses 'meaning' to refer to all of them, and 'sense' to refer to them individually). Now a semantic marker

represents the conceptual constituents of senses in the same way in which phrase markers represent the syntactic construction of sentences. They represent not only the atomic constituents of a sense, that is, the simplest concepts in the sense (analogous to the morphemes in a sentence) but also the complex ones.[11]

As an example he gives the semantic markers (i.e. conceptual constituents) corresponding to 'chair' as (Object), (Physical), (Non-Living), (Artifact), (Furniture), (Portable), (Something with legs), (Something with a back), (Something with a seat), (Seat for one). These markers could in turn be broken down so that the first would for example give us 'organization of parts that are spatio-temporally contiguous which form a stable whole having an orientation in space'.[12]

Now it appears that several markers are redundant: if some marker M_1 occurs in a description of the sense of an expression (i.e. in the set of semantic markers which make up this sense), some M_2 will occur as well (e.g. let M_1 be 'artifact' and M_2 be 'physical object'). In this case we will say that M_1 makes M_2 redundant. It will then appear convenient to introduce a couple of redundancy rules in order to simplify the expression of senses. For example we could have

$$(Artifact) \longrightarrow \left\{ \begin{array}{l} (Object) \wedge \\ (Physical) \wedge \\ (Non\text{-}living) \end{array} \right\}$$

or

$$(furniture) \longrightarrow (artifact)$$

That is, whenever we come across the semantic marker (Artifact) in some description, we know that the markers (Object), (Physical), and (Non-living) are also present. Similarly the presence of (furniture) entails the presence of (artifact).

Katz assumes the set of redundancy rules of a given language to be presented in the following normal form:

---

[11] Katz (1972: 37).   [12] Katz (1972: 40).

$$M_n \vee M_o \vee M_p \dots \longrightarrow M_x$$
$$M_r \vee M_s \vee M_t \dots \longrightarrow M_y$$
$$\vdots$$
$$M_u \vee M_v \vee M_w \dots \longrightarrow M_z$$

Obviously rules like the above can be translated into normal form by considering that there might be only one disjunct on the left and that different redundancy rules may have the same antecedent.

We can then define 'ontological categories' as 'those semantic markers appearing on the right-hand side of some semantic redundancy rules but not on the left-hand side of any such rules'.[13] Similarly we are able to say that the markers appearing only on the left and not on the right constitute the least general concepts of the language.

Not everything appearing on the right is a semantic category since there will be reduction rules like

$$(father) \vee (uncle) \vee (nephew) \vee \dots \longrightarrow (male)$$

and we would not want to call e.g. (*male*) an ontological category. The specification ensures that the markers on the right must not in turn make other markers predictable (since they do not occur on the left), i.e. we take ontological categories to be those semantic markers which are predictable but do not allow us to predict others.

§10   A graph-theoretic view of redundancy rules

It can be shown that the structure fixed by the set of redundancy rules is a particular kind of graph, namely either a tree (if there is only one ontological category) or a disconnected tree (a forest) (if there is more than one).

It is instructive to look at this in a bit more detail. Let us first fix some simple mathematical vocabulary we need. A *graph* consists of a set $V = \{v_1, \dots v_n\}$ of *vertices* and a set E of pairs of members of V which is the set of *edges* connecting the vertices. v_j is a *successor* of v_i if $\{v_i, v_j\} \in E$, and a *predecessor* if $\{v_j, v_i\} \in E$. A *path* is a finite sequence of edges $\{v_{i0}, v_{i1}\}, \{v_{i1}, v_{i2}\}, \dots \{v_{ir-1}, v_{ir}\}$. It is *open* if its initial and terminal endpoints are distinct, otherwise it is a *cycle*.

---

[13] Katz (1972: 100).

A *tree* is a graph such that

- it contains no cycles;
- it contains no *joins*, i.e. every vertex has at most one predecessor;
- one vertex v_t, which will be called the *top vertex*, has no predecessor.

First of all it is important to see that all redundancy rules, whether in normal form or not, can be brought into the canonical form $M_i \longrightarrow M_j$ such that there is only one marker on each side of the arrow. This is done by splitting rules like $(artifact), (furniture) \longrightarrow (physical\ object)$ into $(artifact) \longrightarrow (furniture)$ and $(furniture) \longrightarrow (physical\ object)$ and those of the form $(father) \longrightarrow (male), (living)$ into $(father) \longrightarrow (male)$ and $(male) \longrightarrow (living)$.

We can then argue that the semantic markers correspond to the vertices and the edges to the redundancy rules in their canonical form.

It is now possible to discuss the properties of trees. To say that it should contain no cycles is to say that there are no redundancy rules of the form $M_1 \longrightarrow M_2$, $M_2 \longrightarrow M_3$ and $M_3 \longrightarrow M_1$. Katz does not explicitly rule this possibility out, but it seems as if he could not sustain his conception of meaning in terms of 'breaking down' the semantic markers if such cycles could occur. Note, however, that although a structure consisting only of such cycles would not contain any ontological categories, the presence of only some of them does not exclude this.

Secondly we want to exclude joins, that is canonical rules of the form $M_2 \longrightarrow M_1$ and $M_2 \longrightarrow M_3$. We want the meaning to become more and more differentiated as we break down some semantic markers. Thus the total number of semantic markers should increase at each stage of the process of analysis. It should not happen that some marker reduces to two others, which in turn reduce to a common marker.

Finally we want to show that the top vertex corresponds to the ontological category (if there is only one) or the top vertices correspond to the ontological categories (if there are more than one and we are thus talking about a forest of disconnected trees).

If A is an ontological category, it must be a member of the set of top vertices. For suppose it was not, i.e. there was an A' which was higher. Then whenever some a had marker (A) it would also have marker (A').

But then there would be a reduction rule $(A) \longrightarrow (A')$. So (A) would be on the left of this rule and so A could not be an ontological category. Conversely, if A is a top vertex it will be an ontological category. There will be some x such that if it has some marker (X) it will also have marker (A). So $(X) \longrightarrow (A)$ will be a reduction rule. But *ex hypothesi* there is no Z such that whenever x is A it is also Z. So (A) is not on the left of any reduction rule, and so it is an ontological category.

§11 Advantages and problems of Katz's account

Katz's account of ontological categories has a number of advantages. It provides us with a precise criterion for picking out the ontological categories and makes it possible to construct a taxonomic tree of kinds. Moreover, we can employ this approach to formulate a precise way of spelling out the notion of generality, thus improving Norton's approach, which was not able to do this. This works as follows. Reduction rules can form chains: for example the rules $M_2 \longrightarrow M_1$ and $M_3 \longrightarrow M_2$ form the chain $M_3 \longrightarrow M_2 \longrightarrow M_1$. Now clearly in this example M_1 will be at a higher level in the tree (and thus more general) than M_2, which is in turn higher than M_3. We can say that a marker M_n is *more general* than a marker M_m iff the chain from M_n to the onto-logical category M_n belongs to is shorter than that from M_m to the category M_m belongs to. An advantage of this formulation is that it is not applicable only to markers sitting on the same branch/belonging to the same ontological category (such as $(metallic)$ and $(physical)$), where we could simply say that the second is more general than the first because it can be reached by going up the tree starting from $(metallic)$; it is applicable also to markers on different branches (such as $(table)$ and $(abstract\ object)$).

Unfortunately, there are also several problems. On a very general level we will have to ask whether we have to buy Katz's entire semantic the-ory in order to get our definition of ontological category. His theory has been severely criticized,[14] but mostly for assuming that even the bits of semantics which one would generally count as parts of logic can be for-mulated in terms of semantic markers. Katz introduces separate entries

---

[14] Bar-Hillel (1970: 182–205, 347–53).

for truth-functional connectives like negation[15] or for structural facts about relations. But this criticism is not connected in any way to his definition of ontological categories. In fact, we need surprisingly little from Katz's theory in order to run his definition. It has been argued that his notion of conceptual elements is reminiscent of 'a philosophy of language of antiquity or the Middle Ages'[16] and in fact we can reproduce his definition with nothing more than the venerable notion of conceptual containment. We let concepts play the rôle of semantic markers and have the primitive operation p such that $C_1 p C_2$ is interpreted as 'concept C_1 is a proper part of concept C_2'. So a redundancy rule like $M_1, M_2, \ldots \longrightarrow M_{1'}, M_{2'}, \ldots$ will simply mean that for each of the corresponding concepts $C_1, C_2, \ldots$ and each of the corresponding $C_{1'}, C_{2'}, \ldots$ it is the case that $C_{n'} p C_m$. The ontological categories (simple concepts) will then be simply those C_i such that there are no C_j which are proper parts of them.

§12 The further persistence of the problem

Thus we see that whether we accept Katz's account of ontological categories depends not so much on whether we buy his semantic theory, but more on whether we take a theory of conceptual containment like the above to be plausible.

But even if we do this, the problem is not solved. In fact Katz's account is vexed by a problem which turns up in all attempts to define ontological categories in terms of some order $>$ on them. This order can be spelt out in terms of set-theoretic containment, dependence, generality, or conceptual containment. The question is then whether we can define ontological categories in terms of maximal elements of these orderings, that is by taking them as the 'most inclusive sets' (if $>$ is set-theoretic containment), as categories which do not depend on others (in the case of dependence), as the 'most general sets' (if $>$ means 'is more general than'), or as the 'most primitive concepts' (if $>$ is conceptual containment).

Note that all the examples of systems of ontological categories we discussed in chapter I agree on the existence of some such order. Fur-

---

[15] Bar-Hillel (1970: 187, 353).   [16] Bar-Hillel (1970: 186).

thermore, if we look at the examples there seem to be two fundamental assumptions at work.

First of all they assume that if some ontological category is 'above' some other category (contains it, is more general/more primitive than it) the first category is also an ontological category. That is, the set of categories is *upwards closed* by the ordering $>$ relative to the property of being an ontological category, i.e. for any x, if x is an ontological category and if $y > x$ then y is an ontological category as well.

The second assumption is that the ontological categories are well-founded, i.e. that there is no infinitely descending chain of ontological categories. Every sequence of categories $A > B > C \ldots$ ordered by $>$ eventually terminates in a *minimal category*; that is, there is some ontological category such that anything 'below' this relative to $>$ (included in it, less general/less primitive than it) is an ontological category no longer. We will call this ontological category the *cut-off point* or a *least inclusive category*. Intuitively we might want to say that these contained categories are 'too specific' to count as ontological categories themselves. In all the examples discussed earlier these assumptions are satisfied. Although it is argued that one will stop encountering ontological categories if one goes 'too far' down the ordering,[17] nobody thinks that something similar happens when going up.

It is now clear what the problem is. Assuming an ordering $>$ of categories makes it possible to define ontological categories as $>$-maximal items. But given that the $>$-maximal categories properly include the ontological categories, how far down the ordering shall we go? Where is the cut-off point for ontological categories? Given the second assumption there must be some such point. Clearly, on Katz's analysis it is after the highest node or nodes of the tree of kinds. But this seems to be unsatisfactory, especially if there is one universal marker (as for example in CHISHOLM, LOWE, GROSSMANN, HOFFMAN/ROSENKRANTZ, and CYC), which would then have to be considered as the only ontological category and would make ontology a rather boring discipline.

The cut-off point problem reappears in an account sketched by Charles Caton which bears certain similarities to Katz's proposal.[18] He introduces the notion of an *essentially arising question*, that is a question relating to a statement which must have a non-negative answer,

---

[17] Hoffman and Rosenkrantz (1997: 46–7).
[18] Caton (1971), see also Keil (1979: 157–8).

given that the statement is true.[19]   Suppose we have the statement
'Peter played the violin'. Then there are several questions one could
ask, for example 'When did he play the violin?', 'Who accompanied
him?' or 'Where did he play?'. Caton's point is that the first and third
are somehow special. In the case of the second question we can give an
answer denying the presupposition ('There was nobody who accompanied him'), which Caton calls a negative answer. But in the case of the first
and third, there *must* be a positive answer. If it is true that Peter played
the violin he must have played it at some place and at some time. Here
we could not give a negative answer and for example say that there was
no time at which Peter played the violin. The idea is then that essentially arising questions are linked to the notion of ontological categories.
If you ask a set of essentially arising questions about some thing x mentioned in certain sentences, you can then determine which ontological
category x must belong to (thus playing the violin must be located both
in space and time and by this belongs to the categories of things 'being
in space' and 'being in time').

   Problems start to arise when we consider such sentences as 'Peter
bought a knife', 'Charles wrote a story', or 'George went to a party'.
Clearly, questions like 'What kind of blade does it have?', 'How many
words does it contain?', and 'How many people were there?' are then
essentially arising questions—they must have non-negative answers. But
it would be strange to regard 'having a blade' or 'containing words' as
ontological categories.

   The source of the trouble is easy to spot: if a depends on b and some
sentence mentions a, questions about b will be essentially arising. They
must have a positive answer, since if there was no fact of the matter, a
could not exist because it presupposes the existence of b. So the essentially arising questions tell us about what a thing depends on. But this
is useful for our ontological inquiries only if we are 'high enough' in the
ordering by generality. If we are below the cut-off point, we get information about what 'being of a certain kind' depends on or presupposes
(if it is a knife, it will have a blade), but we would not want to take this
as information about ontological categories.

   There have been attempts to bite this bullet and declare that the cut-
off point problem is not really a problem. Keil argues that all it amounts
to in terms of categories is that 'the only ontologically interesting ones

---

[19] Caton (1971: 29).

are near the top of the tree'.[20] The fact that there would be no exact level at which the ontological categories stop is not in itself troubling, he says. A recent introduction to ontology concurs:

At some point in the hierarchy we reach the limit where we stop to make ontological distinctions and no longer talk about the fundamental structures of being, because the distinctions we draw have become too specialized. However, this limit cannot be defined precisely. Are we still dealing with general metaphysics, or are we already talking about special metaphysics, or even about a particular non-philosophical discipline? This can only be decided arbitrarily.[21]

But despite these claims the problem reported is very disconcerting indeed. It implies that we do not have a clear answer to the question why certain distinctions are ontologically important while others are not. From an ontological point of view it makes no difference whether something takes ten seconds or ten minutes, but it *does* make a difference that it has a duration at all. On the other hand it makes no difference whether something is a spoon or a fork, *nor* whether it is some piece of cutlery or other. If we admit that there is no clear answer to the question why 'having a duration' is an ontologically relevant feature while 'being a piece of cutlery' is not, we may as well say that we do not know what we are talking about when doing ontology. This would be just as problematic as it would be for logic if we had no story to tell about the fundamental difference between logical and non-logical notions.[22]

The point is not that there could not be problems which are located between ontology and another discipline (such as logic or physics), in the same way as there are problems just at the intersection between biology and chemistry. We do, however, have a sufficiently clear grasp of the respective subject-matters of biology and chemistry to appreciate that there are points of contact. But this is entirely different from the above conception of ontology, where what holds the discipline together is left completely in the dark.

We thus see that determining a cut-off point is an essential feature of accounts of ontological categories. No definition which does not satisfy

[20] Keil (1979: 141).

[21] Meixner (2004: 19–20). As other writers on the subject Meixner claims that this difficulty can be circumvented by appeal to 'clear cut examples' of ontological categories (20).

[22] For example in terms of invariance properties as discussed by Tarski (1986), McGee (1996), van Benthem (1989).

this could be adequate, because there would then be no clear distinction between ontologically important and ontologically irrelevant properties.

§13   A list-based account

The final account of ontological categories based on the notion of generality we are going to discuss gets around the cut-off point problem but fails in other respects. It constitutes a part of Hoffman and Rosenkrantz's account of substance.[23] They claim that

> [the] notion of an ontological category needs to be explained, since every entity is of many different kinds of categories of varying degrees or levels of generality. Thus [. . .] we must specify the *degree* of generality of the ontological categories we have in mind.[24]

They propose to develop a definition of level of generality such that a category satisfying this definition is an ontological category.[25] Further conditions are then introduced to distinguish the category of *substance* from the other ontological categories. Our discussion will only consider the first condition, which is supposed to tell ontological categories from other categories. Since we have a slightly different purpose, we will present a somewhat modified version of this condition. However, all our criticisms will apply to the original version as well.

Their definition rests on two notions. The first is the idea of one set being *as general as* another set. Given our reservations about their formulation of subsumption and generality expressed in §7 we assume either that some more satisfactory definition of 'as general as' in terms of the definition of generality provided at the end of §7 has been given[26] or else that the notion is taken as primitive.

The second notion is a list L of 'core categories'[27] which are at the required level of generality. They assume the list contains the categories at the third level of Figure I.5 given above, i.e. property, relation, proposition, event, time, place, limit, collection, privation, and trope.

[23] (1994: 16–21).
[24] Hoffman and Rosenkrantz (1994: 16).
[25] Hoffman and Rosenkrantz (1994: 20).
[26] For example we could say that A is as general as B iff 1) $A \cap B = \emptyset$ and 2) the number of $C >_G A$ is the same as the number of $D >_G B$.
[27] Hoffman and Rosenkrantz (1994: 18).

It is then possible to define a category to be on a level of generality which characterizes it as an ontological category iff 1) it is in L or 2) it is more general than some member of L or 3) it is of the same level of generality as some member of L.[28]

Now it might strike the reader as somewhat circular to have a definition of ontological categories which makes use of a *list* of such categories. After all, the list is what we want to get out. In fact, however, this is not as bad as it sounds. The list L is supposed to be quite flexible. Firstly, not all of the categories in L must be instantiated, so it might be the case that some members are just empty and thus that the list is smaller than it actually appears.[29] Secondly, it might be the case that not all ontological categories turn up in L—and this is what the above condition is for: it allows us to enlarge L in a way which guarantees that all new members will be ontological categories. Thus the above condition generates an *open-ended* account of ontological categories, rather than giving a fixed list (as e.g. in Aristotle's account). This seems to be quite attractive, since it tries to tell us *why* we regard certain categories as ontological categories, while making clear that ascertaining *whether* the condition for being an ontological category is fulfilled in a particular case is another matter.

But there are also a couple of difficulties which cannot be ignored. First of all, despite its flexibility, L cannot be completely empty. So the definition only works if you already have some definite example of an ontological category, so that the above condition enables you to get more of the same. Furthermore, you have to be sure that the members of L are ontological categories of the least degree of generality (since the above condition only gives you categories of the same or a higher level of generality). This seems to be rather problematic, since if you already have an argument why any category less general than this one cannot be an ontological category, you will have a solution to the cut-off point problem and thus will not need the above account anyway.

A second problem is that the above condition makes rather heavy assumptions about the structure of systems of ontological categories. For it to work it has to presuppose that *all the minimal ontological categories are on the same level of generality*. This is satisfied for example by CHISHOLM and GROSSMANN, but not by LOWE or TEGTMEIER

---

[28] Hoffman and Rosenkrantz (1994: 19).
[29] Hoffman and Rosenkrantz (1994: 140).

and, strangely enough, not even by HOFFMAN/ROSENKRANTZ itself. Suppose the category of spirits (in HOFFMAN/ROSENKRANTZ) had been in our L. There would not have been an ontological category less general than it, so the first problem would have been avoided. By the above account, everything on the same or a higher level of generality than 'spirit' would have to be considered as an ontological category. But we notice that the minimal categories on the 'abstract' branch are one level of generality higher up than the minimal categories on the 'concrete' branch. Thus the categories directly below 'property', 'relation', and 'propositions' (whatever they are) would have to count as ontological categories, contrary to the situation represented in the diagram. It is thus evident that Hoffman and Rosenkrantz's approach manages to escape the cut-off point problem but is confronted with other difficulties which prevent it from being a convincing account of ontological categories.

We have now seen that the notion of generality has given rise to a number of different and quite ingenious ways of solving the problem of defining ontological categories. Most of them share the cut-off point problem, i.e. they are too inclusive and do not manage to keep out certain unwanted cases. This provides us with some evidence that the greater generality of ontological categories is a sufficient but not a necessary feature. It is something our account of ontological categories should *imply*, but cannot be what our account is *based on*, at least not without combining it with some other feature to guarantee necessity.

3 ACCOUNTS BASED ON INTERSUBSTITUTABILITY

The second kind of intuition we consider is that of intersubstitutability. The fundamental underlying idea is that objects belonging to the same ontological category can somehow be exchanged for one another in certain contexts. Let us now inquire whether this intuition can be made precise enough to provide us with a satisfactory definition.

The notion of intersubstitutability has been employed in both grammatical investigations (for finding out what the *grammatical* categories are) and in ontological inquiries (for finding out what the *ontological* categories are). Since the idea of using the notion of substitution to define grammatical categories was there first and was only later extended to deal with matters ontological, we will start our discussion with a look at the rôle of intersubstitutability in grammar.

§14   Notions of intersubstitutability

Before we embark on this, however, we should note that people do not always mean the same thing when appealing to substitution in order to pick out categories of a certain sort. The rough idea is straightforward enough: two expressions belong to the same category if you can substitute one for the other. But once we try to make this precise, we realize that there is more than one way of spelling it out. A bit of formalization makes it easier to see how many there are. Consider the following formula:

$$\underbrace{(\forall\Phi)}_{\forall/\exists}((\underbrace{G}_{G/M}(\Phi[x/y]) \wedge \underbrace{G}_{G/M}(\Phi[y/x])) \equiv (x \underbrace{\approx_G}_{\approx_G/\approx_M} y))$$

To understand what this says first ignore everything below the braces. Φ is an expression in which either of the expressions x and y occurs, and $\Phi[x/y]$ denotes the result of exchanging x for y in Φ. G denotes grammaticality and $\approx_G$ means that the relata of this relation belong to the same grammatical category. So the above means that for all contexts, the result of intersubstituting two expressions in the context preserves grammaticality, iff the two expressions belong to the same grammatical category. This is one way of employing the intersubstitutability criterion, but far from the only one. Other formulations can be found by replacing parts of the above formula by the material below the braces. For example, we might just want to demand intersubstitutability in some, and not in all contexts. To do this we exchange the $\forall$ above the first brace for an $\exists$. Perhaps we do not want to talk of grammaticality but of meaningfulness: exchange the two Gs for an M. Perhaps we do not want to define grammatical categories, but categories of meaning/ semantic categories/ontological categories: write $\approx_M$ instead of $\approx_G$.

Taking all these variations into account we are left with eight different ways of understanding the notion of intersubstitutability. Formulae beginning $(\forall \Phi)$ . . . will be called the *strong* versions, those beginning $(\exists \Phi)$ . . . the *weak* versions. For each version there will be four possibilities of employing the notion of intersubstitutability:

– for defining *grammatical* categories

expressions belong to the same grammatical category iff they are intersubstitutable preserving *grammaticality*

expressions belong to the same grammatical category iff they are intersubstitutable preserving *meaningfulness*

– for defining *ontological* categories

expressions belong to the same ontological category iff they are intersubstitutable preserving *grammaticality*

expressions belong to the same ontological category iff they are intersubstitutable preserving *meaningfulness*

Most of these possibilities have actually been endorsed somewhere in the literature. We will now have a look at them in greater detail.

§15   Grammatical categories: The standard account

The grammaticality criterion for grammatical categories is certainly the most straightforward and the most standard.[30] The idea behind this is that two words belong to the same grammatical category if you can take a sentence in which the first word occurs and substitute the second for it (and vice versa) and the result is still a grammatical sentence. Thus we see that only a certain group of words will go into the blank to make '. . . can be very annoying' a grammatical sentence. Another group will go into 'Many people like to . . .' and yet another into 'Joe buttered the toast . . .'. Members of the first group will be words like 'linguistics' or 'satsumas', while those going into the second blank will be e.g. 'swim' or 'live', while those in the final one are expressions like 'quickly' or 'carefully'. We will call the first group nouns, the second verbs, and the third adverbs. Of course the idea is not that for example *only* words which go into the first blank constitute the grammatical category of

---

[30] Bradford (1988: 60, 62), Oliver (1999: 250–1).

nouns, but rather that we can construct enough similar contexts which will *all together* allow us to pick out the nouns by intersubstitutability.

Unfortunately this criterion does not always work as well as in the above example cases. Words which intuitively belong to the same grammatical category, such as 'Boolean algebra' and 'Wednesday', which are both common nouns, can be shown to belong to different categories by suitable sentence-frames. 'I visited my aunt last Wednesday' is grammatical, while we would be hard pressed to say the same of 'I visited my aunt last Boolean algebra'. (One way out would be to say that this shows that we need a more fine-grained analysis which lets common nouns referring to abstract objects and those referring to days come out as different *grammatical* categories. But it is not clear whether there is any independent reason for such a distinction.) Of course this is just a problem for the strong reading of the criterion ('two expressions belong to the same grammatical category iff they are intersubstitutable preserving grammaticality in *all* contexts'). So what about restricting to the weak version ('. . . in *some* contexts')? Obviously a single context cannot do, else 'the violin', 'while it is raining outside', and 'because he is bored' would all turn out to belong to the same grammatical category since they can all be plugged in for the blank in the sentence-frame 'Peter plays . . .' to produce grammatical sentences. Thus we need more than one context. Unfortunately it is very difficult to give a precise answer as to how many one needs if intersubstitutability is to work as a criterion for picking out grammatical categories.

§16 Unsatisfying solutions

Because linguists realized the difficulties with the above criterion, they employed various other approaches. A relatively straightforward one is the *notional* criterion.[31] This tries to pick out grammatical categories in terms of the denotations of words. So one will say that verbs are words which denote actions, that nouns denote objects, adjectives states, adverbs manners, prepositions location, and so forth. This is obviously very imprecise and often leads to unwanted results. 'Assassination' is a noun yet stands for an action, so is 'blindness' yet it stands for a state.

Much more popular with linguists is the *morphological* criterion. It is based on the idea that certain types of inflections are attached to

[31] Bradford (1988: 57).

certain grammatical categories only.[32] In English it is only adjectives and adverbs which have a comparative form ending in -er, it is only nouns and verbs that have a plural inflection, and it is only prepositions which are never inflected at all. Unfortunately there are also numerous problems which trouble this approach. There are many adjectives (like 'intelligent', 'annoying') whose comparative is not formed by adding -er. Furthermore, we are presumably talking about the same grammatical category when we are talking about English, French, or German adjectives, but the last two can actually have a plural inflection. If we relied just on the morphological criterion we would then find it difficult to say what makes the classes of English and German adjectives the very same grammatical category.

There are a couple of other approaches, based on such features as stress, pitches, or pauses, but none of these enjoys widespread popularity as a form of determining grammatical categories. Furthermore, given that our interest here is in ontological categories, we are going to disregard accounts such as the preceding ones which either already presuppose ontological distinctions (as the notional criterion) or employ features of the objects characterized which are too specific to be readily generalized (as in the case of the morphological criterion).

Since none of the above ways of defining 'grammatical category' really works, linguists have hit on the somewhat desperate idea that many of them combined will do the trick. For example we find the following definition in Bradford (1988: 63):

A *word-level* category is a set of words which share a set of linguistic (especially morphological and syntactic) properties.

This will do very well as an informal account of what talk about 'grammatical categories' is all about. It will not, however, give us anything like a general definition. First of all, the 'especially' tells us that there are other (linguistic?) properties which have to be taken into account when picking out grammatical categories. How many of them there are and what we should conceive them to be is unclear. More importantly, what happens if the different criteria deliver different results, that is if one criterion says that a set of expressions constitutes a grammatical category and the other says it does not? Combining different obviously deficient criteria does not seem to be the solution.

---

[32] Bradford (1988: 50-7).

§17 Grammatical categories: Husserl's account

It is strange to see that the very first discussion of intersubstitutability as a criterion for picking out grammatical categories, which can be found in Husserl (1922), uses intersubstitutability preserving *meaningfulness* rather than grammaticality to pick out grammatical categories.[33] This has led to much confusion and resulted in interpretations which described his procedure as a device for picking out either grammatical[34] or ontological (often called 'semantic') categories.[35] This is partly to be blamed on Husserl, who rather misleadingly talks of *Bedeutungskategorien* while these are in fact nothing like the 'ranges of significance' which we usually associate with semantic categories. But let us have a look at how he goes about presenting the criterion of intersubstitutability. Discussing the sentence 'This tree is green' he writes:

Within the framework of this form [of 'this *S* is *p*'] we can change our example 'This tree is green' into 'This gold', 'This algebraic number', 'This blue raven etc. is green'. Any nominal material—in a wide sense of nominal material—can be inserted here and so plainly can any adjectival material replace the *p*. In each case we have a unified meaningful signification, i.e. an independent sentence of the prescribed form, but if we depart from the categories to which the meaning-material belongs the unity of sense vanishes. Where there is nominal material we can put any other nominal material, but no adjectival, relational or propositional material. [...] If we freely exchange material from the same category, we might get wrong, stupid or ridiculous meanings, but these are still unified meanings, that is, grammatical expressions the sense of which can be understood. But if we leave the boundaries of the categories this will no longer hold. We can concatenate words like 'this careless is green', 'more intense is round', 'this house equals' [...], but all we achieve is a string of words, such that every word in itself has a meaning, but we do not get a unitary meaning of the whole expression.[36]

Despite the unfortunate use of terminology (he calls the relevant section '*A priori* laws of the combination of meaning') it should be clear that what Husserl is after is to draw a line between a group of sentences which incorporate both normal sentences as well as sentences which we

[33] See Bar-Hillel (1970: 89–97).

[34] Ajdukiewicz (1978: 95), Bar-Hillel (1956–7: 364–5), Gardies (1985: 39–42), Hiż (1960: 311–22), Quine (1986: 18–19).

[35] Lehrberger (1974: 11), Oliver (1999: 254–5).

[36] Husserl (1922: IV: 10: 319–20) (my translation).

usually call semantically anomalous (or sortally incorrect) and a group of sentences which do not have a unified meaning at all. These latter are actually not even sentences but mere concatenations of words which lack a meaning because material from the wrong categories has been substituted in the wrong place (nominal material stands in the place of adjectival material and so on). Thus the purpose of his intersubstitutability-preserving-meaningfulness criterion is to give a procedure for deciding whether a sentence is grammatical (although it may be 'wrong, stupid or ridiculous') or ungrammatical.

Unfortunately Husserl's account does not seem to do any better when confronted with the criticism against the standard account, which uses intersubstitutability preserving *grammaticality* rather than meaningfulness. There are problems for the strong version of Husserl's criterion since the sentence mentioned in § 15 ('I visited my aunt last Boolean algebra') is not just ungrammatical but meaningless. Similarly the weak version is troubled by problems since the substitutions mentioned in the preceding section did not just produce grammatical, but also meaningful sentences.

It should also be noted that any application of the intersubstitutability criterion so far presented relies either on a grammatical or a semantic primitive. On the standard interpretation we need a way of deciding for an arbitrary sentence whether or not it is grammatical. On Husserl's account we need a procedure for telling of any string of expressions whether it is meaningful or not. Needless to say, neither of these should in turn refer to 'grammatical categories' in any way. Thus the impression of creating categories *ex nihilo* to which the intersubstitutability criterion sometimes gives rise is certainly not justified. However, it is not clear whether this is damaging. It might be that the notion of grammatical category is just a systematization of which sentences we intuitively consider to be grammatical.

§18   Ontological categories: getting ontology from grammar?

The third criterion from our above list, namely using intersubstitutability preserving grammaticality to pick out ontological or semantic categories seems never to have been discussed in the literature. This is partly due to a number of problems which such an account would inevitably meet. If we assume the strong version ('two expressions belong to the same ontological category iff they are intersubstitutable in every context') there are obvious simple counterexamples. Presumably 'Queen Elizabeth' and 'the most popular British woman over seventy' belong to the same ontological category (given that they pick out the very same person), but they are not intersubstitutable preserving grammaticality in such contexts as 'Our dear old Queen Elizabeth is a symbol of the unity of the United Kingdom'. Matters do not improve if we go for a weaker version. Certainly intersubstitutability in *one* context will not do in order to guarantee co-categoriality. ('My new haircut' and 'The proof of Fermat's last theorem' both go into the blank in '. . . was the favourite topic of yesterday's conversation over dinner', but this does not show them to belong to the same ontological category.) So again we need more than one context, while it is far from clear in what contexts intersubstitutability is required in order to establish that the corresponding objects belong to a common ontological category.

In fact it should not be too surprising that nobody has yet tried to get a definition of ontological or semantic categories out of the notion of grammaticality, since it is normally assumed that grammar more often hides than reveals such matters and thus is not a good guide to the underlying ontological (or for that matter logical) form.

In fact neither of the two 'mixed' criteria (the second and third in the above list) for picking out grammatical or ontological categories has enjoyed widespread popularity. The grammaticality criterion of ontological categories has never been employed at all, while Husserl's method for trying to get at grammatical categories via the notion of meaningfulness derives all the plausibility it has from a highly non-standard understanding of meaningfulness. For him, all semantically deviant sentences (e.g. 'This blue raven is green') are meaningful. The only things which are not meaningful are combinations of words which fail to link up to a sentence since they cannot express a 'unity of sense'. Only by taking the extension of the property of being a meaningful sentence to be so wide as to include most of what is usually considered to be meaningless can Husserl make his case that meaninglessness coincides with ungrammaticality.

By contrast the final criterion on our list ('defining ontological categories via intersubstitutability preserving meaningfulness') has been quite extensively developed. To the discussion of this we will now turn.

§19   Ontological categories: The Ryle-Sommers account

The most detailed and systematic account which claims to give 'a formal theory of ontological categories and ontological features' based on the notion of intersubstitutability (where ontology is taken as 'the science of categories')[37] is due to Fred Sommers and was presented by him in a number of papers.[38] He draws on material developed by Russell on types[39] and work on category-mistakes first discussed by Ryle (1938) and later famously employed by him in Ryle (1949).

Russell's theory of types, which was conceived as a means for avoiding paradoxes in the foundations of mathematics, is based on the idea of a *significance-range*:

[. . .] whatever function ϕ may be, there will be arguments x with which ϕx is meaningless, i.e. with which as arguments ϕ does not have any value. The arguments with which ϕx has values form what we will call the 'range of significance' of ϕx. A '*type*' is defined as the range of significance of some function.[40]

Ryle's informal account of categories (or types, as he sometimes calls them) rests on an extension of this idea to natural language. Ryle argues that certain substitutions in a sentence just affect its truth-value (that is they turn it from a true sentence into a false sentence or vice versa) while others affect its meaningfulness: they turn it from a meaningful sentence into a meaningless one. Or, to put it differently, only certain ways of filling the gap in a sentence-frame will produce something which can be true or false; for other substitutions the result will not have a truth-value.

To ask the question To what type or category does so-and-so belong? is to ask In what sorts of true or false propositions and in what positions of them can so-and-so enter? Or, to put it semantically, it is to ask In what sorts of non-absurd sentences and in what positions in them can the expression 'so-and-so' enter? and, conversely What sort of sentences would be rendered absurd by the substitution for one of their sentence-factors of the expression 'so-and-so'? [. . .] Two propositions are of different categories or types when the expressions for

---

[37] Sommers (1963: 350–1).
[38] Sommers (1959; 1971).
[39] See e.g. Russell (1903: Appendix B) for a first sketch, Russell (1924), and Whitehead and Russell (1925: I: 37–65) for later developments.
[40] Whitehead and Russell (1925: I: 161).

those factors are imported as alternative complements to the same gap-signs, the resultant sentences are significant in one case and absurd in the other.[41]

Sommers develops this idea by introducing the notion of U-related terms, a notion which he claims 'forms the formal heart' of his account of categories,[42] which is supposed to be 'the systematic attempt to say what categories are, how they are determined, and how they are related to one another'.[43] Two expressions are U-related if they can be used together to form a significant sentence, i.e. if their combination is not nonsensical. Thus we have U(philosopher, confused) but not U(Monday, confused). If one of the two expressions is a predicate and the other a name we may also say that the predicate *spans* the individual and that in general members of ontological categories are spanned by the predicates truly or falsely applicable to them. This is the same as saying that an ontological category is defined by an absolute predicate (if Px is an ordinary predicate, the corresponding absolute predicate $|P|x$ is the predicate which picks out all those objects of which it can be either truly or falsely asserted that they are P).[44] Of course several absolute predicates will pick out the same category, as in the case of $|sad|$, $|alert|$, or $|angry|$. The ontologist is only interested in *kinds* of things, which are picked out by the absolute predicate, and not in their specific characteristics. In this sense, for him $|red|$ means the same as $|green|$.[45]

---

[41] Ryle (1938: 201–3).

[42] Sommers (1963: 334).

[43] Englebretsen (1990: 4).

[44] Sommers (1963: 351).

[45] Some might argue that sentences like 'Monday is confused' or '17 is green' are not meaningless but plainly false. The problem with such an account in the present context is that it will then be necessary to explain why such statements are somehow more grave mistakes than for example 'Monday is the day after Saturday', 'Monday is the third day of the week', or '17 is even'. All of latter are false ('17 is even' arguably even analytically false) but somehow less false than the former. Judgements that one statement is more false than another one and judgements to which extent it is so are undeniably vague, so that people's intuitions on these matters differ. This, however, does not alter the fact that such distinctions exist. They arise from the fact that objects which are very much like Monday or 17 (namely the other days of the week; other natural numbers) do indeed have such properties as being the day after Saturday, being the third day of the week, or being even. The mistake could thus be attributed to our confusing Monday with some other day or 17 with some other number. But no such explanation is forthcoming in the case of 'Monday is confused' or '17 is green'. It is not just the case that Monday fails to be confused, and 17 fails to be green, but all other days of the week fail as well. Monday is just not the *kind* of thing which could be confused, 17 not the *kind* of thing

§20   Smart's criticism

Ryle's informal account of categories has been criticized by J. J. C. Smart in a short paper.[46] In essence the criticism also applies to Sommers, since he employs the same fundamental idea as Ryle. According to Smart there are two main problems with the Ryle-Sommers account:

- We get unintuitive categories. Take the predicate 'has a green back door'. The absolute predicate derived from it will determine an ontological category. But it seems as if the only things of which one could meaningfully affirm or deny that they have a green back door are buildings of one sort or another. Yet we would hardly want to say that 'building' is an ontological category.

- We get too many categories. Consider the property of natural numbers 'can be divided by itself minus 2'. It is clearly true of 4 to say that it has this property, and similarly it is false to say it about (amongst others) 5, 6, and 7. But what about 2? $\frac{2}{0}$ is not defined. So we might say that the sentence '2 can be divided by itself minus 2' is nonsensical. So then there will be a category which contains every natural number apart from 2. But of course we can then repeat the argument for 3. In fact for any pair of natural numbers x, y we can show that they belong to different categories by considering the predicate 'is divisible by itself minus x'. So we can show that every natural number belongs to an ontological category of its own!

The second of these criticisms, which tries to give an arithmetical equivalent of meaningless predications seems to be rather less successful than the first. The sentence '2 can be divided by itself minus 2' claims that there is some natural number that is identical to $\frac{2}{0}$. But since there is no such number, this sentence is just false, not meaningless. The predicate 'can be divided by zero' can be meaningfully applied to all number-terms in the same way in which 'was opened by a move with White's

which could be green. But now we see the appeal to ontological categories already on the horizon, and such an appeal will indeed explain the difference in gravity between the two kinds of mistakes. But of course the point of the present exercise is to *get out* an account of ontological categories, whereas it appears that any treatment of the above kind of meaningless statements which regards them as false needs to assume that this notion is somehow already present.

[46] Smart (1954).

King' can be meaningfully applied to games of chess: it just fails to be true of any of them.

Nevertheless, the first criticism on its own manages to establish that whatever kind of categories Sommers' notion of meaningful and nonsensical expressions manages to pick out, they are at best a superset of the set of ontological categories. The system resulting from Sommers' account contains categories which are much too fine-grained to qualify as ontological.

Ryle's response here seems to be simply to bite the bullet:[47] for him, 'building', 'furniture', and the like all form types. But if we accept this then it will undermine Sommers' idea that results of Ryle could 'be construed as a formal ontology',[48] i.e. that the Rylean types are just the ontological categories.

It is an essential property of any theory of ontological categories that it should not permit kinds which are *too specific*. This is implied by one of the major purposes of constructing such a theory. It is not supposed to be a theory of everything, a detailed outline of the world down to the finest details, but rather an account of the most general (and thus also most fundamental) kinds of things there are. The Rylean account clearly overgenerates in this respect. This is because whenever we have a group of objects which have a property nothing outside the group could share, this group will count as an ontological category. Any definition which has this consequence will therefore have to be rejected as an unsatisfactory account of what an ontological category is.

§21 Carnap's concept of ontological statements

A criterion which bears some similarity to the Ryle-Sommers account (although presented in much less detail) was constructed by Rudolf Carnap when he tried to develop a procedure for distinguishing ontological from non-ontological statements.[49] He considered ontological statements and questions to be those statements or questions about existence which contained expressions which were ultimately general, that is, those which contained a *universal word*.[50]

---

[47] Drange (1966: 75–6).   [48] Sommers (1963: 327).
[49] Carnap (1937: 292–315).   [50] See Norton (1977: 22, 62–5).

Examples of universal words mentioned by Carnap include thing, object, property, fact, condition, process, event, action, spatial point, spatial relation, temporal point, temporal relation, number, function, aggregate or class, and expression.[51] For Carnap, universal words were the natural-language equivalent of *universal predicates*. The notion of a universal predicate can be precisely defined for artificial languages.

Take a set of expressions such that any two members of it can be intersubstituted in any sentence containing either of them preserving grammaticality (Carnap calls such a set a *genus*). A universal predicate for a particular genus is then defined as follows: if Px is any predicate of that genus, a universal predicate P^*x is simply $Px \lor \neg Px$. In a many-sorted language universal predicates make it possible to pick out the various 'sorts' since a universal predicate will apply to all the objects of a particular sort, while applying to no other object. So no matter which predicate of some object of the genus you take, if you form the universal predicate, the set of objects it is true of will always remain the same.

Carnap considered many-sorted languages as the ideal form of expression for ontological theories.[52] In such languages, category-mistakes could not even be expressed.

If grammatical syntax differentiated not only the word-categories of nouns, adjectives, verbs, conjunctions and so forth, but within each of these categories made the further distinctions that are logically indispensable, then no pseudo-statements [like 'Caesar is a prime number'] could be formed. If, for example, nouns were grammatically subdivided into several kinds of words, according as they designated properties of physical objects, of numbers etc., then the words 'general' and 'prime number' would belong to different word-categories and 'Caesar is a prime number' would be just as linguistically incorrect as 'Caesar is and'. Considerations of grammar would already eliminate them as it were automatically, i.e. in order to avoid nonsense, it would be unnecessary to pay attention to the meanings of the words over and above their syntactical type.[53]

A universal word in a natural language, corresponding to a universal predicate in a formal one, is supposed to express a property which belongs analytically to all objects of the genus. Carnap gives the example of the four predicates 'is a dog', 'is an animal', 'is a living being', and 'is a thing'. If we applied these to the dog Caro, he argues, only the last

---

[51] Carnap (1937: 293–4).   [52] See Norton (1977: 21–5).
[53] Carnap (1959: 68).

sentence would be analytic. If we replace 'Caro' by any other thing designation, we get another analytic sentence; if we replace it by a non-thing designation we do not get a sentence at all. Thus something is a universal word iff it applies to all objects in the genus but to none outside.

How does this procedure help us in finding out about various ontological categories? The ideal case would be something like the following. We observe that 'red', 'square', 'heavy', and so on can all be substituted for the last word in 'The bed is soft'. So these properties form a genus. We can now define the universal predicate for this genus (say, 'red or not-red') which has the same extension as a natural language ontological category (say, 'property of concrete objects').

Of course, this crucially depends on our being able to determine which expressions constitute a genus and which do not, and this in turn presupposes a procedure for telling sentences from non-sentences. In many-sorted languages, this is straightforward: the formation-rules will tell us that we may not use particular predicates together with names of a particular sort if we want to produce something which is to count as a sentence. But in natural language the situation is somewhat different. Suppose the formation rules of natural language (namely grammar) allowed us to tell apart mere concatenations of words from sentences (which probably will not work in all cases, but let us ignore this complication here). Then grammar would not tell us that for example 'The bed is converging to zero' is not a sentence, since it is perfectly well-formed, though meaningless. So direct application of Carnap's criterion would let 'converging to zero' come out as a concrete property, which is false.

The obvious alternative would be to take not grammaticality but meaningfulness of a sentence as a criterion (which quickly gets us into something similar to Ryle's and Sommers' analysis). Suppose we say that anything which can complete the sentence-fragment p into a meaningful sentence constitutes a genus (and thus, at the end of the day, an ontological category). Apart from the fact that criteria for telling whether a sentence is meaningful are even more hazy than those for telling whether it is grammatical, we encounter the above problems again if we consider such sentence-fragments as 'has a green back door'. The results are far too fine-grained to function as ontological categories.

But suppose we finally accept *building* and the like as a genus (and perhaps also a lot of others, amongst them *extended object*). We then realize that we can define the universal predicate only for some genera, and not for others. Take any property of buildings (say, 'being less than two metres high') and construct the universal predicate from this ('being less than two metres high or not less than two metres high'). This clearly applies to all buildings but it does not fulfil the other condition on a universal predicate, namely that it cannot be applied to anything outside that genus. It is perfectly true to say of *any* extended object that it is less than two metres high or not less than two metres high. Would it then be possible to select the 'proper' Carnapian genera from the collection of those produced by the Ryle-Sommers account, by using the concept of a universal word as a filter?

We could modify Carnap's distinction by talking of proper and improper genera. A proper genus would be a collection of objects satisfying the criteria for being a genus such that for every predicate Px true of some object in the collection, $P^*x := Px \lor \neg Px$ is a universal predicate, that is P^*x cannot be applied to any object outside the collection. This allows us to filter out all the spurious genera and leaves us only with those which do not share their P^*x with any other.

§22 Metaontological implications of this

However, this procedure also makes evident two problems of Carnap's approach:

- It does not allow there to be proper containment between genera, that is, ontological categories. For if some category A contains other categories B and C, B and C cannot be proper genera since there is at least one predicate ('being a subcategory of A') which cannot be used to construct a universal predicate.

- It does not allow different genera, i.e. different ontological categories, to share a property: if they did, they would not be proper genera since we could not construct the universal property from the shared property.

Whether the Carnapian analysis is successful will thus depend on whether both of the following two metaontological principles are true:

1. No ontological category contains another one.
2. No object in an ontological category shares a property with an object in any other ontological category.

If we deny the first (i.e. say that at least some ontological categories contain others) we also have to deny the second (i.e. say that some objects in different ontological categories can share properties). For clearly if two categories B and C are subcategories of some category A, there is at least one thing they have in common (namely being A) so that B and C could not be categories in the first place.[54] Obviously, Carnap's account is in harmony with this, since it denies both 1 and 2.

§23   Containment of categories

The above two metaontological principles are sufficiently implausible to make Carnap's account unsatisfactory. First of all they contradict examples of systems of ontological categories we actually encounter, where for example the categories of events, material objects, and tropes are included in the category of objects in time, or where facts, sets, and propositions are contained in the category of abstract objects. It is evident that Carnap's principles are not satisfied by the examples of ontological systems given in § 1. In CHISHOLM the category of individuals includes boundaries and substances, so that members of both have the common property of being individuals. For GROSSMANN, sets and facts are contained in the category of complex entities, and thus particular sets and particular facts share the property of being complex. Similar points can be made about HOFFMAN/ROSENKRANTZ, LOWE, and CYC.[55]

Secondly it is hard to see the justification of the above metaontological principles independently of the job they do in fixing problems of the Ryle-Sommers account. We argued above that systems of ontological categories are systematizations of our intuitions about generality, intersubstitutability, and identity. Clearly none of these manage on their own to enforce the metaontological principles 1 and 2. Considering generality, it is clear that two most general sets can share a property, as can two objects having the same criterion of identity. The metaontological principles 1 and 2 were a consequence of an attempt to cut back the

---

[54] The reverse does not hold: objects from different ontological categories can share properties without any category containing any other.

[55] For intuitive counterexamples against principle 2 which are independent of our reservations against principle 1 see § 25.

radically proliferating collection of ontological categories churned out by the Ryle-Sommers account. But in order to show that this cure is not worse than the disease it is surely necessary to show that the fact that systems of ontological categories are systematizations of certain intuitions about generality, intersubstitutability, and identity supports—contrary to the evidence provided by the examples of systems of ontological categories presented above—the restrictions on containment and shared properties; or else we must give some independent argument for the truth of them.

Such an argument is not forthcoming.[56] We therefore conclude that the Carnapian way of repairing an account of ontological categories in terms of intersubstitutability is not satisfactory. This does not bode well for attempts at constructing a theory of ontological categories based on the notion of substitution—at least not in the form in which they are presented above. Nevertheless, the notion of intersubstitutability seems to be at the heart of the concept of a category, and it is therefore not without justification that it is employed in influential accounts of grammatical and ontological categories. Our positive account described in chapter IV will use it at an important point. Nevertheless, as we have just seen, this notion, like that of generality, is not on its own able to provide us with a satisfactory account of ontological categories, be it because it includes categories that are too special (as in the case of the Ryle-Sommers account), or be it for structural reasons (as in Carnap's case).

We will therefore conclude our examination of different accounts of ontological categories by considering in the next part a further family, based on the notion of identity. Before we do this, however, let us look briefly at another example of a possible structural constraint on systems of ontological categories.

[56] The only plausible argument I can think of for an exclusive picture of categories as enforced by Carnap's principles comes from the principle of homogeneity forming part of the Russellian theory of types. This principle says roughly that if some function is significant for two different arguments, the set of *other* functions which are significant for the first is the same as the set of functions which are significant for the second: it therefore enforces that any two types which have a common member coincide and that any two different types are mutually exclusive. But the principle of homogeneity is fraught with so many difficulties (see e.g. Halldén (1949: 72–9), Black (1944), Routley and Routley (1969: 22)), and is moreover not even necessary as a paradox-blocking device within the theory of types (Potter (2000: 146)), that I do not think a good defence for Carnap's metaontological assumptions can be based on it.

§24 Sommers' law

We just saw that the constraints Carnap's principles imposed on the structure of systems of ontological categories could not be integrated into a plausible account of such categories. There is another constraint, however, for which the situation is different. This constraint is discussed by Fred Sommers in his treatment of types and is sometimes referred to as *Sommers' law*.[57] It says that two ontological categories cannot overlap, they are either disjoint or one properly includes the other. This means that the containment structure of a system of ontological categories is a tree, rather than a lattice. If we picture the containment relation by a descending arrow, then Sommers' law rules out that three categories A, B, and C can be related in the following 'V-shaped' way:

But why should Sommers' law be taken as a plausible constraint on the structure of systems of ontological categories? There are three main reasons for this.

The first is that the tree structure is fairly widespread in the examples of systems of ontological categories presented in chapter I, § 1. Of the examples which allowed containment of categories, all had the structure of trees (TEGTMEIER constituted a forest) with the exception of CYC. This, however, may well be attributed to the fact that CYC is trying to produce not just a system of ontological categories but, more importantly, a workable basis for knowledge engineering within an extremely complex computer program. This may well force one to adopt otherwise undesirable structures to ensure that the system runs smoothly.

Secondly Sommers' law allows us to prove a number of nice technical results about the structure of systems of ontological categories in which it holds. Amongst other things we can show that every set of categories ordered by containment has exactly one maximum and some minimal elements. This is again a property which is very common in the examples of systems of ontological categories we discussed.

[57] Sommers (1963: 355).

A final reason is derived from work of the developmental psychologist Frank Keil, who conducted a series of empirical investigations into what he calls the 'M constraint' (i.e. the fact that containment structures on ontological categories do not contain M- or W-shaped substructures and are therefore trees, not lattices).[58] These studies, conducted with both children and adults, seem to confirm that people's intuitions about copredication of terms do not generate structures which violate the M constraint and thus Sommers' law. In the studies conducted with adults, between 80 and 90 per cent of the subjects made judgements in accordance with Sommers' law.[59] It could also be shown that the probability of generating graphs obeying the M constraint by chance rapidly decreases when the number of terms exceeded about 7×7.[60] Experiments with speakers of different languages confirmed that 'different syntactic formats and a different language had little effect on the patterns of development'.[61]

It could thus be argued that categorizations with non-overlapping categories (which are hierarchies and not lattices) are particularly psychologically natural.[62] Keil also suggests that a preference for a non-overlapping categorization could be regarded as an *a priori* constraint on the acquisition of complex, structured knowledge, similar to the putative constraints linguistics appeals to in explaining the acquisition of language.[63]

Unlike the structural demand for disjoint categories implied by Carnap's principles, excluding overlapping ontological categories therefore seems to be both in accordance with the examples of systems of ontological categories discussed in chapter I, and independently justifiable. It would thus be attractive if an otherwise successful account of ontological categories also obeyed Sommers' law.

After having thus discussed a plausible constraint on the structure of systems of ontological categories, let us consider a final family of

---

[58] Keil (1979: 17–18).
[59] Keil (1979: 31, 42).
[60] Keil (1979: 177-9).
[61] Keil (1979: 117). For the rôle of this principle in lexical semantics see Cruse (1986: 152–3).
[62] Keil (1979: 18).
[63] Keil (1979: 64–5).

approaches trying to account for the notion of an ontological category, this time based on the notion of identity.

4 ACCOUNTS IN TERMS OF IDENTITY

It seems to be uncontroversial that the notion of an ontological category is closely connected with that of identity. There have been attempts at exploiting this connection in order to construct an account of ontological categories. The idea here is that two objects belong to the same ontological category if their criteria of identity are the same.[64] This seems to be an attractive position for

> we are surely inclined to say of rabbits and dogs, battles and weddings, even numbers and odd numbers that these are six sorts of things, but of only three categories or ultimate sorts.[65]

Conversely, we would want to claim that if objects have different criteria of identity, they belong to different categories. For example, we could argue on this basis that sets and clubs belong to different categories. Sets have a very clear criterion of identity, encoded in the axiom of extensionality: two sets are the same iff whenever something is a member of the one, it is also a member of the other. But it is obvious that this does not provide an adequate criterion for the identity of clubs: the same club can have different members (at different moments in time) and the very same group of persons can form two different clubs.

§25 The Frege-Dummett account

We shall first examine an account which ultimately goes back to Frege's *Grundlagen*. There he claimed that if we employ a sign a to refer to some object, we need a procedure such that it is in principle possible to tell for any b whether it is the same as a.[66] Furthermore, Frege's attempt to use a criterion of identity to define that which is identical (such as 'having the same direction' to define 'parallel', or 'being equinumerous' to define 'number')[67] seems to imply that different sorts of objects have

---

[64] See e.g. Lowe (2001: 179).
[65] Stevenson (1976: 516).
[66] Frege (1986: § 63), see also Dummett (1981: 179).
[67] Frege (1986: §§ 64–8).

different criteria of identity.[68] If two different sorts of objects a and b had the same criterion of identity, it would obviously not do to try to define one sort by appealing to this criterion, since in this case the other sort would invariably be included in the definition.

This idea has been systematized by Dummett into an account of ontological categories which we will call the *Frege-Dummett account*.[69] Dummett argues that particular names (such as 'man', 'woman', and 'tailor') can have the very same criterion of identity. This, according to him, is due to the fact that 'Peter is the same man (tailor) as Paul' can be spelt out as 'Peter is a man (tailor) and Peter is the same *person* as Paul'.

More precisely, Dummett considers the union of sets of equivalence classes under particular sortal identity relations $=_{\phi_1}, \ldots, =_{\phi_n}$ which are peculiar in the following way: for each expression $a =_{\phi_i} b$ we can substitute $\phi_i a \wedge a =_\chi b$, where χ is a predicate such that for all predicates ϕ_i, and all objects x if $\phi_i x$, then χx, but not vice versa.[70] Furthermore, χ must be the *most general* predicate for which this holds. Obviously this predicate χ will then be applicable to all the objects in this union which constitutes, according to Dummett, an ontological category. The predicate χ is then also the *most general* predicate applicable to any object in the union.[71]

Dummett admits that

it may require discussion to identify these most general terms: one might at first be uncertain, for example, whether or not the criterion for 'same person' was always the same as that for 'same animal', or, again, whether or not there exists a general criterion for 'same organism' to which 'same animal' is subordinate (in the sense that 'is the same animal as' could be equated with 'is an animal and is the same organism as'). But that it must be possible to identify such most general terms, one for each criterion of identity that is employed, it seems impossible to doubt.[72]

---

[68] Dummett (1981: 75–6).

[69] Dummett (1981: 75–80).

[70] Dummett is unclear on whether there will always be such a χ. Sometimes he seems to agree (1981: 75, 552), sometimes he only claims that it will exist 'often' or 'normally' (1981: 546).

[71] He distinguishes categorial predicates from *sortal predicates* by claiming that only objects picked out by the latter can have one criterion of identity at one time and another one at another time (Dummett 1981: 76). There are close connections here to the notion of impredicability discussed in Sayward and Voss (1972).

[72] Dummett (1981: 75–6).

It has been argued by Stevenson that this account is unsatisfactory since 'it presupposes [. . .] that we have a way of telling, in general, whether one sortal supplies the same criterion of identity as another, i.e. that we have a criterion of identity for criteria of identity.'[73]

In fact this question can be answered in the way Dummett proposed. If we have a set of sortals, such as 'battle', 'war', and 'funeral', and want to find out whether the objects falling under them belong to the same ontological category, we can ask whether there is some common χ which allows for a 'reduction' of identity statements involving these sortals in the above way. In a similar way we can try to settle whether all things falling under a certain sortal, such as 'material object', really belong to the same ontological category by trying to find a sortal s which is properly included in 'material object' such that 'is the same s as' cannot be spelt out as 'is an s and is the same material object as'.

Of course the definition does not answer these questions for us. All it does (and all it could be asked to do) is to provide a test which we can apply to settle questions of sameness or difference of ontological category. That it is a further matter to ascertain the outcome of the test is entirely unproblematic as long as determining the outcome of the test does not circularly involve that we already have an answer to the question which we are about to settle (which is not the case with the above definition).

However, one might suspect that 'having the same criterion of identity' is only a symptom of 'belonging to the same ontological category' and cannot be used in a definition covering all cases of the latter. This is due to a problem which we have already met a couple of times in the course of our investigations.

If there are ontological categories which are more general than others, the Frege-Dummett account cannot be satisfactory since it will not deliver all ontological categories. Suppose there is some most general category including all others such as 'entity'. In this case *any* sortal identity statement '$a =_\phi b$' can be spelt out as 'is a ϕ and is the same *entity* as' so that 'entity' comes out as the only ontological category. But even in cases which are not as extreme as this one the problem remains. If there is any category more general than another one the Frege-Dummett account will deliver only the more general one, since we always have to

[73] Stevenson (1976: 516).

look for the most general χ for which the 'reduction' works. The Frege-Dummett account has to presuppose that all ontological categories are on the same level of generality, an assumption which is not justified by the examples of systems of ontological categories we presented earlier. As a theory of ontological categories it fails to account for an important and widespread property of these, namely that some of them stand in containment relations.

Moreover, according to the Frege-Dummett account ontological categories cannot share properties. Suppose there are categories χ_1, χ_2 which have some property ϕ in common. Then consider the category χ_3 'object to which ϕ applies'. χ_3 can be plugged in for both χ_1 and χ_2 in all 'reduced' identity statements in which they occur. But this implies that χ_1, χ_2 could not have been ontological categories.

This last fact does not seem to accord well with what we normally take categories to be for. It seems that we put objects into different categories because there is some fundamental difference between *some* of their properties (numbers have successors, facts do not, events can be interrupted, tropes cannot), but this does not mean that there are *no* properties which they share (numbers and facts are abstract, events and tropes have a spatial location). A fundamental difference between objects does not mean that they differ in every property whatsoever, but that there are certain key properties which only the one but not the other can have.

§26 Ultimate sortals

The same problems come up again in connection with work on the formal structure of sortals, in particular in that of Wiggins (1971: 27–40) and Stevenson (1975). The notion which interests us here is that of an *ultimate sortal*. This is considered 'to give the criterion of identity of everything it applies to, and of all sortals subordinate to it'.[74] As such this kind of sortal, which corresponds to the predicate χ discussed above, has a connection with ontological categories which other sortals lack. It is a kind of 'master sortal' which settles the identity conditions for all sortals included in it.

---

[74] Stevenson (1975: 187). See particularly the discussion on p. 187 and on pp. 195–9.

Two assumptions are generally made about sortals:

[SUBORDINATION]   If two sortals S, T intersect there is a sortal U to which both are subordinate.[75]

[REGULARITY]   There are no infinitely ascending chains of subordination, i.e. there are some sortals which are subordinate to no other sortal. These are the ultimate sortals.[76]

The following facts about ultimate sortals are simple consequences of these two principles:

1. No ultimate sortal can be subordinate to any other ultimate sortal.
2. Any two distinct ultimate sortals are disjoint.[77]
3. Each object cannot belong to more than one ultimate sortal.[78]

Now although the idea of equating ontological categories with ultimate sortals might seem quite attractive because of the rôle ultimate sortals play in identity statements (which are in turn closely connected to ontological categories), the above three facts show that the concept of an ultimate sortal cannot be a satisfactory explication of the notion of an ontological category.

1 is exactly the problem we encountered before in our discussion of the Frege-Dummett account. 3 is also problematic, since usually systems of ontological categories assume that objects can belong to more than one ontological category (for example if one less general category is included in a more general one). 2 is presumably the least harmful, depending on one's position on whether ontological properties can properly overlap.

Given that the same problems we encountered with the Frege-Dummett account turn up in attempts at equating ontological categories with ultimate sortals, we can conclude that the notion of identity—at least on its own—cannot provide us with a satisfactory account of ontological categories.

---

[75] Stevenson (1975: 187), Wiggins (1971: 33).
[76] Stevenson (1975: 187). For a defence see Wiggins (1971: 71).
[77] Stevenson (1975: 3.5.5, 4.1.1).
[78] Stevenson (1975: 4.1.2).

§27   Essential properties

An attempt to avoid the above problems connected with identifying ontological categories with ultimate sortals consists in arguing that 'being an ultimate sortal' is merely a sufficient, but not a necessary condition. In order to get a condition which is necessary as well, the candidate set is enlarged by adding *essential kinds*.[79] For example, given the fact that 'event' is subordinate to 'concrete object', 'event' cannot be an ontological category. However, we might argue that 'event' is an essential kind, which means that anything which belongs to it could not cease to belong to it without ceasing to exist. This has the advantage of enlarging the set of ontological categories and thus allowing for containment between them. Furthermore, it appears to be intuitively plausible that the ontological category some thing belongs to is an essential kind. No thing, one might argue, could 'move' to another category without ceasing to exist.

However, this enlargement of the set of candidates for ontological categories brings with it a problem we have already met. Essential kinds can be very specific, and arguably too specific for our purposes.[80] 'Having a blade or a handle' constitutes an essential kind for knives and 'being colder than 25 degrees Celsius' an essential kind for snowballs. However, we would hardly want to claim that the set of things which are colder than 25 degrees Celsius constitutes an ontological category. Including the essential kinds in our definition solves problems due to the too restrictive nature of the Frege–Dummett account, but only at the price of overgenerating and introducing categories that are too specific.

The accounts based on the notion of identity therefore do not seem to be too promising either, mainly because they imply restrictions on the sets of ontological categories which are not in harmony with structural features of systems of ontological categories discussed in chapter I. But if all the accounts discussed above fail to deliver a satisfactory definition of 'ontological category', what is actually behind this notion? In the following chapter we will discuss a theory of ontological categories which escapes the problems of those previously discussed and gives us some insight into their nature and origin.

---

[79] Stevenson (1977: 283), Wiggins (1971: 32).   [80] See § 20.

III

A world of states of affairs

In the preceding chapter we argued for four main theses:

- The accounts of ontological categories in terms of generality, dependence, and conceptual containment are unsatisfactory because they are faced with the *cut-off point problem*: they do not provide an account of how far down the partial order we are allowed to go and still be sure that we are dealing with ontological categories.

- The Ryle-Sommers account picks out too many categories for them all to be ontological. Even if we agree that it manages to pick out a proper superset of the ontological categories, it is not able to tell us where the line should be drawn.

- Carnap's criterion entails implausible metaontological properties. In particular it is incompatible with the ontological categories being a particular kind of significance-ranges as the Ryle-Sommers account would have it, for these are allowed to contain one another.

- The same is true for the accounts in terms of identity. According to them, no ontological categories can contain one another.

We can summarize these by saying that there are two main problems which trouble the accounts of ontological categories we have encountered so far. They are either not able to draw the line between ontological and non-ontological categories with sufficient precision and hence cannot solve the cut-off point problem (e.g. Norton, Katz, Ryle, and Sommers) or they have to adopt rather unattractive restrictions on the structure of systems of ontological categories (e.g. Carnap).

Our aim is to develop an account of ontological categories which manages to escape these two problems and which also has a number of interesting philosophical implications. This will be done in this and in the following chapter. The present chapter will elucidate and justify the basis of our account, which is the concept of a state of affairs. The next chapter will then give a detailed theory of ontological categories relying on this concept.

1 THE CENTRALITY OF STATES OF AFFAIRS

Our theory will start from the fundamental notion of a state of affairs. Taking states of affairs as primitive is by no means a minority position in ontology. Examples of four fully worked-out very different ontological theories which nevertheless agree in taking the notion of a state of affairs as basic can be found in Wittgenstein,[1] Bacon,[2] Meixner,[3] and Armstrong.[4]

But what is the appeal of such a 'factualist', rather than 'thingist' view of the world?[5]

We can distinguish two major kinds of argument for assigning states of affairs a special rôle in ontology. The first, which we will call the *cognitional* kind, argues from facts about our cognitive contact with the world to adopting states of affairs as the most plausible primitive of our ontological theory. The second kind of argument will be called *semantic*, since arguments belonging to it all rely on the link between sentences and states of affairs assumed by many prominent semantic theories. Amongst the semantic arguments we can distinguish those based on the idea that states of affairs are necessitated by the form of any satisfactory *theory of the world*, and those which argue from the *priority of sentence-meaning* to the privileged status of states of affairs in our theories of the world. As will become clear in a moment, the cognitional argument and the second kind of semantic argument are structurally similar since they try to reason from the alleged plausibility of a particular principle which asserts the priority of the whole over its constituents in epistemology and semantics to its plausibility in ontology.[6] We will discuss both the cognitional and the semantic kind of argument for factualism in turn.

---

[1] Wittgenstein (1989).
[2] Bacon (1995).
[3] Meixner (1997).
[4] Armstrong (1997).
[5] The terms are due to Armstrong (1997: 4).
[6] This 'complex principle' will be discussed in detail in §§ 30–5.

§28 Cognitional arguments

Cognitional arguments are based on a specific account of perception, which assumes that we perceive the world by perceiving complexes, which are then analysed into parts, rather than perceiving it as parts, which are later synthesized into complexes.[7] The conflict between these two different views of perception is exemplified by two opposed psychological approaches which were particularly dominant towards the end of the nineteenth century. One is *associationist* psychology which traces its intellectual ancestry back to Hume and the English empiricists and formed the foundation of modern experimental psychology as developed *inter alia* by Wilhelm Wundt.[8] Its fundamental idea was a sort of perceptual atomism which conceived of psychological phenomena as being made up of discrete, ultimate elements (such as sensations of individual cutaneous spots, points in the visual field, or elementary auditory experiences) which are unified by association, i.e. by the fact that different such perceptual elements are in close spatio-temporal or causal relations, are related as part and whole, resemble one another, and so on.[9]

This view of the constitution of the mental is contradicted by Gestalt psychology, founded by Christian von Ehrenfels in his 1890 paper 'Über "Gestaltqualitäten"'.[10] Gestalt psychology denies that all perception can be explained in atomistic terms. It is based on the idea that in many cases the whole of a perceptual complex is prior to its parts. It argues that the parts of a perception can be *discerned* within the whole experienced, without supposing that the whole is *made up* of these parts.

---

[7] Carnap's system presented in the *Aufbau* famously rests on such an account of perception. He employs the primitive notion of an elementary experience which cannot be subdivided further but constitutes the epistemic foundation of our knowledge of the world. Elementary experiences are 'objects which do not have directly accessible parts or properties but which are only given as compounds and thus can only be treated in a synthetic manner' (Carnap 1928: 94). Their parts or properties can only be determined as *abstractions* from the elementary experiences.

[8] Wundt (1902–1903). Compare for example the following passage in Hume (2000: I: iv: 5): '[. . .] since all our perceptions are different from each other, and from every other thing else in the universe, they are also distinct and separable, and may be considered as separately existent, and have no need of any thing else to support their existence'.

[9] Hamilton (1959–60: lectures 31–2).

[10] von Ehrenfels (1890). See Ash (1995) for a comprehensive history of Gestalt psychology.

The standard example of such a Gestalt complex is a melody or musical phrase. For an associationist, a melody would be an aggregate of individual tones, one following the other. For him our awareness of the melody is based on the process of a gradual addition of individual auditory sensations in our mind. But, von Ehrenfels pointed out, such an understanding of melodies is deeply unsatisfactory. For the associationist, only a single tone would be present in our mind at a single moment. In perceiving a melody, however, we do not just perceive the present tone or perhaps the one immediately before it, but an entire sequence of tones, the musical phrase, is present in our awareness of the present tone simultaneously. We do not hear the sequence of tones one by one but rather identify it as a structural feature in the unitary complex of auditory perception. Perceiving a melody as a sequence of tones (for example in order to write it down in musical notation) is something we have to practise explicitly.[11]

An argument for the privileged status of facts, based on such a Gestalt-theoretic view of perception can be found in Erik Stenius's commentary on Wittgenstein's *Tractatus*.[12] He argues against an atomistic picture of perception which understands the perception of an object as putting together distinct perceptions of the parts of the object. For Stenius, perception of the whole is both temporally and conceptually prior to the perception of its parts.[13] He calls this complex our 'field of perception', and assumes that it is at first perceived in an unanalysed form and later structured by distinguishing different bits within it. This structuring is not always unique. Stenius discusses the example of a diagram consisting of eight parallel lines, which can be seen either as consisting of eight lines, or of four narrow bands, or three broad brands flanked by two lines.[14]

Stenius then draws a parallel between the field of perception and states of affairs.[15] In the same way as the field of perception is primary in epistemology and constitutes the basis of subsequent structuring, he argues, so the state of affairs is primary in ontology and its constituents are determined by abstraction from it. The idea is to move from the priority of one sort of complex to the priority of another one. If the complex is prior to its constituents in our perception, Stenius argues,

---

[11] See Katz (1951: 38–9).   [12] Stenius (1960: 23–8).   [13] Stenius (1960: 24).
[14] Stenius (1960: 24, fig. 1).   [15] Stenius (1960: 26–7).

the closest equivalent to such a complex in the world (namely the state of affairs) can plausibly be considered to be prior to *its* constituents as well.

I think the parallel between the concepts of a field of perception and of a state of affairs is indeed sufficiently close to allow such a transition. Whether Stenius's argument is convincing then hinges on whether our perception does indeed work in the way described by him, rather than in an atomistic fashion, which assembles complex perceptions from simpler ones.

The plausibility of this view of perception depends on the senses we consider. Stenius confines himself to vision, and indeed it seems to be the case that an atomistic account of perception makes little sense in the case of sight. If we perceive a painting (for example a still life) we do not first perceive that it depicts a glass, and a plate of cakes, and a bunch of flowers, and that it depicts them as arranged in a certain fashion on a table; rather we perceive the whole arrangement and subsequently identify its different parts. The same can be argued for the perception of sounds (in fact, as noted above, the perception of melodies is usually taken to be *the* example of the perception of Gestalt properties).

An atomistic model of perception appears more plausible in the case of touch, taste, and smell. If we feel a pointed shape, do we not perceive something simple rather than something complex? And how could smelling strawberries or tasting something bitter possibly be regarded as a complex perception? Of course it may be argued that perception by touch is indeed complex, not only giving us information about shape, but also about texture, temperature, and vibration at the same time. Smell similarly leaves the possibility of such complexity open, at least in the case of organisms with a more sophisticated sense of smell than humans. Taste perception seems to be genuinely atomistic, but is hardly something we would want to select as a representative example of how we perceive the world.

Let us try to construct a perceptual scenario as close as possible to an atomistic one. Consider how a blind person would perceive the bronze model of the Cambridge city centre which can be found on Senate House Hill by touch. He might first determine the shape of King's College Chapel, then that of Great St Mary's, then the distance between the two, and so on, until he has a complete mental image of the city and its main buildings. Clearly this is a case where the constituents of a complex are perceived first, and the complex is only perceived temporally and conceptually *after* its constituents. Therefore genuinely atomistic perception can and does happen. But it is not evident that this invalidates Stenius's argument for the existence of the complex principle relative to human perception. All that seems to be required for this is arguing that the non-atomistic form of perception is the most common or most important one.

It indeed seems reasonable to argue that those senses for which a non-atomistic interpretation is most plausible (i.e. sight and hearing) are the dominant ones. Most information about the world comes to us through sight or hearing, rather than through touch, smell, or taste. Vision dominates all of the other senses: the informational capacity of sight is about 500–600 times that of hearing.[16] Stenius is therefore justified in concentrating on cases of vision. Even if not all our perception of the world proceeds in the same fashion, visual perception (and thus perception satisfying the complex principle) accounts for the greatest part of our information about the world.

There also seems to be an argument that an atomistic account of perception could not even in principle account for all our perceptions. While information about some visual aspects of the world can be delivered in atomistic form (as in the case of the bronze model), certain Gestalt properties could not properly be perceived in an atomistic fashion. There is no tactile equivalent to visual ambiguities such as the Necker cube.[17]

Similarly it is interesting to note that sight and hearing allow us to track and reidentify objects through time, while touch, taste, and smell are not very well equipped to do this. We might argue that this is because touch and taste cannot operate at a distance, while the sense of smell is not very well developed in humans. However, it might also be that this is because sight and touch primarily perceive complexes rather than 'atomic' sensations, which enables them to reidentify objects through the interrelations with other objects in the visual field perceived.

[16] Ditchburn (1987: 795).

[17] See Hoffman (1998: ch. 7) for a possible example of a tactile ambiguity in the case of patients with phantom limbs. The example described there could, however, also be described as the patient's experiencing two different tactual perceptions in rapid succession. This seems different from the visual case: seeing a circle and a square projected onto a wall in quick alternation is not an example of a visual ambiguity—in this case we would not assume to be dealing with *the same* object which somehow had two different shapes.

Although both of these points are far from being a conclusive argument for the correctness of Gestalt theory they might serve as a starting point for arguing that human perception is not just contingently non-atomistic, because it primarily relies on sight and hearing, but that there might be a reason why non-atomistic forms of perceptions are more successful means of representing the world than atomistic ones.

After the first wave of 'classical' Gestalt theory in the initial half of the twentieth century Gestalt theoretic considerations appear to become increasingly important in contemporary cognitive science. Work on 'naive physics' as a theory of the commonsense world given to us in pre-theoretic experience provides interesting links between Gestalt theory, ontology, and Artificial Intelligence,[18] Gestalt aspects become increasingly important in contemporary theories of vision,[19], and attempts have been made to integrate them into theories of parallel distributed processing considered in neuroscience.[20] Despite its occasional portrayal as an account of mainly historical interest Gestalt theory is an important theoretical approach in current theories of cognition, even though its implications for a theory based on states of affairs have not been much discussed elsewhere.[21]

Let us note finally that if we argue for the centrality of states of affairs on such cognitive, Gestalt theoretic grounds by proposing that states of affairs provide the primary epistemic point of contact between us and the world we have to be aware what implications this has for the *kinds* of states of affairs we are justified in postulating. One important case is that of merely possible states of affairs. No plausible epistemology I am aware of provides us with a good account of direct acquaintance with non-actual states of affairs. All that comes into contact with our five senses is what is, rather than what is not, but could (or should) be. All of our frequent references to merely possible states of affairs should therefore be understood as a mere manner of speaking about *rearrangements* of bits of actual states of affairs.[22] When I refer to a state of affairs

---

[18] Smith and Casati (1994).

[19] See Spillmann (1997) for an overview.

[20] van Leeuwen (1989). For some critical assessment of 'neo-Gestalt' theories see Henle (1989).

[21] With the possible exception of Barwise and Perry (1983); for more on this see § 95.

[22] See Armstrong (1990).

in which it is snowing in Oxford on the 23rd of March (while it is in fact dry) I talk about a recombination of the elements of two states of affairs, that in which it is dry on the 23rd, and that on which it snows on some other day. We just regard merely possible states of affairs as the ontological analogue to anagrams: recombinations of bits of complexes we are directly acquainted with. This also implies that talk about merely possible *objects* should be construed in the same way. If I refer to the merely possible state of affairs in which a unicorn is walking down Merton Street, what I have in mind is a recombination of objects from obtaining states of affairs (such as Merton Street and the property of walking) together with one object which is constructed from properties found in actual states of affairs (horseness, whiteness, having one horn . . .). The only states of affairs our cognitive argument justifies are therefore actual states of affairs. By constructions like the above, however, we can make sense of merely possible states of affairs and merely possible objects in a fictionalist manner by regarding them as constructions from their actual counterparts.

§29   Semantic arguments

Semantic arguments for factualism agree in accepting two premisses: firstly, that sentences are somehow privileged when compared to their constituents, and secondly that sentences are to language what states of affairs are to the world. It is then concluded that the privileged status of sentences is transmitted to states of affairs, thereby supporting factualism. Of course neither of the premisses is uncontentious; we will, however, refrain from challenging the second (as we refrained from challenging Stenius's connection of fields of perception with states of affairs). In fact the second premiss is intuitively quite plausible. States of affairs have a certain structural similarity with sentences (at least on the Bloomfeldian picture of sentences). Just as sentences are the largest grammatical unit which cannot be embedded into an item of another grammatical category, states of affairs cannot form parts of an ontological category other than themselves. Even states of affairs consisting of other states of affairs are still states of affairs.

But let us consider the first premiss more closely and investigate the reasons for assigning a privileged status to sentences. As noted on page 66 there are two kinds of reason usually discussed; one based on the idea of a satisfactory theory of the world, the other on the priority of sentence-meaning. We will discuss these in turn.

In his commentary on the *Tractatus* Max Black considers the problem of giving a comprehensive description of the entirety of the actual universe.[23] One way of doing this would be to give a list of all the things which exist. But such a list of names would not yet be a comprehensive description of the world.[24] We would want to add one or more of the following statements:

- All the things mentioned in the list exist.
- The things mentioned in the list are *all* the things which exist.
- The things mentioned in the list stand in a number of relations, which can be specified as follows: . . .

Since all these statements incorporate the list of names, we can restrict our comprehensive account of the world to one or all of the three statements. And since statements like the above are indispensable, our account of the world will necessarily be formulated as a set of sentences, rather than as a list of names. Since sentences correspond to states of affairs, our world has to consist of states of affairs, rather than of individual things (in which case our theory of the world *could* have taken the form of a list of names).

Black does not seem to have been too impressed by his own argument, which he considered as somehow question-begging.

One might be inclined to say that a special use of 'universe', to *mean* an aggregate of facts, rather than an aggregate of things, has somewhere been smuggled in. If you start by thinking of the universe as a thing, *summa rerum*, the all inclusive list will seem perfectly adequate; only if you somewhere find yourself induced to think of a universe as a fact, will the idea of the list seem unsatisfactory.[25]

I fail to see the temptation of regarding the universe as an 'aggregate of things' in this context. The only sense I can make of this is as a mereological fusion of all the objects in the universe. But the description of this will clearly not do as a comprehensive description of the universe, since mereological composition notoriously disregards most of the structure of the items summed: a Lego house and a Lego car made from the

[23] Black (1966: 29–31).   [24] Griffin (1964: 31).   [25] Black (1966: 30).

same blocks will be the same fusion of blocks.[26] Regarding the universe as a fact thus does not appear to be 'smuggling in' dubious assumptions, but rather does justice to the structured nature of the world, which is more like a wall built from bricks than an unstructured heap of stones.

The above argument from the form of a comprehensive theory of the world therefore seems to be a good reason for introducing states of affairs into our ontology. It also provides us with a reason for taking them as a primitive, since the sentences in our world-description (corresponding to states of affairs) incorporate the names (corresponding to things), but not vice versa. What it does not do, however, is to serve as evidence for the epistemic priority of states of affairs. That sentences are indispensable for a comprehensive description of the world and that therefore states of affairs must be parts of the world does not imply that these are prior in the order of cognition. It may equally be the case that we know the things in the world first, and only subsequently put together information about the states of affairs in the world which they constitute.

We will show in the remainder of this section how a second semantic argument also manages to support the claim of the epistemic priority of states of affairs. This second argument is based on a *molecular theory of meaning*.[27] Such a theory holds that the sentence, the complex, is the primary bearer of meaning, while the meaning of its constituents is only determined derivatively according to the rôle they play in the sentence.

Quine subscribes to such a molecular theory of meaning in his account of stimulus meaning. For him, language is connected with the world via the link between observation sentences and perceptual stimuli. This connection is primitive and fundamental for Quine, not the result of associating parts of the sentence with parts of the perceptual stimulation. It is the entire sentence which acquires its meaning via the association with the stimulus. Without this there would be no possibility of talking about the meanings of its constituents in any way.[28]

---

[26] For some arguments regarding the adequacy of mereology as the only composition operation see Lewis (1986b).

[27] Molecular theories of meaning find their obvious syntactic counterparts in molecular theories of grammar which consider 'sentence' to be the primary syntactical category, from which all other categories are derived. This is done for example in certain versions of categorial grammar. See Ajdukiewicz (1967).

[28] See Quine (1960: 26–30).

Davidson's philosophy of language has similar implications. He argues that language and the world are linked via the notion of truth, and as only entire sentences can be true or false, the semantically primitive language-world contact is made at the level of sentences:

Words have no function save as they play a rôle in sentences: their semantic features are abstracted from the semantic features of sentences [. . .]. If the name 'Kilimanjaro' refers to Kilimanjaro, then there is no doubt there is *some* relation between English (or Swahili) speakers, the world, and the mountain. But it is inconceivable that one should be able to explain this relation without first explaining the rôle of the word in sentences [. . .].[29]

Thirdly it is important to note that a molecular theory of meaning is also directly involved in familiar attempts to construe sentences or propositions in terms of sets of possible worlds.[30] If we conceive of the meaning of a sentence as a function from worlds to truth-values (i.e. as a set of possible worlds) we are not able to attribute any structure to the sentence which could serve as a basis of an account of its meaning in terms of subsentential components. The sentence as a whole must have meaning, and its analysis into different components can only take place as a second step, once this meaning has been established.[31] In fact Lewis claims that there is no 'objective sense' of the assertion that a particular analysis into components is correct—there will always be different, equally satisfactory theories which can explain the genesis of the sentence's meaning from its components. Given this relativity of constituents Lewis argues that they are incapable of serving as the basis of a theory of meaning. This can only be done by entire sentences.

A final example which comes to mind in this context is Frege's context principle claiming that 'only in the context of a sentence do words have meaning'.[32] What precisely this principle says, whether it is about senses or references of words or rather a methodological maxim, is a matter of debate. On one plausible reading, however, it seems possible to understand it epistemologically as a principle which claims the

---

[29] Davidson (1984: 220). For the discussion of molecular theories of meaning see Heal (1979), Borowski (1979), Dresner (2002).

[30] As e.g. in Lewis (1983).

[31] Lewis (1983: 176–8).

[32] Frege (1986: §62).

priority of judgements over their constituents.[33] Frege claims that

instead of combining the judgement from an individual as a subject together with a prefabricated concept as a predicate, we proceed in the opposite way: we split up the judgeable content and thus generate the concept.[34]

I do not think that forming concepts could be prior to judging, since this already presupposes some self-sufficiently existing concept. I think the concept arises from splitting up a judgeable content.[35]

Within Frege scholarship some interpretations have taken the context principle as either purely epistemic (that the context is prior to its parts in the order of cognition), while others read it also in an existential way (that the context is also prior in the order of being). Dummett assumes that both readings have their rôles to play.[36] He argues that the purely epistemic reading applies to thoughts while a combined epistemic and existential reading should apply to functional expressions.

A different interpretation is given by David Bell.[37] He argues that the purely epistemic reading of the context principle should be confined to senses of sentences, whereas the epistemic *and* existential reading applies to thoughts. This position then denies (contrary to Dummett) that 'thoughts have a determinate, intrinsic structure',[38] that is that there is a unique or privileged way of breaking down a thought into its constituents. Frege himself noted in a letter to Marty that he 'did not think that for every judgeable content there is just one way in which it can fall apart, or that one of those possible ways can always demand priority.'[39]

Be this as it may, if we interpret the context principle in a purely linguistic way as asserting the priority of sentence-meaning it seems to be relatively uncontroversial. To consider the sentence rather than the individual words as the primary bearer of meaning is something of a commonplace in linguistics.[40] This is partially motivated by the fact that treating subsentential components as bearers of meaning is vexed

---

[33] Cf. Wittgenstein's claim that 'only propositions have sense' (Wittgenstein 1989: 3.3).

[34] Frege (1969c: 18).

[35] Frege (1976: 164).

[36] Dummett (1981: 261–91).

[37] (1996).

[38] Bell (1996: 596).

[39] Bell (1996: 596).

[40] This idea is challenged in text linguistics, but there the potential bearers of meaning are even larger units, namely entire texts.

by obvious problems. The *Oxford English Dictionary*, for example, lists 317 definitions of the verb 'take'.[41] Considering words as bearers of meaning would imply that 'take' is highly ambiguous. But in fact we do not think that if somebody uses the word 'take' there are 317 different things he could have meant. In everyday speech there is usually nothing ambiguous about 'take' at all. The ambiguity only arises because we restrict ourselves to subsentential components as bearers of meaning. We could easily devise a dictionary arranged according to syllables, so that in this dictionary there would be several meanings for the syllable 'sent': one for 'sent' standing on its own, one for its being preceded by 'dis', one for its being followed by 'inel', one for its being preceded by 'repre' and followed by 'ative', and so on. We would consider this odd, because syllables are not the things which can have meanings on their own, but in fact every argument against syllables as bearers of meaning equally well applies to words. From a linguistic perspective it therefore makes a lot of sense to consider the sentence as the smallest and primary bearer of meaning, both regarding the *ordo cognoscendi* (how we learn the meaning of words) and the *ordo essendi* (how meaning is constituted).

The argument from the priority of sentence-meaning therefore does not only justify attributing an important place to states of affairs in our ontology, but also serves as an argument for their epistemic priority. In the same way as we grasp the meaning of a sentence before grasping the meaning of its subsentential components, it is argued, we get to know the state of affairs, and subsequently analyse it into its different constituents.

2 THE PRIORITY OF STATES OF AFFAIRS OVER THEIR CONSTITUENTS

Having thus argued for the centrality of states of affairs on cognitional and semantic grounds and justified their rôle as a primitive in our theory we must now be a bit more explicit regarding the nature of states of affairs. One particularly pressing issue concerns the structure of states of affairs.

When considering this issue David Armstrong, one of the main contemporary advocates of state-of-affair-based ontologies, immediately

---

[41] Miller (1951: 110).

asserts that their constituents are 'particulars, properties, relations and, in the case of higher-order states of affairs, lower-order states of affairs'.[42] He also claims that these constituents are abstractions from states of affairs:

> We may think of an individual, such as *a*, as no more than an *abstraction* from all those states of affairs in which *a* figures, F as an abstraction from all those states on affairs in which F figures, and similarly for a relation R. By 'abstraction' is not meant that *a*, F and R are in any way otherworldly, still less 'mental' or unreal. What is meant is that, whereas by an act of selective attention they may be *considered* apart from the states of affairs in which they figure, they have no existence outside states of affairs.[43]

Unfortunately Armstrong does not give an argument of why we are justified to proceed from taking constituents of states of affairs to be abstractions from them to identifying the abstractions with particulars, properties, relations, lower- and higher-order states of affairs. For him, these two assumptions seem to go hand in hand. I would prefer to separate the two issues, distinguishing the *way* in which we might come to identify constituents of states of affairs from the *nature* of what we so identify. I hope the preceding cognitional and semantic arguments convinced the reader of the plausibility of assuming states of affairs as a basic primitive. They do not, however, in any way serve as arguments that a structuring of states of affairs in the Armstrongian subject-predicate manner, or indeed in any other specific way, can be derived in an abstractionist manner. In my account I would therefore like to treat states of affairs as unanalysed primitives. This means both taking the *concept* of states of affairs as primitive, without trying to define states of affairs in terms of yet more basic notions, as well as treating states of affairs *themselves* as primitives, without making any preliminary assumptions about their internal structure and only appeal to those properties of their structure which can be derived in the framework of the present theory. The present section attempts to justify this decision.

§30 The complex principle

I want to argue that a *complex principle* is true of states of affairs. I consider a complex principle to be any principle which asserts the priority

---

[42] Armstrong (1997: 1).   [43] Armstrong (1990: 43).

of the whole, the complex, over the parts or constituents which make up the whole. We encounter the complex principle in cases where the parts of some entity are not taken to exist in their own right, but merely as *abstractions* from some preexisting whole. When we talk about the regions of some country for example, the country, the whole, is there first and is subsequently divided up into regions which are agricultural centres, regions with the major universities, regions where the risk of dying of lung cancer is above average and so on. We would not want to say that the country is *made up* of these regions; rather the regions are something we *discern* in the country relative to our specific interests.

Applied to ontology the complex principle asserts the priority of the state of affairs over its constituents. This priority constitutes a good reason for assuming the notion of a state of affairs as primitive without making any prior assumptions about their internal structure.

First of all it is necessary to get the principle itself into sharper focus. There are two major ways of spelling out the complex principle, which we will call the *epistemic* and the *existential* reading. Describing them in detail also makes it necessary to give a brief sketch of the notion of *ontological dependence*. Furthermore, the principle can be applied to different subject-matters; apart from ontology the most prominent ones are epistemology and semantics. In the following I shall briefly explain the concept of ontological dependence in order to spell out the interpretation of the complex principle I have in mind. I shall then discuss whether the plausibility of the principle in different contexts can lend support to its application in ontology.

§31 Analysis, decomposition, and dependence

Dividing a country into regions is interestingly different from taking a watch apart, since in the latter case we think of the different mechanical parts as being 'already there' in the watch, whereas the former act of dividing seems to be what brings the regions into being in the first place. Michael Dummett calls the first kind of division *decompositions*.[44] He contrasts decompositions of wholes with *analyses* by arguing that decompositions are non-unique, interest-relative, and not part of the intrinsic structure of the whole decomposed.[45] The example of an

---

[44] Dummett (1981: 261–91).   [45] Dummett (1981: 263).

analysis Dummett gives is that of dividing a molecule into atoms: there is only one way to do this, it does not depend on our specific interests, and the atoms constitute the intrinsic structure of the molecule. Therefore

we may say that the molecule is *built up* out of the component atoms, [...] [while] it is [...] preferable to say that the country may be *divided* or *broken down* into those regions, rather than as describing it as *built up* out of them.[46]

On this analysis there seems to be some sense in saying that the country is prior to the regions, but that the molecule is not prior to the atoms. In fact this claim, that in one case the complex principle applies whereas in the other it does not, seems to be a much greater contrast between the two cases than the difference between the two ways of splitting a whole into parts which Dummett distinguishes. After all, that a molecule has a unique analysis into atoms depends on the fact that we decided to split it *into atoms*, rather than into smaller molecules or subatomic particles.[47] But once we have settled for such a determinate concept of part which we shall refer to when breaking down the whole, surely the division of a country and the division of a molecule are completely on a par regarding uniqueness and interest-dependence. In both cases uniqueness is only relative to a particular kind of part (say, 'atom' or 'linguistic region') and both are interest-dependent only to the extent that we have to decide into what we want to divide the whole, but interest-independent in that once this decision has been made, there is only one way of dividing the whole into parts of this kind. And if Dummett's criterion for 'being part of the intrinsic structure' in the case of the atoms is the fact that

to discover anything about the molecule itself, for instance to explain its properties in terms of its constitution, it is necessary to uncover its structure as composed of atoms of various elements connected in certain way[48]

then for example a division of a country into linguistic regions will be part of the essential structure of the country as well. If we want to explain 'its properties in terms of its constitution', for example certain events in the country's history, we might explain them as a result of its linguistic divisions.

However, Dummett's example brings out the difference between cases where the complex principle applies and where it does not. Whereas it

[46] Dummett (1981: 263–4).   [47] As noted by Oliver (1992: 93–4).
[48] Dummett (1981: 263).

would not make sense to speak of regions without the country being already there, it does make sense to speak of atoms without there being a particular (or indeed any) molecule, just as it makes sense to talk about individuals without there being sets of them—the sets depend on the individuals which are their members, but the members do not depend on the sets containing them.

§32 Kinds of dependence

But what exactly does this mean? The discussion of the complex principle necessarily brings up various questions involving the notion of *dependence*. If the complex is prior to the parts, then this means that in some way the parts depend on the complex, while the converse does not hold. The difference between analysis and decomposition boils down to the fact that in the case of decomposition we think that the parts depend on the complex in a way in which this is not the case with analysis. What exactly is the best way of spelling out the concept of dependence is still a widely debated matter in contemporary philosophy.[49] Although we cannot hope to settle the matter here in any final way, let us at least try to disentangle some of the major senses of dependence.

The most straightforward form of dependence is surely when one object ontologically depends on another one, as a man depends on its father, or a mechanism depends on its essential part. Let us call this *rigid dependence*.[50] It is usual to spell this out in modal terms, so that we have

(RD) *a* rigidly depends on *b* := Necessarily, if *a* exists, *b* exists.

One obvious problem with this notion occurs when we are dealing with necessary existents.[51] In this case everything will rigidly depend on this necessarily existent object.[52] Such a view might be attractive for certain theological positions but ceases to be so when we take particular abstract objects as existing necessarily. I do not consider myself to be ontologically dependent on any natural number whatsoever. Simons solves this

---

[49] One of the most detailed accounts of dependence is still to be found in Simons (1987: ch. 8).

[50] Simons (1987: 295–7), Lowe (2001: 137).

[51] Simons (1987: 295), Fine (1995a: 271).

[52] Suppose n is such an object, and let E be the existence predicate, so that $\Box(En)$. Thus En and so $\Phi \rightarrow En$, for any Φ. By necessitation we get $\Box(\Phi \rightarrow En)$, and, since Φ is arbitrary, for any object m, $\Box(Em \rightarrow En)$.

problem by simply stipulating that the dependee must not be a necessary existent.[53] It is far from clear whether this does the trick, though,
given that statements like '{2} rigidly depends on 2' seem to be unproblematic, as Kit Fine notes. For him, of course, this points at a general
problem with spelling out dependence in modal terms. For the purposes
of our discussion, however, it is sufficient just to note this objection, and
then to ignore it.[54]

Although rigid dependence was taken above to relate particular objects, it is also possible to generalize it. We may have either single objects
or sets of objects on either side of the relationship. For example, a crown
may rigidly depend on two large diamonds which are part of it, and thus
depend on a set of objects. But contrast this with the way in which a particular painting such as Raphael's *Madonna of the Pinks* depends on the
matter which constitutes it. It does not depend, one might argue, on
the particular piece of wood it is painted on; had Raphael chosen a different piece, it would still be the same painting. However, it depends on
the fact that some wood is around: for that painting to be that painting
it had to be painted on wood, rather than on canvas, copper, or porce-
lain. Therefore the existence of the *Madonna of the Pinks* depends on the
existence of wood. This gives us another notion of dependence, which
we will call *generic dependence*:[55]

(GD) *a* generically depends on objects which are *G* := Necessarily, if *a* exists,
there exists something which is *G*.

Rigid dependence can be taken to be a special case of generic dependence, namely by taking rigid dependence to be generic dependence in
cases where the *G* applies only to *b*.

A third and final notion of dependence, which should not be confused with the other two, is *notional dependence*.[56] We want to say that

[53] Simons (1987: 295).

[54] Fine (1995a; 1995b) has pointed out fundamental problems with a modal construal
of dependence like the one described above. He argues that the notion of dependence is
genuinely stronger than what is captured by the modal statement: the latter is entailed by
the former, but does not encompass all aspects of it. While I agree with Fine's criticism,
the present argument would not gain much from introducing his more sophisticated
formal machinery. For the points I want to make the modal formulations, unsatisfactory
as they may appear from a more general perspective, suffice.

[55] For some discussion see Simons (1987: 297–8), Fine (1995a: 287–9), Lowe (2001:
141).

[56] Simons (1987: 297–8).

husbands depend on wives, murderers on victims, the Queen of England on England, and Northern Europe on Southern Europe. But this is not to say that the husband Socrates—that very man—depends for his existence on there being wives. If nobody had ever married, Socrates would still have existed. Similarly Macbeth does not depend on Duncan, Elizabeth of Windsor on England, or Scandinavia on Italy and Spain. We have to distinguish *de re* dependence (dependence for existence) which is constituted by rigid or generic dependence from *de dicto* or notional dependence (dependence for description). We can formulate notional dependence in the following way:[57]

(ND) Objects of sort F are notionally dependent on objects of sort G := Necessarily, if some x belongs to sort F there will be some y distinct from it such that y will belong to sort G.

Unlike rigid and generic dependence this is not a dependence between two objects or between an object and a concept, but between two concepts. We saw above that rigid dependence implied generic dependence. Notional dependence implies generic dependence if the Fs are essentially Fs.

§33 Epistemic and existential dependence

There are different ways of understanding the complex principle's claim for the priority of the complex over its constituents which are intimately connected with the different kinds of dependence distinguished above.

Let us first consider the *epistemic* reading of the complex principle which interprets the priority of the complex to be the constituents' epistemological dependence on the complex. The idea is that the complexes are what we get to know first and only after that do we acquire knowledge about the complex's constituents. Epistemic priority should not be understood as contingent temporal priority relating to the order in which we actually get to know things, but as a necessary fact about our cognitive faculties. Relative to other cognitive faculties such a priority might not hold. Furthermore, the epistemic reading of the complex principle does not mean that the constituents of the complexes are only brought about by our abstracting them from the complexes and thus have no proper life of their own. They may exist independently of the

[57] This definition is adapted from Simons (1987: 298).

complexes in which they occur; the fact is only that we are not able to know them in this way.[58]

That *a* epistemically depends on *b* therefore means that necessarily, if *a* is known, so is *b*. It is thus evident that epistemic dependence is a form of rigid dependence. It differs from the form of rigid dependence described above in that we are here not referring to *existence* but rather to *knowability*.

By putting 'exists' for 'is known' we regain the standard conception of rigid dependence just described, which is also just the notion of *existential dependence* at work in the existential reading of the complex principle. This reading, which can be adopted together with the epistemic reading, claims that it is the existence of the complex which brings the parts into being. Given that the constituents only exist as abstractions from the complex, the complex is to be not just epistemologically but also existentially prior to its constituents. Adopting the existential but not the epistemic reading would not make much sense. If we assume that the constituents of complexes do not exist on their own but only as abstractions, we would not want to conclude that we can have access to these abstractions before knowing the things we have abstracted them from. The existential reading implies the epistemic one.

It is interesting to see that Carnap's distinction between *analysis* and *quasi-analysis* (see pp. 104–5) can be reduced to the difference between these two different readings of the complex principle.[59] They are formally identical procedures which differ only in the conception we have of the underlying complexes. In the case of analysis we assume that there is an antecedent fact of the matter about the constituents of complexes which we *infer* from information about the complexes (this corresponds to the purely epistemic reading of the complex principle). In the quasi-analytic case, however, 'there is no independent or antecedent sense in which the objects standing in the relations have properties; they only have properties which are definable in a quasi-analytic way'.[60] This corresponds to the combined epistemic and existential reading of the

[58] There are close connections between this reading and a reading of the dependence involved in purely *notional* terms. This entails that the constituents only require the complex to the extent to which they are to be *described* as constituents of the complex. It assumes that apart from this description the constituents have an ontological life of their own and therefore exist independently of the complex of which they are constituents.

[59] Carnap (1928: 95–9).

[60] Richardson (1998: 53).

complex principle: the constituents of complexes are not just inferred from the data but rather *constituted* by the data.

Analysis in this sense resembles taking apart a structure made of Lego blocks: the blocks are already there when we start to 'analyse' the complex. Quasi-analysis, on the other hand, is rather like cutting up a bowl of jelly: it is our process of cutting which brings the different portions into being. They are not there before we start cutting.

A parallel from linguistics might make this distinction between the existential and the epistemic reading clearer. A relatively frequent assumption there is that sentences constitute the starting-point for the identification of syntactic components. (Other approaches start from phrases or from entire texts, but let us ignore them here.) Taking sentences as unstructured sequences of phonemes as given, syntactic components are then identified by first determining which elements occur repeatedly in different sentences. Then certain operational procedures are used to group the elements into different types. Such procedures involve substitution tests (Does replacing these elements by those preserve sentencehood?), reduction tests (Can these elements be left out without destroying sentencehood?), commutation tests (Does exchange of two elements preserve sentencehood?) and so on. This sorting of elements into types then constitutes the foundation of a system of grammatical categories and eventually of a grammatical theory of the specific language.

We could now take two very different views of the grammar constructed in such a way. On the one hand we could say that there really are the grammatical categories in question and that our grammar has identified them. Alternatively we could claim that our grammar is only a *theory* of the linguistic data presented to us and that the grammatical categories are abstractions from these data. In the first case the complex principle would only apply on the epistemic level, in the second case both on the epistemic and on the existential level.

§34 Uniqueness of constituents

A question immediately related to the different readings of the complex principle is that of the *uniqueness* of the constituents involved. Here we can distinguish three different positions. *Uniqueness* obviously claims that there is one and only one way of taking a complex apart. *Weak failure of uniqueness* claims that although there might be more than one way, one of them can be singled out as fundamental. For example there are four different ways in which we can take apart the proposition *Cato killed Cato*, namely by analysing it as '*a* killed *b*', '*a* killed Cato', 'Cato killed *b*', and '*a* killed himself'. Nevertheless, Peter Sullivan[61] argues that the first is most fundamental since 'given that one description, all the others are available, whereas this is true of no other account of the sentence'.[62] *Strong failure of uniqueness* finally denies that amongst the many ways of splitting up a complex we can always identify one which is most fundamental.

These three positions match up in an obvious way with the epistemic and existential readings of the complex principle distinguished above. Since the purely epistemic reading assumes that complexes do have a determinate set of constituents, uniqueness or weak failure of uniqueness are the positions to adopt here. Somebody who advocates the epistemic and existential reading, however, will have to adopt the weak or strong failure of uniqueness. This is because only it will ensure that the notion of dependence involved is asymmetric. Such asymmetry is a desirable feature: Jonathan Lowe even argues that it is at the core of our intuitive notion of dependence.[63] This asymmetry is obvious in the epistemic case: if a requires b to be known this does not entail the converse. But on the existential reading this is different. If the constituents require the complex to exist, then surely the complex requires the constituents to exist.

This symmetry disappears, however, if we adopt the weak or strong failure of uniqueness. It is then the case that the constituents rigidly depend on the complex. However, the complex will not rigidly, but only generically depend on its constituents. This is due to the fact that there are different sets of constituents which can be used to assemble the very same complex. A complex like Rab can be assembled from R, a, and b or from Ra and b or from R and ab. Therefore, if we reject the uniqueness of constituents, dependence comes out as asymmetric even on the existential reading of the complex principle.

§35 The complex principle and states of affairs

Assuming we assign a central rôle to states of affairs in our theory, why should we believe that the complex principle holds of them? It appears

---

[61] (1992: 98–9).   [62] Sullivan (1992: 99).   [63] Lowe (2001: 144).

that the cognitional and semantic arguments outlined above can be made to serve a double purpose. They do not only support the theoretical centrality of states of affairs by underlining their epistemological and semantic centrality, but also carry with them certain implications regarding our conception of the internal constitution of states of affairs. If we conceive of states of affairs in analogy to Gestalt-theoretic fields of perception (as we did in the cognitional argument) or complete sentences (as in the semantic one) it is clear that the constituents of states of affairs only come into being as a product of the analysis of the whole. We break the field of perception apart and thereby produce the various items which compose it, we analyse the sentence and thus generate the expressions belonging to different grammatical categories which make up the sentence. The units of perception depend on the entire field of perception, grammatical categories depend on the sentence they constitute, and so constituents of states of affairs depend on the state of affairs they are part of.

For present purposes I want to argue for an epistemic reading of the complex principle regarding states of affairs. The cognitional argument outlined in § 28 supports the claim that states of affairs are prior to their constituents in the order of cognition. This reading may be strengthened by adding a claim of existential priority as well, but such a combined epistemic and existential reading is not necessary for present purposes. For the moment just note that the underlying idea is that we are confronted first with ontological complexes and only subsequently become acquainted with the different ontological categories which make up these complexes. Assuming in this way that states of affairs are our primary point of epistemic contact with the world is part of our argument for granting them a central place in our ontology. Since they are the items on which we base our knowledge of reality, they provide a sensible foundation for a theory of the most general kinds of things there are in the world, i.e. a theory of ontological categories. But this argument also carries with it the implication that we are not acquainted with the constituents of states of affairs before we know the larger wholes they are constituents of. Our knowledge of these has to be abstracted from the knowledge of the whole; we are not able to synthesize this knowledge by prior knowledge of the bits which make up the whole. This is what the complex principle asserts. I remain neutral on whether this epistemic point has any existential impact, that is whether the constituents are *brought about* by this abstraction, or whether they are only *known* by it, but in reality have been there all along. For my account the weaker assumption, that the constituents can only be known by abstraction is sufficient.

A parallel with the philosophy of science can be drawn as follows. We only know microscopic objects (such as electrons) by knowing macroscopic ones (the tracks in a cloud chamber, the readings on a measuring apparatus). Macroscopic objects are therefore epistemically prior to microscopic ones. This has led to various proposals in the philosophy of science which attempted to describe how our knowledge of things like electrons can be accounted for in terms of knowledge of macroscopic phenomena (by regarding microscopic objects as the best theoretical unifiers of our knowledge, by taking them to be parts of effective predictive devices . . .). But such acceptance of the epistemological priority does not yet entail an answer to the existential question: whether electrons are *just* e.g. theoretical unifiers and do not exist otherwise, or whether we can only come to know them as such unifiers, while electrons exist independently, and the properties we ascribe to the unifiers can either apply or fail to apply to them. It is therefore possible to adopt the epistemic reading of the complex principle regarding macroscopic objects while remaining neutral about whether to adopt the existential reading as well.

Let us note in conclusion that accepting the epistemic reading of the complex principle entails that our account of ontological categories must be purely structural. As such it excludes psychological, physical, or linguistic accounts of distinguishing between types. For example, we would have to exclude ways of distinguishing between the types of individuals and properties in terms of different kinds of mental acts, in terms of the ability to be present at more than one place at the same time, or in terms of subject and predicate of well-formed sentences.[64] For such procedures would imply that we already have some distinguished parts of states of affairs in place (such as spatial points, temporal instants, mental acts, etc.) in order to use them to sort the form-sets into different categories. But since such parts will inevitably be parts of states of affairs *themselves*, they cannot be identified *ab initio*, before our ontological classification takes place, without violating the complex principle.

[64] See Ramsey (1990: 9).

The above 'physical' criterion for example assures us that we can distinguish individuals and properties *given that we have already identified some properties* (namely spatial and temporal ones).[65] But according to the epistemic reading of the complex principle we can only get to know constituents of states of affairs (such as properties) by abstraction from them. The purely structural account we shall focus on will not refer to any such privileged constituents but relies solely on information about which items can go together with which other items in states of affairs.

---

[65] This difficulty is also noted in MacBride (1998: 210): 'The proposed distinction between particulars and universals presupposes the notion of space, but that notion itself presupposes the categories of particular and universal. It is therefore circular to ground the distinction between particular and universal in spatial modalities. [. . .] Spatial relations are just themselves a special sort of universal, and particulars have the unique locations they do just because of the totality of spatial relations in which they figure.'

IV

Categories in an ontology
of states of affairs

1 FORM-SETS AND BASE-SETS

In the preceding chapter we presented an argument for the centrality of states of affairs and their priority over their constituents. This chapter will set out to construct a satisfactory account of ontological categories within the framework of a theory of states of affairs. Questions of membership within ontological categories arise primarily once we investigate the various constituents of states of affairs and ask ourselves for example why in the state of affairs denoted by 'the apple is red' the bit picked out by 'the apple' behaves so differently from the one picked out by 'is red'. It is therefore with an investigation of the constituents of states of affairs that we will have to start.

§36 States of affairs and their constituents

Although the arguments presented in the preceding chapter did not support the view that states of affairs are structured in the syntactically inspired subject-predicate manner favoured by Armstrong it seems to be uncontroversial that states of affairs are structured entities. Within them we can identify bits which are put together in a particular way. Consider the state of affairs denoted by 'Albert loves Becca'. We can distinguish at least three different bits in it, the two persons Albert and Becca, as well as 'loving' holding between them. They are combined in a particular way to give *this* state of affairs; putting them together in another way would result in other states of affairs (such as 'Becca loves Albert'). We will call the set consisting of the different bits we can make out in a state of affairs (or in several states of affairs) the *constituent-set*. However, it is not obvious to me without further argument that any or all states of affairs should have a *unique* way of taking them apart and thus a unique constituent-set. And even if they do, *what* the constituents are and whether they belong to the types Armstrong takes them to belong to seems to be something which should be the result of our theory of states of affairs, rather than something which is presupposed from the very beginning.

The first important notion we want to introduce is that of a *form-set* of constituents of states of affairs. The conception of a form-set relies fundamentally on the notion of intersubstitutability. Intersubstitutability in linguistic contexts was discussed at length in §§ 14–24. In order to keep ontological and linguistic issues as separate as possible we will focus in the following discussion on a different notion of intersubstitutability, namely intersubstitutability in *states of affairs*, rather than in sentences. This may sound obscure at first, but the underlying idea is in fact very simple. Suppose someone asserts that 'Albert loves Becca' and someone else replies 'No, it's Charles rather than Albert'. What the second speaker means is that it is not the state of affairs in which Albert loves Becca which obtains, but rather a similar one, in which Charles takes the place of Albert (that is, the state of affairs in which Charles loves Becca). We might also want to say that the latter state of affairs is the result of *substituting* the individual Charles for the individual Albert in the state of affairs in which Albert loves Becca. Similarly we can regard the state of affairs in which Charles admires Becca as the result of substituting the relation of admiring for the relation of loving in the state of affairs in which Charles loves Becca.[1]

We will define form-sets as sets of constituents of states of affairs which can be intersubstituted in states of affairs to form new ones. Thus Albert, Becca, and Charles will be in the same form-set, as will be the relations of loving, admiring, and so on.[2]

---

[1] The concept of substitution in states of affairs is also used in Fine (2000: 26–8). Fine, however, argues that not all constituents of states of affairs can be substituted for one another. In particular he does not think that all relations can be so substituted, a position not shared by us. See Fine (2000: 30, note 19).

[2] Note that we only consider substituting objects within a single world, in the same way as in grammar we only consider substituting expressions within a single language. Thus if we say that two objects a and b can go together to form a state of affairs, we mean that a and b exist in the world under consideration and that e.g. ac obtains in this world

The reader will have noticed that there is an obvious parallel here to Wittgenstein's notion of the *form* of an object discussed in the *Tractatus*.[3] He argues that the form of an object makes it possible that this object can combine with others in states of affairs. Different objects have so to speak different 'logical shapes' which make it possible for them to 'fit together' with other objects to form complexes. Objects with the same logical form are in the same form-set.[4]

§37 The 'fitting' of constituents

It is now important to note that the ability of a collection of objects to 'fit together' in forming a state of affairs is not stable under substitutions. Consider Lego blocks. For some collections of Lego blocks you can build some single Lego structure which uses all the blocks. But if you exchange some blocks for others, this is not necessarily the case any longer. It may be the case that either you cannot build any structure at all, since the new collection of blocks does not fit, or you might be able to build something, but be unable to use all the blocks. The very same thing can happen with states of affairs. Take the three objects Adam, Becca, and the loving relation. They can form a state of affairs together. (In fact they can form two: that Adam loves Becca and that Becca loves Adam.) Now substitute the loving relation by the relation 'have 3 as their greatest common factor'. There is no state of affairs which consists just of Adam, Becca, and *this* relation, no matter which order we arrange the elements in. The relation is of the wrong type: it is a relation between numbers, whereas loving is one between persons. Similarly, consider substituting the loving relation by the property 'is male'. There is no state of affairs consisting just of Adam, Becca, and 'is male' either, since 'is male' takes only one individual, whereas 'loves' takes two. Parts of the collection of Adam, Becca, and 'is male' can go together to form a state of affairs, but the whole collection cannot.

and *ab* (the result of substituting *b* for *c*) obtains in an accessible world. It is essential that *a* and *b* exist in the same world for them being able to form a state of affairs together. It is not sufficient that the 'fitting' *b* exists in some other world, even if it is accessible from the world under consideration.

[3] 'The form of an object is its possibility of occuring in states of affairs.' (Wittgenstein 1989: 2.0141). See in particular 2–2.063.

[4] Some further parallels with the ontology of the *Tractatus* will be discussed in the final chapter.

But how do we know that some constituents of states of affairs cannot go together? I am obviously appealing here to some kind of 'ontological intuition' about what fits together with what. What does such an intuition amount to?

We can first of all characterize it purely negatively by saying what it is not: it does not just reduce to intuition about meaningfulness. The idiom of constituents of states of affairs fitting together is not just a *façon de parler* for words fitting together to form meaningful sentences. We could not just transpose the discussion of what states of affairs could obtain to what sentences make sense. States of affairs and meaningful sentences are closely related but differ in important ways. It is not the case that if some objects $a, \ldots, n$ fit together to form a state of affairs there is a meaningful sentence containing expressions referring to the $a, \ldots, n$: our language might not contain names for all the constituents. It is not even the case our language always *could* contain such names. Depending on the extent of one's Platonist inclinations one might want to claim that all relations between the real numbers (or some other set of the same cardinality) constitute states of affairs. But names being finite strings of symbols, there are not enough of them to go around for every real number. Nor is it the case that if a sentence picks out a state of affairs with constituents $a, \ldots, n$ there are expressions referring to $a, \ldots, n$ in the sentence (none of the parts of an equation a Gödel number picks out correspond to the digits in the Gödel number). States of affairs and sentences stand in a close structural relation, but not in one which is so close as to make them identical for our purposes.

This does not mean, however, our ontological intuition (about whether certain constituents of states of affairs fit) cannot be informed by linguistic intuitions. Our intuitions about *grammaticality* (or rather the lack of it) are one such source of information: that the relations of loving and sitting between belong to different types can be inferred from the fact that 'sits between' cannot be plugged in for 'loves' in 'Adam loves Becca' *salva congruitate*. Although not reducible to them, intuitions about *meaninglessness* can also inform our intuitions about ontological fitting: we can argue that being prime and being green belong to different types since 'green' cannot be intersubstituted with 'prime' in '17 is prime' *salva significatione*. Note that the meaningless sentences we consider for these purposes are a very restricted class, namely just those sentences which are *grammatical* and where *the meanings of all the constituent expressions are clear*, but which still lack meaning as a whole.

There is yet a further source of our intuitions about fitting the existence of which further underlines that fact that our exposition of the notion of an ontological category is not fundamentally linguistic. This is our ability to *imagine* possible but not actual states of affairs. None of us has ever encountered states of affairs featuring pink elephants, talking donkeys, or worlds with four spatial dimensions. But we find it quite possible (with a bit of practice in the last case) to imagine what such states of affairs would be like. In other cases, however, we fail no matter how hard we try: even considerable practice does not supply us with a sufficiently clear impression of what a state of affairs containing a green prime number or the square root of a symphony would be like. In cases like these we do not get behind the mere words to ascertain the referents of the respective sentences.

There are thus at least three sources which feed into our ontological intuitions about fitting of constituents of states of affairs: intuitions about grammaticality, intuitions about meaninglessness, and intuitions about our imaginative capacities. This will have clarified the idea of our ontological intuitions about fitting a bit, but I have not said anything about what underlies the fitting *in the world*. I have described ways in which we can *acquire knowledge* about it, but I have been silent about what is actually *behind* the whole thing. What makes it the case that only certain bits of states of affairs fit while others do not?

One possible answer could appeal to *essential properties* of objects. Numbers, it could be argued, are essentially non-spatial, and since everything which has a colour must be spatially extended the property 'being green' cannot apply to any number in a state of affairs. Which object goes together with which other objects in states of affairs then would be taken to be a direct consequence of the different objects' inner nature. But this is not the only possibility of explaining joining behaviour.

Another explanation could appeal to *neurobiology*. The assumption would be that our brains are set up in such a way that certain concepts just cannot be combined. Our inability to imagine certain states of affairs would then not have anything to do with the essential properties of the objects involved, nor would it be a reflection of lack of imagination on our part. It would be the case that it is biologically impossible for us to make a connection between certain mental representations. This could be explained by the fact that particular representations necessitate certain codings in the brain, and that the neuronal structures brought about by these codings cannot be merged, due to the way our brain is constructed. The impossibility of imagining a particular state of affairs would be the same kind of impossibility as that of learning a language which violated certain language universals: an impossibility resulting from the hard-wiring of our brains.[5]

Finally we could try to explain the different kinds of fitting on purely *linguistic* grounds. Once we have expressed the 'deep structure' or 'logical form' in a suitable way we see that the sentence 'The number seven is green' is just as ungrammatical on the 'deep' level as 'Caesar is and' is ungrammatical on the surface level.[6] That only certain bits of states of affairs fit together would then have nothing to do with either the essences of objects or with the way our brains work, but would be a result of facts about the 'deep grammar' of the language employed for speaking about the world.[7]

Now which of the three explanations, if any, is the right one? This is a deep and difficult question to which I do not pretend to know the answer. It is intimately connected with the question regarding the kind of modality involved when some constituents of states of affairs fit or fail to fit. If we are opting for an essentialist explanation it is plausible to conceive of it as some sort of metaphysical necessity; if, however, we go for the neurobiological variant it will be some weaker notion, which we might want to call biological or cognitive necessity.

I therefore set up my theory in such a way that answering this question is not necessary for arriving at an account of ontological categories. I treat the 'fitting relation' between constituents of states of affairs as

[5] I do not claim that there is actually any neurobiological evidence for such a foundation of inconceivability in brain structure. The sole purpose of this hypothesis is to show that appeal to essences is not the only possible way of explaining information about joining behaviour acquired via considerations of imaginability.

[6] Such a view of formal languages was famously held by Carnap (1959: 68).

[7] Note that whichever option we go for, we can explain what our judgement that the number seven and the colour green cannot go together in a state of affairs is about without appealing to the ontologically rather problematic notion of an impossible state of affairs. In the first case the objects of our judgements are the respective essences of the number seven and the colour green, in the second case we talk about the structure of neuronal representations and how they relate to the structure of our brain, and in the final case we refer to consequences of the 'deep' grammatical rules of the language we speak.

primitive and develop a theory on this basis.[8] Given the fundamental epistemic and semantic rôle of states of affairs argued for previously this relation seems to be sufficiently well-entrenched in our cognitive lives to make it an interesting object of study. Since I was able to describe some possible ways in which knowledge about this relation could be acquired its epistemological background should be sufficiently clear for further investigations. But its ontological background is far from clear. It could be a manifestation of facts about essence, or brains, or deep structure, or something else completely. It is therefore so important for my account that it relies on information about this primitive 'fitting relation' only.

§38 Form-sets and base-sets

After clarifying the concept of the 'fitting' relation which is fundamental in identifying form-sets a central point for our ensuing discussion is that not all form-sets are alike. Some of them (intuitively speaking, the 'more fundamental' ones) can be used to *construct* other form-sets. What I mean by 'construct' will be explained in detail in § 3 of this chapter. For the moment just note that the conception of construction I have in mind here is the same which is used when saying that the rational numbers can be constructed from the natural numbers, or that physical objects can be constructed from sense-data, or properties from tropes. In a very imprecise manner we could say that only the resources used in the construction, but not the objects constructed, have any ontological weight.

We will call a minimal subset of a set of form-sets which can collectively construct all the remaining form-sets in the set a *basis* of the set of form-sets, and its elements *base-sets*. The complement of the basis will be called the *surplus*, and its members *redundant sets*. The notion of a basis employed here (which is, as we shall see, essential for avoiding the cut-off point problem) is of course precisely that of a basis of a set relative to some collection of generating operations. For any set X such a

---

[8] This is analogous to the way in which linguistics treats intuitions about 'grammatical fitting' as primitive and constructs theories to account for them. Both grammatical and ontological intuitions should be regarded as being replicable under controlled experimental conditions (for some work on ontological intuitions see Keil (1979)) and as arising from our unconscious knowledge of grammar or ontology, respectively. Note that we are able to develop linguistic theories without knowing which kind of modality corresponds to 'grammatical fitting'.

basis is a minimal subset B of X which generates X. That B generates X means that there is a certain set of operations which can be applied to the members of B to obtain any member of X. That B is minimal means that there is no proper subset B' of B which generates X. For example, the set of natural numbers including 0 has the singleton of 0 as its basis relative to the successor function, since all the other natural numbers can be generated from 0 via iterated application of this function. The set of natural numbers greater than one has the set of prime numbers as its basis relative to multiplication, since all other numbers can be obtained from the prime numbers by multiplication.

Note that the fact that some object is in a basis does not mean that there are no members of the surplus which can generate it. This follows simply from the fact that a set can have more than one basis. If we take implication as our generating operation then the logical closure of the set $\{x, y, x \wedge y\}$ has two bases, namely $\{x, y\}$ and $\{x \wedge y\}$. Thus relative to the first basis the second set is a surplus, and relative to the second basis the first set is a surplus.[9]

Note furthermore that we are *not* claiming that the base-sets are the form-sets which cannot be generated or constructed from other form-sets (i.e. those form-sets which are members of the intersection of the bases of a set). This is because we shall later want to identify base-sets with ontological categories, and this intersection can sometimes be empty (the above example is a case in point). We would thus be left with the possibility of there being no ontological categories in certain circumstances, something which does not at all harmonize with any of the conceptions of ontological categories generally discussed.

Base-sets can be compared to the axioms of a particular theory, while the redundant sets can be compared to its theorems.[10] We can also think of the different form-sets as being like different chemical substances, so that the different substitution behaviour in different states of affairs would correspond to the different properties chemical substances exhibit when put together. Natrium, Chlorine, and Natriumchloride have quite different properties, so that the chemist regards them as different chemical substances. However, some of these substances are less fundamental than others since they are just the result of putting certain elements together (as in the case of Natriumchloride). We can

[9] This point will be explored further in § 50.
[10] See § 55 for a more detailed exploration of this comparison.

therefore understand the distinction between form-sets which are base-sets and those which are redundant sets analogously to that between chemical substances which are atoms and those which are molecules. If suddenly all the Natriumchloride disappeared from the world, it would not be qualitatively poorer from a chemical perspective, since as long as Natrium and Chlorine were there, Natriumchloride could still be 'constructed'.

While this example is helpful it can be misleading to some extent. There is only one way to split a molecule into atoms, but this is not necessarily the case for splitting a set of form-sets into base-sets and redundant sets (as we have just seen). Better examples for the division of form-sets into base-sets and redundant sets therefore come from propositional calculus. Consider the set of formulae S:

$$\left\{ \begin{array}{c} p \\ q \\ p \rightarrow r \\ p \rightarrow s \\ q \wedge q \\ r \wedge r \\ \neg s \end{array} \right\}$$

Let us say that formulae belong to the same form-set if they have the same logical form.[11] Thus S can be divided into four form-sets: $F_1 = \{p, q\}$, $F_2 = \{p \rightarrow r, p \rightarrow s\}$, $F_3 = \{q \wedge q, r \wedge r\}$, and $F_4 = \{\neg s\}$. We just said that some form-sets could be constructed from the members of other form-sets. If we read 'construction' as 'implication' it is clear that F_3 can be 'constructed' from F_1 and F_2, since the members of these together entail all the members of F_3. However, no other set can be constructed in such a way: therefore F_1, F_2, and F_4 together form the basis of S and are base-sets, while F_3 is the only member of the surplus and thus a redundant set.

---

[11] As with most examples, this example is not perfect either, something which is particularly apparent in the case of this identification of 'belonging to the same form-set' and 'being of the same logical form'. A set of formulae all of which have the same logical form is very much unlike the notion of a form-set determined by intersubstitutability criteria just sketched: formulae of propositional calculus are not good models of the constituents of states of affairs. The reader is asked to ignore this imperfection and to concentrate on the relation between base-sets and redundant sets instead, which *can* be faithfully modelled in terms of propositional formulae.

Another way to draw the distinction is this. Consider a consistent set of formulae L and let $\overline{L}$ be its deductive closure. A minimal subset L' of L will be a basis if $\overline{L'} = \overline{L}$. F_1, F_2, and F_4 are therefore base-sets since $\bigcup F_1, F_2, F_4 = \bigcup F_1, F_2, F_3, F_4 = \overline{S}$.

It is clear that the base-sets constitute the fundamental and important elements of the set S: they fix the logical consequences of the set, whereas the redundant sets are (like the base-sets) members of the logical consequences of the set, but do not determine them.

§39 Motivation for introducing base-sets

If we employ linguistic information to tell us when some constituents of states of affairs can be intersubstituted, we encounter an obvious problem: some form-sets which are picked out in this way are too restricted to be the kind of thing ontology inquires into.

Consider the state of affairs denoted by the statement 'Peter was gated'.[12] We cannot simply intersubstitute the name of any other person *salva significatione*, since the predicate 'to gate' is only sensibly applicable to Oxbridge undergraduates. Just as it is not meaningful to apply the property of loving anything to something which is not a person, a non-Oxbridge undergraduate could not be gated. But if we identify form-sets on the basis of this linguistic information, it will turn out that since any Oxbridge undergraduate (and nothing else) could take the place of Peter in the state of affairs that Peter was gated, there is a form-set consisting of all and only the Oxbridge undergraduates. But we will hardly want to say that these form an ontological category.

In fact this is quite a widespread phenomenon. There are numerous properties which give rise to very restricted form-sets. 'Having a green back door' is a property only a building can have, 'being abelian' can only be meaningfully applied to groups or categories, 'having a hard seat' can only be true or false of chairs of some kind or the other.

§40 Weak and strong form-sets

The relative frequency of these very restricted form-sets depends on the precise way in which the form-sets are constructed. The reader may have

---

[12] The verb 'to gate' means, according to the *OED*, 'to confine an undergraduate at the Universities of Oxford or Cambridge to the precincts of the College, either entirely or after a certain hour'. See also Stubbings (1991: 26).

noted that I was deliberately vague about this when I claimed on page 91 that form-sets are sets of constituents of states of affairs which can be intersubstituted. Does this mean that *each particular* state of affairs with a blank generates a form-set containing all the constituents which can be plugged into this blank? Or do I want to say that two constituents belong to the same form-set if they are intersubstitutable in *all* states of affairs? Let us call the former the *weak* and the latter the *strong* conception of form-sets. Opting for the strong conception of form-sets means that we end up almost entirely with very restricted form-sets. Demanding intersubstitutability in all contexts we will for example not get a form-set containing all the abstract or all the concrete objects (since there will always be states of affairs (such as '. . . is abelian', '. . . has a green back door') where not all, but only some of the objects from the respective sets can be plugged in). This problem is avoided by opting for weak form-sets. Here a single state of affairs is sufficient, so that for example '. . . is extended' would deliver the form-set containing all the concrete objects.

Nevertheless I adopt the strong conception of form-sets in the rest of this inquiry. *Prima facie* this may appear as a strange choice, since apart from leaving us only with the very restricted form-sets, division into strong form-sets generates a partition on the set of constituents of states of affairs (whereas weak form-sets commonly generate a containment structure). Since we want to construe ontological categories as particular form-sets this means that there would not be a containment structure on the set of ontological categories, something we explicitly demanded in our criticism of Carnap. But in fact there is a procedure for generating both the less specific form-sets and a containment structure on the basis of typing the constituents of states of affairs into strong form-sets. It will be described in § 48. This procedure will allow us to have the benefits of the weak form-sets (a containment structure on the form-sets and the existence of less specific form-sets) without its disadvantages, namely overlapping categories. The procedure will imply that the containment structure on the set of form-sets is always a hierarchy, so that Sommers' law is obeyed. It will furthermore license us in assuming that there are less restricted form-sets (such as abstract object and concrete object), as well as very restricted ones (such as group and building). The latter is crucial for dealing with the puzzling phenomenon of *semantically anomalous sentences* and for solving the problem of too specific categories.

§41 Dealing with too specific categories

Semantically anomalous sentences are sentences containing expressions denoting properties which give rise to very restricted form-sets. As we have seen above, these sentences present a problem for many accounts of ontological categories since there has to be some way in which to distinguish them from category-mistakes proper. Typical examples of such anomalous sentences are

1. The man is pregnant.
2. The lake has a hardcover binding.
3. The typewriter is five minutes fast.

These are very similar to category-mistakes (such as 'The number four is green', 'The fact that I have got a red armchair in my room is in Beijing') but with the important difference that they violate quite specific categories (such as 'female mammal', 'book', or 'watch') which do not qualify as ontological categories. It is of principal importance for any account of ontological categories to be able to tell the difference between category-mistakes and semantically anomalous sentences. In fact the problem of drawing this distinction is just the cut-off point problem (which the accounts by generality faced) and the problem of too specific properties (of the Ryle-Sommers account) in disguise.[13]

Now there is a sense in which form-sets containing the Oxbridge undergraduates, or buildings, or groups are parasitic upon other form-sets, namely those containing persons, or material objects, or sets. They rely on these other form-sets for their existence. These very specific sets are also in a certain sense redundant: if all the Oxbridge undergraduates, all buildings, and all groups suddenly vanished overnight, but persons, material objects, and sets were still around, the loss would not be considered fundamental. It would not have affected the ontological richness of the world. We could still regain the lost form-sets from the ones which are still there.

The fundamental idea we are going to exploit is that certain form-sets can be *constructed* from others, and that properties which give rise

---

[13] An overview of different ways of dealing with this problem, some of which have been discussed above, can be found in Keil (1979: 139–47). Keil admits that 'the sceptical reader may not find any one argument [of those presented] completely convincing' (1979: 147).

to the kind of semantically anomalous sentences discussed above generate precisely such form-sets. What the notion of construction is going to amount to will be discussed in more detail below, but for the moment note that there are a couple of very straightforward and uncontroversial senses of the word. It is clear how groups (and many other mathematical objects) can be constructed from sets, simply by specifying which particular kinds of sets (which fulfil specific conditions) will be regarded as groups. In an equally direct way buildings can be regarded as constructions from material objects: they are what results when material objects are put together in a particular way.[14]

Other form-sets are used in the construction of form-sets, and these are very often those for which there is no easy way of constructing them in turn. There is no obvious procedure for constructing abstract objects from other kinds of things, or temporally extended things from things which have no temporal extension, or propositional things (things which can be *about* other things) from non-propositional things. At the same time abstracta, objects with a temporal duration, or propositional contents are often used to construct other kinds of objects. For example, if we wanted to consider speech acts to be ordered triples of persons, time-instances, and propositions, we would have used items of all three kinds in our construction. We call these form-sets which are employed in the construction of other form-sets base-sets, and it is these base-sets which we want to take as an explication of the concept of ontological category. All members of such a set have the same logical form, while the set is fundamental and general enough to be regarded as an ontological category.

Intuitively this presents us with quite an attractive picture. On this account ontological categories—the base-sets—are responsible for the categorial richness of the world. They constitute the qualitative basis of phenomena: all there is is reducible to them, and thus constructible from them. The constructible or redundant sets, on the other hand, have customarily been denied the status of ontological categories. When the set nominalist claims that properties can be constructed in terms of sets of individuals, the point is not that properties are somehow not

[14] This picture might strike some as a bit simplistic, and indeed it could be the case that we cannot successfully specify what a building is by describing only its physical shape, but also have to take into account the purposes it is supposed to fulfil for human beings and so on. However, this will not change the fundamental underlying idea of the argument but at most entails that there are other components involved in constructing buildings than just material objects.

there, but that they do not constitute a fundamental or ontological category; this status belongs only to individuals and sets. According to the nominalist it is these which provide the basis for the phenomenal plenitude of the world.

§42   A simple model

If we follow the account outlined above, a picture of ontological categories emerges which fundamentally relies on a two-stage process. First we want to identify the different form-sets by applying intersubstitutability criteria. This gives us a necessary but not sufficient condition for being an ontological category. In a second step we then filter out those form-sets which are too specific (the redundant sets) until we are left with the base-sets. In order to do this we invoke the notion of constructibility, that is we check which form-sets can be constructed from other form-sets and thus do not qualify as genuine ontological categories. Both steps require substantial spelling-out which will occupy us during the ensuing sections and will give rise to a number of philosophically interesting questions as we go along. Before we proceed to this, however, we will have a look at a simple model of the above process.

Strings of symbols will function as substitutes for parts of states of affairs in our model. These strings consist either of capital 'A's and 'B's or of lower-case 'a's and 'b's. We will say that two strings can be combined ('form a state of affairs together') if one is shorter than the other and is a proper substring of the other in case capital 'A's and 'B's are exchanged for lower-case 'a's and 'b's, or the other way round. Thus for example 'AABA' and 'aba' can be combined since if you switch 'aba' to capital letters you get 'ABA' and this is a proper substring of 'AABA'. Strings like 'BBABB' and 'baa', however, cannot be combined, nor can 'abbab' and 'bba'. We also assume that by concatenation new strings can be constructed from old strings.

Now consider the following list of strings:

ABABAA
BAABA
AAB
abaaba
aba
baa

These strings can be sorted into form-sets such that any member of such a set can be substituted for any other member in any combination of strings ('state of affairs'). The result will look like this:

$$F_1 = \{\text{ABABAA}, \text{BAABA}\}$$
$$F_2 = \{\text{AAB}\}$$
$$F_3 = \{\text{abaaba}\}$$
$$F_4 = \{\text{aba}, \text{baa}\}$$

As the reader is invited to check, any two members of F_1 and F_4 can be combined, as can the only members of F_2 and F_3. There are thus four different kinds of strings (four different form-sets) in our collection of six strings. But not all of them are equally fundamental, since the content of one form-set can be constructed from members of another form-set: concatenating two copies of 'aba' (which is in F_4) gives you 'abaaba', which is the entire content of F_3. This construction is combinatorially equivalent to 'abaaba'. Every string which can be combined with 'abaaba' can be combined with the construction from two copies of 'aba'. There is therefore a sense in which F_3 does not contribute to the combinatorial richness of the set of strings in the way in which the other three form-set do. F_3 is therefore a redundant set while the other three are base-sets.

2 FORM-SETS

After arguing at length for the centrality of states of affairs in the previous chapter, and sketching the notions of form-set and base-set, we are now faced with two immediate questions. First we must address the question how we can refer to the constituents of states of affairs. This is far from straightforward, given that we want to treat states of affairs as primitives, making no assumptions about their internal structure. We therefore cannot claim any direct acquaintance with the constituents of states of affairs; we can only regard them as being somehow derivative entities, based on the more fundamental notion of states of affairs. Secondly, we have to describe the way in which these constituents can be sorted into the different form-sets they belong to. Both of these questions will be answered in the present section.

The problem of identifying the constituents of states of affairs in our framework is essentially a problem of quasi-analysis. The term quasi-analysis was introduced by Carnap[15] for a procedure which obtains information about the constituents of some objects[16] not by direct acquaintance with the constituents but on the basis of information about some relation *between* the objects. Quasi-analysis can be applied if the objects in question do not have any constituents (as in the case of Carnap's elementary experiences) so that they have to be constructed as 'logical fictions',[17] or if the objects do have constituents or properties but we want to give some rational reconstruction of the epistemic process by which we might come to know these. The quasi-analytical method is thus applicable regardless of whether we think of the complex principle in existential or in epistemic terms.

Another example of a quasi-analytical problem arises in Arnold Koslow's structuralist theory of logic.[18] There the class of items which are supposed to stand in implication relations (a class which includes but is not exhausted by the class of propositions) is taken as prior in a way which implies that we do not have any immediate access to their constituents (i.e. their truth-functional make-up); in fact we do not even have to suppose that they have any particular structure at all. Their syntactical structure is rather determined on the basis of information we have about the implication relations between the different complexes. Koslow sets out to define the logical constituents of the primitive objects, such as the truth-functional operators, from the way in which the objects imply one another. The familiar picture is thus reversed: rather than starting with the truth-functional components and then seeing how they generate implications between compounds, we consider the components of the primitives to be detected (if not produced) by the implication relation between the primitives.[19]

§43 Mereology and states of affairs

The relation we are considering in our inquiry is the relation 'has a part in common with' on states of affairs and parts of states of affairs. This might require some motivation. After all we usually only speak of parts

---

[15] Carnap (1928: §69).

[16] 'Constituent' is here taken in a wide sense so as to include properties of objects. See Carnap (1928: §69).

[17] That is, they are constructed as sets of objects. Carnap therefore calls quasi-analysis 'synthesis appearing as analysis' (1928: §74).

[18] Koslow (1992).

[19] For a related project in the context of belief dynamics see Gärdenfors (1988: ch. 6).

of material objects of some sort or other. So what sense can we make of
the idea that states of affairs can have parts as well? Is it unproblematic
to say that states of affairs can have parts in much the same sense as
flowers, trees, houses, and garden sprinklers do? And just as adjacent
houses share a wall, can states of affairs share parts, that is have parts
which are at the same time parts of another state of affairs? Let us look
at some examples.

The state of affairs that there is an apple on top of the table and the
state of affairs that there is an apple near the edge of the table share
the apple, which is involved in both cases. The state of affairs that the
banana is yellow and the state of affairs that the lemon is yellow share
the occurrence of yellowness. The state of affairs that Peter is eating beef
and the state of affairs that Peter is eating pork are both states of affairs
such that Peter is eating meat. The apple, being yellow, that Peter is eating meat—these can be regarded as objects which are part of a number
of different states of affairs. There seems to be nothing inherently mys-
terious or obscure about this notion.[20] One state of affairs being part
of two others implies that the two sentences corresponding to the latter
entail that corresponding to the former. But parthood is more general
than entailment, since entailment holds between sentences and could
thus only inform us about the *states of affairs* which are part of states of
affairs. But not all the parts of states of affairs have to be states of affairs
themselves.

Let us note once again that we are not talking about language here. If
something is a part of two states of affairs there need not be an expression all (or indeed any) pairs of sentences picking out those two states
of affairs have in common which refers to the part in question. The
apple can be referred to in all sorts of ways, for example by definite
descriptions, by pronouns, or by indexicals. Similarly there need not be
an expression referring to the fact that Peter is eating meat in any of the
sentences picking out the state of affairs in which he is eating pork. As
stressed in § 37, talk about parts of states of affairs is not just a funny
way of talking about words, but a way of talking about the world: it is
talk about the represented, rather than the representation.

This attitude towards states of affairs also influences our conception
of logically complex states of affairs. On the traditional understanding

---

[20] See Meixner (1997: 23–129) for a comprehensive ontological theory employing a
mereology of states of affairs.

a state of affairs picked out by the sentence Fa is regarded as logically atomic, while that picked out by $Fa \wedge Gb$ is taken to be a logically complex, molecular, conjunctive state of affairs.[21] This might then lead to the question how we should understand the sharing of parts of states of affairs in these complex cases. For example, do two conjunctive states of affairs somehow have the conjunction in common? If so, what kind of object is this? Do we have to admit that the logical constants denote? Fortunately we can circumvent all these difficulties by conceiving of the complexity of states of affairs not in terms of the syntactic complexity of the sentences in some language (such as predicate calculus) which pick them out, but solely in terms of the sharing of parts between states of affairs. A state of affairs is *complex* if it has some part it shares with another one, otherwise it is atomic. A state of affairs is the *conjunction* of two other ones if it is the smallest state of affairs which has both as parts. A state of affairs s' is the *negation* of a state of affairs s if s' is the largest state of affairs which does not have s as a part. All the familiar logical operations can be accounted for in this manner.[22] The reader familiar with Koslow's work will realize that our position is the ontological equivalent to his conception of the logical form of propositions in terms of relations between propositions, rather than in terms of the syntax of the system representing them. Questions of complexity and atomicity, and more generally questions of the ontological form of states of affairs are addressed by reference to relations between states of affairs or their constituents, but not by reference to the form of their representations.

§44 The overlap relations

Let us now make the mereology on states of affairs more precise by introducing an overlap relation between them. Like the standard 'overlaps' relation familiar from mereology overlapping of states of affairs is reflexive, symmetric, and not transitive. Of course we want to use the

---

[21] There is no philosophical consensus about what kinds of logically complex states of affairs (if any) we might want to admit. Wittgenstein in the *Tractatus* does not allow for any, Russell in his lectures on logical atomism assumes negative and quantified states of affairs (1972), Armstrong admits only conjunctive states of affairs (1997). We might take this disagreement as an indication that there is something problematic about the conception of logically complex states of affairs when construed along the traditional linguistic lines.

[22] For a detailed theory of this see Meixner (1997).

'overlaps' relation to define the constituents of states of affairs, but this is not as straightforward as one might think. Although it is generally unproblematic to define the 'part of' relation in mereology in terms of the 'overlaps' relation,[23] in the mereology of states of affairs we are presently considering that does not give us exactly what we want. This is because, as the above examples suggest, states of affairs can overlap in more than one way: what they have in common might itself be a state of affairs (as in the states of affairs involving Peter) or it might not be (as in the two preceding cases). For this reason it will not do to identify *constituents* of states of affairs with their *parts* (defined in terms of overlaps), since some parts of states of affairs are not constituents but states of affairs themselves. In usual mereology, the parts of the objects considered are of the very same kind as the objects themselves. In our mereology of states of affairs this is not the case: some states of affairs have states of affairs as parts (which will result in a standard mereological picture), but they also have parts which are quite a different kind of thing, namely constituents of states of affairs.

It is therefore important to note that there are two possible ways of understanding the overlapping relation between states of affairs. One is a form of overlapping in which the overlap is a state of affairs (or several states of affairs) ('*s-overlapping*'), the other one in which not all of the overlap is (which we call '*c-overlapping*', '*c*' standing for 'constituent').

For example the states of affairs $Fa \wedge Gb$ and $Fa \wedge Hc$ s-overlap but do not c-overlap (all they have in common, Fa, is a state of affairs itself), Fa and Ga c-overlap but do not s-overlap (their common a is no state of affairs), and $Fa \wedge Gb$ and $Fa \wedge Hb$ s-overlap (they have a state of affairs, Fa, in common), and c-overlap (not all of the overlap is a state of affairs, b is not).[24] Both c- and s-overlapping have the familiar properties of overlap relations, i.e. they are symmetric and reflexive.

We can now define a *constituent* of two states of affairs as any c-overlap of two states of affairs which is not also an s-overlap. Based

---

[23] a is a part of b iff the two overlap and every c which overlaps a also overlaps b.

[24] Note that we use the familiar notation of predicate calculus to denote states of affairs, both atomic and molecular. These illustrative examples should be taken with several grains of salt. I do not observe the use-mention distinction precisely (strictly speaking a is a syntactic object, a name, the constituent being the referent of a), moreover I use a framework which implies assumptions about the internal structuring of states of affairs I do not want to make. Despite these defects, however, this is the most succinct framework for getting my point across.

on this we can employ the quasi-analytical procedure Carnap uses in the *Aufbau*[25] to let particular *sets* of states of affairs play the rôle of the constituents of states of affairs in our system. The way to do this is to consider sets of states of affairs such that every pair of states of affairs in the set shares a constituent, and no state of affairs in the set shares any constituent with any state of affairs outside the set. (This is just the Carnapian concept of 'similarity circles'.) These sets will go proxy for the constituents of states of affairs.

The point of quasi-analysis is that it allows us to develop a procedure for referring to the constituents of objects which we consider to be primitive, i.e. about the constituents of which we do not want to make any assumptions. This is done by relying exclusively on relations between these primitives (s- and c-overlapping in our case). Based on these we can then define sets which act as formal substitutes of the constituents which can be used in the further course of our investigation.

As we saw in the discussion of Dummett's example in § 31 there is usually more than one way of splitting up a whole, sometimes even if the part-concept involved is settled in advance. For example, if we consider a whole of the form Rab we realize there are three different ways of splitting it up: into R, a, and b, into Ra and b, and into Rb and a. However, if we adopt the weak failure of uniqueness (which is compatible with both the epistemic and the existential reading of the complex principle) we can divide up wholes in a unique way if we always divide them into their smallest parts. (Of course this presupposes that the whole is well-founded, otherwise there will be no smallest parts.) The quasi-analytical treatment of states of affairs considered above will entail (together with some assumptions specified below) that our similarity circles correspond to the atomic constituents of states of affairs.[26]

---

[25] Carnap (1928: §§ 61–74).

[26] See Goodman (1951: 158–60) for a fully worked-out example. The reader might want to notice that c-overlapping also gives us the resources for defining atomic constituents of states of affairs directly, assuming we are prepared to apply the c-overlap relation not just to states of affairs but also to their constituents (i.e. to c-overlaps themselves). The intuitive interpretation of this is unproblematic. When we say that what 'Peter loves Becca' and 'John loves Becca' have in common ('loves Becca') has something in common with what 'Albert loves Gill' and 'Bertrand loves Gill' have in common ('loves Gill') we are taking about c-overlaps of c-overlaps. If we do this we can define an *atomic constituent* of two states of affairs as any c-overlap which is not also an s-overlap *and* which does not c-overlap with any other constituent. For example ab is a constituent of

It is important to note that sometimes determining whether two states of affairs overlap presupposes certain ontological assumptions. Consider the philosophical position of monadism, which holds that all relations are monadic. For the monadist the states of affairs that John loves Kate and that John loves Becca only share one part, namely John. For him both are states of affairs in which John has different properties, in the one that of loving Kate, in the other that of loving Becca, and he will not assume that they have any other parts in common. Somebody accepting relations, however, will regard both states of affairs as relational and will not just assume that John is a part of them, but that loving is as well.

A related dispute could arise between defenders of a Davidsonian and an anti-Davidsonian conception of events. The Davidsonian will claim that the event of buttering a piece of toast slowly contains one more part than that of simply buttering it (the slowness being taken as an additional property of the event constituting the buttering), whereas someone who takes the buttering and the slow buttering to be two completely distinct relations between John and the toast will not agree on this view of the mereological relation between the two events.

This presupposition of certain ontological assumptions for determining the overlaps between states of affairs does not appear to be too problematic. After all even given particular assumptions about the constituents of states of affairs the main questions regarding the nature of ontological categories (i.e. how to distinguish them from other categories and how to understand their relations with one another) remain still open. The theory of ontological categories sketched below will be able to deliver an account of constituents of states of affairs, and thereby a theory of ontological categories, compatible with specific prior assumptions about these constituents, such as monadism. Obviously such assumptions will not *be entailed* by the account we are about to describe, so that someone like the monadist will have to find additional arguments for his conviction that all *prima facie* relational states of affairs are in fact monadic. But then the aim of our inquiry is to address the metaontological problem of the nature of ontological categories, rather than to provide justifications of particular object-level ontologies.

Gab and *Hab*, but it is not an atomic constituent because it overlaps with a constituent of *Fac* and *Hac*.

§45 Problems with quasi-analysis

Since the publication of Nelson Goodman's *Structure of Appearance* with its criticism of quasi-analysis this method is now often considered to be vexed by so many problems that it is wholly unfit to achieve its purpose. Goodman discusses cases where particular distributions of the constituents of the complexes to be analysed lead the method astray in that it identifies the constituents wrongly. There are two main difficulties, which Goodman calls the *companionship difficulty* and the *difficulty of imperfect community*.[27] In the first case some constituent is always in the company of another, and therefore cannot be identified; in the second case although every pair of elements of the set has some constituent in common, there is no constituent which all the elements of the set have in common. In this case the set obviously cannot go proxy for any constituent.

Given problems like the above we will of course require some justification for employing the quasi-analytical method in discussing ontological questions. There have been numerous ways of refining the quasi-analytical procedure which, although they did not lead to a complete disappearance of the Goodmanian problems, at least drastically reduced the probability of their occurrence.[28] None of these were ultimately successful, because for every refinement of the quasi-analytical method it seems possible to devise some peculiar distribution of the constituents among the complexes which leads that method astray.[29]

The route to achieving a workable form of quasi-analysis therefore does not appear to lie in constructing more and more refined versions of the quasi-analytical procedure, but rather in making certain background assumptions regarding the data on which the method will be employed which will be jointly sufficient for ruling out the counterexamples. These assumptions will be:[30]

[CARDINALITY]   The cardinality of the sets of elements the quasi-analytical method is supposed to operate on should be fairly large.

---

[27] Goodman (1951: 160–4).
[28] See Brockhaus (1963: 98), Lewis (1969); and Kleinknecht (1969) for an overview.
[29] Moulines (1991: 281–2).
[30] See Moulines (1991: 283).

[UNIFORMITY]   The number of constituents should be considerably
                 smaller than the set of elements.

[VARIETY]   Every constituent should appear in a number of different
                 elements and together with different other constituents.

A brief look at the structure of the Goodmanian and related counterexamples shows that they systematically violate the above assumptions.
Furthermore, all of the three assumptions seem to be plausible in the
context of our discussion, where the elements we have in mind are states
of affairs. Obviously the total number of states of affairs observed will
be very large, in any case much larger than the dozen or so elements
considered in Goodman's counterexamples. Similarly the world as a collection of states of affairs is fairly uniform: a large number of states of
affairs is made up by rearranging a rather small number of constituents;
these constituents, moreover, come up in a considerable variety of combinations, rather than in just one or two.[31] Thus given that these three
assumptions rule out the above counterexamples and appear furthermore to be plausible, employing the quasi-analytical method in our discussion of states of affairs turns out to be justified after all.

§46 Some formalism for the notion of a complex

Having described a procedure for referring to the constituents of states
of affairs by using particular sets of states of affairs to go proxy for them
in § 44 our second task is to describe how to sort these constituents into
different form-sets.

We can formulate much of this discussion in a more perspicuous
way by introducing some formalism designed to capture aspects of the
notion of a complex which we are going to need in the further course
of our inquiry. This notion comes up in a variety of contexts but has up
to now received hardly any discussion of its own.[32]

We start by considering a set **A** of complexes $A_1, \ldots, A_n$. Complexes are encountered in a wide variety of contexts. Examples from
chemistry come to mind most readily: a considerable part of it is concerned with the study of which chemical elements can form compounds
with which other elements and which cannot. For example, two

[31] See Black (1966: 115) who interprets Wittgenstein's *Tractatus* as claiming that every
object must be the constituent of at least one state of affairs.

[32] A notable exception is Tzouvaras (1995).

hydrogen atoms can form a compound with one oxygen atom while we cannot have a compound consisting of four hydrogen atoms and one oxygen atom. Here the notion of complex involved is that of a molecule.

Less scientifically, we can also find examples of complexes in the world of *artifacts*. Different blocks of a Lego toy fit together, nuts fit into bolts and pegs into holes. A set of tiles can be considered as a complex if it manages to tile a plane.

Admittedly neither molecules nor Lego blocks are major topics of philosophical inquiry. Other kinds of complexes, however, are. Frege introduced the notion of predicate-senses which could fit together with name-senses to produce a complex which is a thought. Such a thought is a complex entity located in the Fregean 'third realm'. There is of course also a more down-to-earth and purely linguistic way of understanding the formation of a complex out of predicates and names, simply in terms of functions awaiting completion by an argument which produces a complex expression (a sentence or phrase).

Another example of a complex (which is probably best described as a *semantic* complex) is discussed by Stenius in his interpretation of Wittgenstein.[33] This is the notion of a sentence-radical. The radical is supposed to constitute the 'content' to which can then be joined different operators for different moods (the 'forms') to yield a complex which is either a declarative sentence, a question, a command, or a modal statement (all of which have the same content).

A final example are individuals which fit together with properties into a complex which is a state of affairs. Unlike linguistic or semantic complexes they do not belong to the level of representation of the world, but rather are *in* the world. On the other hand they differ in important respects from complexes like molecules or artifacts.

The formal properties of complex formation depend to some extent on the kind of complex we have in mind. For example, in the case of complexes consisting of material objects we will want to say that if some object forms part of some complex it is 'taken' and cannot simultaneously be used to form part of another non-overlapping complex.[34] If we consider linguistic complexes, however, we would not make this assumption. The fact that a word is used in a particular sentence does not imply that it cannot be simultaneously used in another sentence. The complexes we are most interested in for the sake of our

[33] Stenius (1960: ch. 9).   [34] Tzouvaras (1995: 459).

investigations, however, are not chemical, linguistic, or semantic complexes, but *ontological complexes*, that is states of affairs.

Let us now introduce some further notation. We use strings of lower-case Roman letters $a, b, c \ldots$ to denote complexes. Thus some complex A_i, for example, will be represented by the string $\phi = (aba)$, another one by $\psi = (abbca)$ and so on. In accordance with our discussion in § 44 the lower-case letters will go proxy for the constituents of states of affairs and will denote sets of states of affairs which overlap in a particular way. Thus the as in (aba) denote a particular set of states of affairs (a 'similarity circle', to use Carnap's terminology) and go proxy for a particular constituent of states of affairs. The structure of a state of affairs is thus modelled in terms of strings of sets of states of affairs. This construction allows us to do justice to the assumption that knowledge of the complex, the state of affairs, is prior to knowledge of its constituents and that knowledge of the constituents is generated by abstraction from knowledge of the states of affairs and their interrelations.

The critical reader might object that strings are not particularly suitable as models of states of affairs, since we would not want to suppose that states of affairs are structured in a linear way, with one element following the next one. Complexes which are sentences are certainly very straightforwardly represented by strings: the $a, b, c, \ldots$ represent the words while the linear arrangement of them in the string represents the order of the words in the sentence. The structure of a state of affairs, it might be argued, is more similar to the way chemical molecules are structured than to the way sentences are structured. Just because the state of affairs in which a has R to b can be expressed by the sentence Rab this does not mean that the structure of the state of affairs it refers to is of a similar linear structure. All we need to claim is that in that state of affairs the a and the b are in some way linked or connected by the R. States of affairs could therefore be much more perspicuously represented by a two-dimensional notation (for example one along the lines of the 'existential graphs' used by Charles Sanders Peirce).[35] I agree with this criticism insofar as I do not want to suppose that states of affairs have a linear structure, nor would I want to argue that the linear structure of *language* can serve as an argument for the existence of such a structure

---

[35] Hartshorne et al. (1958: 4.347–4.584); for a good survey see also Burch (1991: 123–36).

within the states of affairs.[36] Unfortunately, though more conspicuous, a two-dimensional notation is far more complicated to handle than the familiar one-dimensional one. Furthermore, information about other, non-linear forms of putting together elements to form complexes can be encoded in a linear form as well. Introducing strings in order to model states of affairs does not commit us to assuming that they have a linear structure (in the same way as the fact there is a unique linear translation of every structural formula of a molecule does not imply that the molecule *itself* has a linear structure), while at the same time providing a system of notation which can easily be manipulated.

We will assume that all strings are finite. The idea here is that all complexes can be split up into a finite number of smallest parts and are thus well-founded. We call the *multiplicity* of an element in a string the number of times it occurs in it. Thus the multiplicity of a and of b in $(abbca)$ is 2 while that of c is 1. Later we will need the operation of forming the *concatenation* $\phi^\frown \psi$ of two strings ϕ, ψ. The multiplicities of elements in the new string will be the sum of the multiplicities in the individual strings. For example, $(abc)^\frown(abbca)$ is $(abcabbca)$. The set of all the elements of all the complexes $A_1, \ldots A_n$ will be called the *basis* of the set of complexes **A**.

We then introduce the monadic predicate **C** of strings of members of the basis. We say that **C**ϕ if there is some A_i in **A** and some permutation π_i of ϕ such that $\pi_i(\phi)$ denotes A_i. The intuitive meaning of **C** is thus that the members of the basis in ϕ 'fit together' so that they can form a complex. The members of the basis in ϕ are such that some way of arranging them (some permutation) makes them fit together, that is there is some complex in **A** which is identical with putting them together in this way.[37] Information about this predicate **C**, that is information about which members of the basis fit together to form a complex, will be crucial in the further course of our investigations.

---

[36] For a discussion of the relation of the linear structure of language to the structure of thought see Simons (1997).

[37] We could also have chosen an alternative formulation by letting **C** stand for a property of multisets of elements. Multisets are just like ordinary sets apart from the fact that they allow for repetitions. Thus while $\{a, b\} = \{a, a, b\}$, $[a, b] \neq [a, a, b]$. They are distinguished from ordered sets in that the order of elements does not matter, i.e. while $\langle a, a, b \rangle \neq \langle a, b, a \rangle$, $[a, a, b] = [a, b, a]$. For the formal properties of multisets see Blizard (1989).

Of course it will generally not be the case that there is just one such complex. Members of the basis which manage to fit together can fit together in different ways, thus producing different complexes. If we consider the complexes to be sentences and take the string $\phi =$ (*Alfred, Bertrand, chases*) then there are two different ways in which the elements of this string may be put together, i.e. two permutations of ϕ which are identical with elements of the set of complexes **A** under consideration, namely 'Alfred chases Bertrand' and 'Bertrand chases Alfred'.

Isomers (chemical compounds containing the same atoms but arranged in different ways such as HCN and HNC) and anagrams (such as 'Tokyo' and 'Kyoto') are further examples illustrating this point. However, there are strings that can only be put together in one way. For example $(\neg, \phi)$ gives only one complex (here to be understood as a wff), namely $\neg\phi$. There is no other possibility for just these two objects to be joined in a complex of this kind. However we cannot rely on this always being the case, as we have just seen.

§47   Typing data

After this discussion of complexes we are now in a position to describe how constituents of states of affairs can be sorted into different form-sets. The general idea is as follows.

We partition the basis into different subsets, each of which constitutes a strong form-set or *type*. The idea is thus that elements of the same type can be intersubstituted in all complexes in which they occur without destroying the ability of the whole to form a complex. Often when we say that two objects are of the same type or kind we mean that for any collection of objects which fit together (can form a complex) one of the objects being in the collection, you can also take the other object instead and everything will still fit. Thus two parts of a mechanism belong to the same type if each can be used as a spare part relative to the other in all mechanisms under consideration. Similarly, two expressions belong to the same grammatical type if in any grammatical sentence where the one occurs you can also use the other without destroying grammaticality.

We will be operating under the assumption that for every string ϕ of elements of the basis we know whether $\mathbf{C}\phi$ or not $\mathbf{C}\phi$ (we call this the *information assumption*).[38] We thus have some way of deciding

---

[38] See p. 204.

for every collection of objects from the basis whether or not they go together. This collection of objects (of constituents of states of affairs) can be very small. The information assumption does not demand that we know many states of affairs, but that we know those we do know very thoroughly.

We can then produce a set of *complex descriptions*. These complex descriptions tell us which types go together with which other types to form complexes. For example one complex description might tell us that if we put together one member of one type and two members of another type and nothing else these can form a complex together.

The information present in the complex descriptions can be reformulated to give us a *type description* for every type discussed. These indicate what we have to 'add' to elements of this type in order to get a complex. Part of the type description of the first type just mentioned would be that we have to add exactly two members of a specific other type to get a collection of objects which can form a complex together. The reader who is interested in a small formal example of complex descriptions and type descriptions is referred to § 96 in the Appendix.

§48   Containment of types

In § 40 I claimed that there was a procedure for constructing a containment hierarchy on the partition generated by splitting up the set of constituents of states of affairs into strong types which would also provide us with a sufficient amount of relatively comprehensive form-sets (such as abstract and concrete object) to act as base-sets for constructing the very restricted form-sets (such as group or building). Let us now describe this procedure.

The basic idea is very simple. We start by partitioning the basis of a set of data A into types. We then *restrict* A to A^- by deleting some of the data and divide it into types. Depending on the elements of A we delete, we end up with a typing which is less fine-grained. We then proceed by restricting A^- still further to A^{--}, type this again, and continue in this manner. We then 'link' the types produced in the typings of the different restrictions of A to form a containment-hierarchy.

The intuition behind this procedure is clear. Strong form-sets or types gave us a partition since they demand intersubstitutability in *all* complexes. Restricting the set of data (the set of states of affairs considered) obviously has the same effect as considering intersubstitutability in *some* complexes only. In this way we can achieve the containment structure generated by dividing **A** into weak form-sets, *while guaranteeing that the structure is hierarchical,* thus satisfying Sommers' law. The strong form-sets at the top of this hierarchy will also function as plausible candidates for base-sets for constructing the very restricted form-sets.

Some readers might find it helpful once again to look at a worked out formal example of such a generation of a containment hierarchy from a partition. This is given in § 97 in the Appendix.

A final point we might want to note in this context is that the containment structure we generate might be the very same we would have got had we used weak, rather than strong form-sets for our typing. (In fact this is the case in the formal example.) That applying the procedure described results in exactly this containment structure (rather than in another one, which would have also been a hierarchy), however, is not necessary—it depends on the order in which we consider different restrictions of the initial set to be typed. But it is possible to show that whenever a division of the basis of some set of data into weak form-sets generates a hierarchy, this structure can be reconstructed by applying the above method. Not all sequences of restrictions of a set will result in a containment structure according to the procedure described, but whenever this set *can* be divided into a hierarchy of non-overlapping types there is such a sequence resulting in a hierarchical structure.

3 BASE-SETS

On the basis of the preceding remarks we are now equipped with a more precise understanding of form-sets. In order to understand how they can be systematized by being constructed from base-sets, it is now necessary to have a closer look at the notion of construction involved.

§49 Constructing categories

In the different branches of knowledge we often encounter projects which attempt to construct certain classes of entities from certain others. They are particularly widespread in mathematics and the mathematical sciences, but can also found in philosophy, in law, and in many other disciplines. For the theory of ontological categories presented here it is particularly important that we develop a clear conception of what such 'construction' of some categories from others amounts to. Let us therefore begin by considering three examples.

The construction of different kinds of *numbers* is a central part of the familiar set-theoretic foundational theories in mathematics. Having constructed the natural numbers in terms of sets one then proceeds to construct the rational numbers from the natural numbers, then the reals from the rationals, and so on. Let us focus on the construction of rationals as pairs of natural numbers. Rational numbers behave quite differently from natural numbers (after all, this is why they have been introduced) but there is a sense in which this difference of behaviour which makes them into a different kind of number is not mathematically fundamental. It does not mark a diversity which could not be achieved in a world in which there are only natural numbers and the pairing function. The different behaviour shown by the rationals is the very same thing as the different behaviour shown by equivalence classes of pairs of natural numbers. Because the rationals are so constructible we might be inclined to say that they do not constitute a genuinely new kind of entity in a world with integers and the pairing function.

Similar considerations apply when mathematicians construct points as sets of volumes or as pairs of lines, volumes as sets of sets or sets of points, or sets as mereological sums. *Prima facie* points are very different from sets of volumes (for example they have members, which points do not), but all the important mathematical properties of points are retained by sets of volumes. Were the mathematician stranded in a strange possible world in which some objects were missing, he could make up for the loss of points by taking sets of volumes instead. Afterwards, the world would not be any poorer.

Constructing some categories from others also forms the basis of many philosophical theories. Work in epistemology has endeavoured to reduce physical objects to sense-data, metaphysicians developed constructions of properties from sets, or from mereological sums, or constructed individuals as collections of tropes or bundles of properties. A particularly interesting project of a similar nature is the construction of the category of *events* from other categories, discussed by Jaegwon Kim.[39]

[39] Kim (1976: 161).

Kim equates events with ordered triples of individuals, properties, and time-instances. The individual is the bearer of the property which is exemplified by that individual when the event occurs. Thus the event of me lighting a candle is spelt out as the triple consisting of the candle, the property of its being lit by me, and the particular time when this happened. Kim uses this account amongst other things as a basis for a theory of criteria of identity for events and for analysing their rôle in causal contexts. We are here interested not so much in whether this account is completely satisfactory,[40] but rather in the underlying thesis that if it is and if we have form-sets containing individuals, properties, time-instances, and the set-theoretic membership relation, the form-set of events is a redundant set. The idea is therefore that the existence of events does not contribute anything genuinely new to the kinds of things there are: events are just a special configuration of other kinds.

A final set of examples of constructions of categories can be found in law. The motivation behind many legal definitions is the attempt to take some intuitively unified category of things or actions (such as 'property', 'theft', 'contract', or 'assault') in order to describe the construction of some other entity, which has a clearly delineated set of properties and can for all intents and purposes be used instead of the original one. Take for example the case of *murder*. Different legal systems construct this category in slightly different ways, but the minimal common core seems to be that it is a) an action which takes the life of another human being, b) intentional, and c) motivated by malice. No lawyer will deny that this legal category of murder is distinct from the everyday variety. There are notorious tricky cases we are inclined to ascribe to one category, but not to the other. Moreover, the legal category of murder only comes into existence together with the legal code which defines it, the everyday category was there already. Nevertheless, there is an important sense in which these differences are not crucial. The legal concept is taken to incorporate all the important properties of murder. A morally better world than ours in which all acts of murder had magically disappeared would lose its ethical preferability as soon as we managed to construct the category of intentional malicious killings in this world.

So how do these three examples of constructing categories from others relate to the notion of ontological construction mentioned earlier?

---

[40] See Runggaldier and Kanzian (1998: 188–92) for some discussion.

The reader will recall that I defined a collection of base-sets to be a minimal subset of some set of form-sets or categories such that the minimal subsets can construct all the remaining forms-sets in the bigger set. Now in the examples of constructing the category or form-set of rational numbers from the natural numbers, constructing events from ordered triples of individuals, properties, and time instances, and constructing the category of murders from that of killings, which are additionally qualified by intention and malice the categories of *natural numbers*, of *sets*, *individuals*, *properties*, and *time instances*, and that of *killings* are all potential base-sets. Whether they are actual base-sets depends on whether they are not just able to construct the category or form-sets in question (i.e. rational numbers, events, or murders), but also *all other* form-sets.

In the cases of natural numbers and killings there do not seem to be bright prospects for this. But in the case of sets, individuals, properties, and time-instances the chances seem to be a bit better. At least a significant chunk of the variety of form-sets we usually meet, such as macroscopic objects, structural properties, states of affairs, and mathematical structures could be constructed from these. If we were thus successful in basing a satisfactory ontological theory on these four form-sets and construct all others in terms of them, this would imply that our ontological needs would not have to extend beyond these four. All the variety there is in the world can be conceived of as a more or less complicated arrangement of these four basic categories.

So events will still be identified as a form-set by noting that certain parts of states of affairs such as 'the battle', 'the funeral' and so on can form states of affairs with other parts of states of affairs such as 'was interrupted twice' or 'lasted for two days' and that this fact distinguishes them from other parts of states of affairs. But they will not be regarded as base-sets or ontological categories because they can be constructed from a set of form-sets which is also able to construct everything else there is. Events, and similarly all other form-sets apart from the special set of four just mentioned, do not contribute to the ontological plenitude of the world.

Two of the three constructions described above were explicit set-theoretic constructions. However, this should not be taken as suggesting that set theory was somehow an indispensable part of constructions of categories or indeed of the basis of a set of form-sets. As is evident from its wide employment the category of sets is a very versatile constructive tool, but it is not the only composition operation available.[41] Operations like mereological composition or physical composition, which puts objects into direct spatial adjacency are similarly able to play a part in constructing categories from others. Because all these composition operations have different formal characteristics[42] it is not possible to give a generalized account of the form of constructions of categories beyond the discussion given above. This is comparable to the case of replacing an artifact, say a screwdriver, with an equivalent one. There are a variety of ways in which we can 'construct' a replacement screwdriver: we can put together a metal part and a wooden handle, we can carve the whole object from a solid block of metal, glue together several metallic parts, cast it from molten metal, and so on. None of these will involve the same constructional operations, nor the same raw materials these operations operate on. Apart from describing several characteristic examples there is thus no way in which we can give a generalized theory of constructions of screwdrivers which would cover all possibilities of manufacturing a replacement. The same applies to the construction of categories: we can elucidate the notion by pointing out important specimens of constructions, but cannot provide a generalized formal account which would subsume all categorial constructions.

At this point one might raise the following worry: if there are categories which can be adequately constructed from others, does this not imply that systems of ontological categories are not exhaustive? Do the constructed categories not end up as ontological waifs, unattached to any ontological category? But this is surely problematic, given that it seems to be one of the central points of constructing systems of ontological categories that everything can be placed in some category or other.

I agree that this would be an unwelcome result, but we should note that the above conception of events, for example, does not entail that different particular events (such as the battle of Leuthen or Victor Hugo's funeral) do not belong to any ontological category, since the category of events is not granted such a privileged title. Everything belongs to some ontological category. If we follow Kim's line, these events can all be constructed of sets of some sort. And therefore the category of sets, being a

---

[41] A taxonomy of different kinds of composition operations can be found in Westerhoff (2004).

[42] Westerhoff (2004).

base-set, is the ontological category they belong to. This holds for members of redundant sets in general: the ontological category they belong to is one of the form-sets the redundant set has been constructed from.

Note furthermore that my theory is not just committed to the constructability of relatively general types, such as events, but also to that of more particular ones, such as tables, chairs, or buildings. Given their greater specificity the constructional processes for these are much more intricate than those required in the case of events. Constructions of tables, chairs, and buildings cannot be just regarded as complexes of physical objects, but will presumably also have to include some psychological items, such as the human *intentions* that the lump of physical stuff is to serve as something to sit on or to live in. This, however, is not a qualitative, but only a quantitative difference. In the same way in which the construction of imaginary numbers out of pure sets is more complicated than that of the integers, that of more specific categories is more complicated than that of less specific ones. There is, however, no difference in the *nature* of the different constructional processes involved.

Having gained a more precise conception of what is meant by ontological construction, the critical reader might raise the following objection at this point. Surely the fact that some set can be constructed from others does not stop it from being a base-set. After all we explicitly claimed on page 97 that we did not want to identify base-sets exclusively with all the form-sets which *cannot* be constructed from other form-sets (although all of these are obviously to be counted amongst the base-sets). But how do we then find out whether a base-set is a redundant set and thus not an ontological category? Given the fact that there can be multiple bases for a set, it seems that relative to one basis a form-set such as the set of events is a redundant set, whereas relative to another basis it is not.

§50 Local relativism

If we consider a set of form-sets, there are several ways in which its members may be constructionally related. It may be the case that no subset is able to construct any other one, in which case all form-sets in the set are base-sets. Precisely one subset may be able to construct all the other form-sets, so that it constitutes the basis, while all the other form-sets constitute the surplus. The situation is a bit more complicated if there are several sets which can construct all other sets and thus several bases and several sets of redundant sets. There may be some form-sets which belong to the intersection of all bases (and which are thus not constructible from anything), the set of which will be called the *core of the basis*. Equally there might be form-sets which are members of every surplus, which are always constructed, never used to construct other form-sets. We will call the set of these the *core of the surplus*. By means of illustration we might want to say that form-sets like sets or mereological sums, which turn up in a number of ontological constructions belong to the core of the basis for most sets of form-sets, whereas other form-sets, such as culinary implements or kinds of furniture, which are not usually employed to construct any other form-sets, but can in turn be very well constructed, belong to the core of the surplus.

If we want to decide which of the form-sets are base-sets and which are redundant sets, the cores of the basis and surplus are obviously to be included in the two. (If they exist, that is. There may be radically different bases which can construct an entire set of form-sets so that there is no core of the basis, or it may be the case that every form-set can be employed to construct some others, so that there is no core of the surplus.) When allocating any other form-set to the basis or the surplus there is room for negotiation. Depending on which basis is taken as most plausible, some form-set which is neither in the core of the basis nor in the core of the surplus may come to lie on either side of the divide between base-sets and redundant sets. This fact is what we call the *local relativism of ontological categories*. It is local because relative to a given world (a given set of form-sets) there may be more than one set of form-sets which can be chosen as a basis, and thus more than one plausible candidate for the set of ontological categories in that world.

But how do we settle which of the different bases of the set of form-sets under consideration is to be regarded as the set of ontological categories? There are certainly cases where this is a matter of argument. Considering the two form-sets of individuals and properties it is evident that there have been attempts to construct the first from the second and the second from the first. Constructing properties from individuals is usually associated with different forms of nominalism, while constructing individuals from properties (sometimes called 'universalism') is what bundle theory sets out to perform.[43] For the nominalist,

---

[43] See Armstrong (1978: I: §§ 2–9) for an overview.

individuals would be base-sets and properties redundant sets. For the universalist, it would be exactly the other way round. Similarly, the firm believer in events may well argue that in a world in which there are sets, individuals, properties, time-instances, and events, it is not the events which should be constructed from other form-sets. Rather should sets and events be taken as base sets, while individuals, properties, and time-instances could be conceived of as set-theoretic constructions from events.

If both accounts worked, and worked equally well, this would indeed leave us in a tie regarding which of the form-sets in question are base-sets and which redundant sets. But in ontology the situation is usually not like this. Apart from the fact that it is relatively hard to provide a satisfactory construction even in *one* direction, the two constructions would presumably differ enough in their internal details to provide some criterion for accepting the one but not the other.

It is apparent that there is no determinate procedure for selecting the 'best' of the bases. We rather employ pragmatic criteria, such as the size of the basis, the nature and simplicity of constructions and so forth in order to rate some bases as more plausible than others and then pick one of the most plausible ones. It should be noted, however, that the fact that it may in this way be relative whether some particular form-set constitutes a base-set and thus an ontological category is no deficiency of the metaontological account described here. What we were looking for was a satisfactory account of ontological categories; whether a particular class of objects fulfils that definition is then a further question, and it is ontology rather than metaontology which is required to answer it.

Turning from the question of how to tell apart base-sets and redundant sets to the concept of 'constructing' one form-set from others, it should be clear from the examples given in the above pages that there are other senses of 'construction' apart from the set-theoretical one which are relevant for the distinction between base-sets and redundant sets. Particularly prominent is the notion of mereological construction, which is especially important in nominalistic systems such as those developed by Goodman. Mereological construction crucially differs from set-theoretic construction in giving rise to a transitive containment relation: a part of a part is a part of the whole, but a set which is a member of a set which is a member of a set is not necessarily a member of the last set. Furthermore it entails that distinct entities cannot be made up from the same items: the fusion of a with the fusion of b and c is the same as the fusion of the fusion of a and b with c, but $\{a, \{b, c\}\}$ is not the same as $\{\{a, b\}, c\}$. Indeed Goodman claims that this second property is essential to all notions of construction employed in nominalistic systems.[44]

We can imagine still other kinds of constructional operations. For example, to show that the form-set 'building' is not a base-set it would presumably be sufficient to show how members of this set could be constructed from physical objects with the help of some aggregation operation.

It is important to note at this point that all the constructions we consider are complexity *increasing*, rather than *decreasing*. Roughly speaking, a construction is complexity increasing if it constructs more complex objects out of less complex objects, rather than the other way round. Obvious examples of increasing constructions are constructing sets from their members, constructing the concept 'bachelor' from 'male' and 'unmarried', or constructing molecules from atoms. Decreasing constructions work the other way round: they construct members from the sets containing them, 'male' and 'unmarried' from 'bachelor' and atoms from molecules.

The difference between increasing and decreasing operations can be made more precise by considering the complexity of algorithms or instructions for generating objects.[45] It is straightforward to calculate the complexity of these algorithms in terms of the number of computational steps and the memory capacities needed. For each object call the least complex algorithm generating it its *recipe*. Now a constructional operation is increasing if the recipe of its input is always less complex than the recipe of its output, and decreasing if it is the other way round. For an example consider the following two simple constructional operations O_1 and O_2 which take pure sets as inputs. O_1 returns for any set ϕ the output $\{\phi\}$, O_2 makes ϕ out of inputs of the form $\{\phi\}$. Now clearly if the complexity of the recipe of some set is n, that of the recipe of the result of applying O_1 to it will be greater than n and that of the recipe of the result of applying O_2 to it will be smaller than n. Constructions which use O_1 are therefore increasing, those which confine themselves to O_2 decreasing.

---

[44] Goodman (1971: 295–301).   [45] See e.g. Chaitin (1987b), (1987a).

If not straightforwardly pathological, decreasing constructions seem to represent a particularly non-standard kind of construction. In fact we would not want to call them constructions at all, but rather reductions or dissections. We will demand that all the constructions of form-sets out of form-sets we consider are complexity increasing. This has the advantage of constraining the relativism just discussed to some extent. If all constructions must be increasing, only fairly inclusive form-sets can be chosen as base-sets. If we allowed decreasing operations as well, *every* form-set would be a possible base-set (even a very specific form-set such as that of buildings might be used in constructing the more general form-set of material objects, which might be done by forming the union of many such form-sets). The predominance of fairly inclusive form-sets in systems of ontological categories which have been proposed can then be explained by a preference for increasing over decreasing construction operations.

§51 Constructs and originals

An important problem in this context is the relation between the construct and the object which the construct is supposed to replace (the *original*). The most straightforward position seems to be to demand an extensional identity of the expressions referring to the construct and the original. This was advocated by Carnap, who argued that the fact that some a can be constructed from b and c meant that each expression referring to a can be replaced by one referring to some construct from b and c *salva veritate*.[46] For example, Carnap argues that whenever we refer to prime numbers we can also refer to natural numbers having the property of being divisible only by 1 and by themselves. But in fact this demand is far too restrictive. As Goodman has shown, this is obvious in the case of identity-statements involving constructs and originals.[47] To know whether replacing 'point' by 'set of volumes' in 'a point is the same as a set of volumes' changes the truth-value of the statement we first have to know its truth-value. Once we do know it, however, we no longer need to appeal to the notion of extensional identity to see whether they really are the same. Thus the 'test' presupposes what it is supposed to show. It is furthermore important to note that this problem

---

[46] Carnap (1928: 47).　　[47] Goodman (1951: 8). See also Quine (1976).

will not just arise in the case of identity-statements but also in the case of all statements depending on such identity-statements. To determine whether replacing 'point' by 'set of volumes' in 'a point has no members' changes the truth-value of the statement, for example, we first have to know whether points really are the same as sets of volumes.

The failure of extensional identity of construct and original is in harmony with the fact that we often give different extensionally non-identical constructions of the same original, as in constructing a point as a set of volumes or as a pair of intersecting lines. We can thus agree that far from being identical with the originals the constructs are in many respects quite different.[48] The point of devising a construction 'consists not in showing that a given entity is identical with a complex of other entities but in showing that no commitment to the contrary is necessary'.[49] The important point in determining whether something is a construction of an original is therefore, as Goodman notes, that the truth-value of the sentences we 'care about' is preserved.[50] The existence of extensionally non-identical constructions of the same objects is evidence enough that there are always some sentences we do not care about. In the above case, for example, we do not care about whether points have members. Similarly in the case of set-theoretical constructions of the natural-number sequence we do not care about whether the number 2 is a member of the number 4 (which is the case with von Neumann's but not with Zermelo's construction).

§52 Adequacy of constructs

The properties of originals and constructs properly overlap: there are some properties which the original has but the construct lacks, some the construct has but the original lacks, and some which are shared by both. The properties they share will determine whether a construction of an original is adequate or not. To give a precise specification of the amount or nature of the properties the two must share to make something an adequate construct is surprisingly hard in the general case.[51] The extent to which one can give precise criteria for the adequacy of a construct

[48] See Gottlieb (1976: 59).
[49] Goodman (1951: 29).
[50] Goodman (1951: 23).
[51] See Gottlieb (1976: 67–9) for some attempts.

depends crucially on how precise our understanding of the original is. In the case of arithmetic, for example, nothing is an adequate construction of the natural numbers which does not satisfy the Peano axioms. A construct containing only finitely many items, or one where two items could have the same 'successor', can under no circumstance count as an adequate substitute for the natural numbers. The Peano axioms thus provide us with a necessary condition for the adequacy of constructs in the case of natural numbers. Unfortunately, such necessary conditions cannot always be formulated with this degree of precision. However, we might get something less precise but still useful. It seems evident that any construct which is supposed to act as a substitute for events must somehow incorporate the fact that they exist in time. Similarly anything which can go proxy for the category of murder must at least be a killing. The notion of an *essential property*, of something an object cannot lose without ceasing to be that very object, suggests itself here. The natural number structure cannot lose the properties described in the Peano axioms, events cannot stop being in time without ceasing to be events, and so on. We might therefore say that something is an adequate construct of some original if it shares all its essential properties with the original. This criterion is of course only as clear as our conception of the essential properties of the original under consideration. If these are relatively well-defined we seem to get round problems such as the 'unicorn-construction' discussed by Gottlieb.[52] The idea there is that we have a set-theoretic construction of the natural numbers which is completely standard apart from the fact that the successor-function $S'xy$ is defined as $(x = y \land (\exists x)(Ux)) \lor Sxy$, where U stands for the property 'being a unicorn'. This construct is extensionally equivalent to the standard one: all sentences true in it are also true in the unicorn-construct. The problematic thing about the unicorn-construct is that it *entails* things the standard construct did not entail. For example the truth that no number is its own successor $((\forall x)\neg(x = x \land (\exists x)(Ux)) \lor Sxx)$ entails that there are no unicorns $(\neg(\exists x)(Ux))$. It is clear that we must find some way of ruling out this kind of construction. If the natural number structure has any essential properties at all, not entailing anything about unicorns is one of them. The unicorn-construct therefore cannot be an adequate construct of the original natural number structure.

[52] (1976: 64).

The reader will have noticed from my discussion of essences here and in § 27 that my theory admits them only so far as they are properties which could be shared between different objects. To be colder than 25 degrees Celsius is a property a snowball and a piece of rock can share, but it is an essential property only of the latter, the rock could warm up without ceasing to be what it is. I am therefore not committed to the position that essential properties of objects are properties *which only this object could have* (such properties are often referred to as haecceities). I do not agree with Plantinga in assuming that 'being identical with that snowball' names a property which is that snowball's haecceity.[53] Indeed I do not see why talk about the snowball being self-identical should commit us to anything else but assuming the existence of the snowball and of the relation of self-identity,[54] where the latter is something which can be shared by different objects (in fact it is plausible to assume that it is shared by *every* object).[55] I do therefore not include for example 'being the number 7' or 'being this particular event' amongst the essential properties a construct must share with its original. That the number 7 is the number 7 does not ascribe a particular unique property of sevenness to the number 7 which would constitute its essence, but rather asserts the (boring) fact that the number 7 reflexively bears the identity relation to itself. This, however, is nothing which distinguishes 7 in a fundamental way from any other object.

§53 Construction and paraphrase

Let us also note that there is an obvious language-based equivalent to the above talk about 'construction' of form-sets. Instead of speaking about constructing one kind of thing from another, we speak about *paraphrasing* certain sentences by others. This way of approaching the matter has been somewhat more popular in philosophical discussion, although the problems involved in formulating both accounts have a substantial

[53] Plantinga (1979).

[54] This point is also argued for in Chisholm (1989: 47–8).

[55] We might want to note at this point that this is also the most plausible analysis of all reflexive statements of sortal identity. If I say of John the tailor that he is the same tailor as himself, all I am referring to is John, the relation 'is the same tailor as', and the fact that it holds reflexively of John. I would not want to say that this statement ascribes some special property, which we might call 'tailor self-identity', to John.

intersection. Since speaking in terms of construction is more congenial to my way of dealing with the analysis of ontological categories, I will not say a great deal about its language-based counterpart, the paraphrase approach. I will mention just one point which helps to serve as a useful contrast in order to clarify certain aspects of talk in terms of construction.

The underlying idea of the paraphrase approach is of course that for a group of sentences referring to some object a we try to find paraphrases which do not refer to this a. Now it has been argued that this approach is obviously defective, for either the paraphrase says the same as the paraphrased sentence, in which case it entails the same sentences so that there has been no ontological gain in passing from the one to the other, or else the paraphrase does *not* say that same as the original sentence, it which case it is not a proper paraphrase.[56]

If we follow the above argument, however, it becomes evident that it is not problematic to accept the second horn of the dilemma. We do not have to assume that a paraphrase has to say the same as the original sentence in the sense that it shares all entailments with it. Rather we want to say that if ϕ is a sentence involving a, and ϕ' is like ϕ, except that all occurrences of a have been replaced by some expression referring to something else (so that ϕ' is supposed to be a paraphrase of ϕ), then ϕ and ϕ' have the same truth-value if and only if ϕ makes an essential statement about what a refers to.

Jackson seems to think that offering such a paraphrase which is not supposed to be extensionally equivalent and thus 'a surrogate, rather than an analysis'[57] entails that we consider the original sentence to be false and the paraphrased version to be the only *really* true one:

the offending sentences are eliminated as false and allegedly true and ontically inoffensive surrogates are put in their place.[58]

While this is true of certain kinds of paraphrases (e.g. those paraphrasing statements about 'the average man') it is not true of all of them. In particular this position is not adopted by our account. That we consider something to be a construct of some original does not mean that we want to eliminate the original or somehow claim that it is not *really*

---

[56] Alston (1957: 9–10).   [57] Jackson (1980: 307).   [58] Jackson (1980: 308).

there.[59] If we discover that a certain chemical compound can be used as a surrogate for some substance, this does not affect the existential status of that substance in the slightest—it is there whether or not we discovered that there is a surrogate for it. What *is* affected by the discovery of the surrogate, however, is our *dependence* on the original substance. If the surrogate is worth its salt, that is if it has all the essential qualities of the original, we are no longer forced to employ the substance itself; we can achieve the same result by using the compound. Ontological construction is therefore not aimed at eliminating originals, as Jackson seems to think, but is rather a procedure which allows us to determine ways in which to achieve the most comprehensive results with the most restricted resources. Knowledge about ontological constructions provides us with possibilities for *systematizing* collections of kinds of things, i.e. collections of form-sets.

§54 Global relativism

In § 50 we discussed the local relativism of ontological categories, namely the problem that relative to one world, one set of form-sets, there might be several plausible candidates for sets of ontological categories. There is another relativism to consider, which we may call *global relativism regarding ontological categories*. This implies that even the most certain candidates for base-sets and thus ontological categories (the members of the core of the basis) are not base-sets in all worlds (relative to all sets of form-sets). Every base-set's being a base-set depends on what *other* form-sets there are. In the presence of certain form-sets it might be constructible and redundant; in the presence of others it might be a base-set and thus an ontological category. Therefore no kind of thing is *essentially* an ontological category.

We can draw a parallel here with the distinction between atomic and molecular significance-ranges developed by Brady in the context of his

---

[59] Cf. Armstrong (1997: 33):

And just as one day natural science may give us reason to think that the fundamental particulars have been identified, so also it may give us reason to think that the fundamental universals—the fundamental properties and relations—have been identified. But even then, what is non-fundamental is not therefore non-existent. Macroscopic particulars do not fail to exist if they turn out to be assemblages of fundamental particulars!

significance logic.[60] His theory of significance-ranges is based on a weak notion of intersubstitutability. These significance-ranges are constructed by abstraction from predicates. For example, the significance-range generated by the mereological predicate of overlapping ○ is the class X such that $(\forall z)(z \in X \equiv (\exists x)(\exists y)(z = \langle x, y \rangle) \wedge S(x \circ y))$,[61] where S is a primitive monadic operator on propositions the intuitive reading of which is 'is significant'. Since Brady claims that statements like $(x \circ y)$ are only significant if the x and y stand for individuals, the significance-range generated by ○ is the class of ordered pairs of individuals.

The idea is then that certain significance-ranges can be understood as logical constructions from others.[62] These significance-ranges are then called *molecular*. Consider for example the significance-range generated by the predicate 'owns a car'. Clearly this will include people, but it will also include things like companies, since they are capable of owning cars. Thus this significance-range can be taken to be the union of two other significance-ranges, that containing persons (generated by such predicates as 'works in a library') and that containing companies (generated by such predicates as 'is liked by its shareholders'). This significance-range is therefore molecular. *Atomic* significance-ranges are of course those which cannot be constructed in this way. It is now easy to see that 'it depends on the different predicates in a language [. . .] whether a significance-range is atomic or not'. [63] Consider the case of the significance-range containing material objects. Clearly this can be partitioned into the sets of animate and inanimate objects. But whether this means that it is therefore constructible as the union of the two depends on whether our language contains predicates which have just these two sets as significance-ranges. 'Being an atomic significance-range' (in the same way as 'being a base-set') is thus a property which can be possessed by something in one language (world) but not in another. It is the background, the other significance-ranges or other form-sets, which determine whether a particular one is primitive or can be reduced to others.

It is thus apparent that our answer to the question *what* an ontological category is entails that—due to the local relativism described in § 50—there is often no clear answer to the question whether x is an

---

[60] Brady (1980).   [61] Brady (1980: 328).   [62] Brady (1980: 329).
[63] Brady (1980: 329).

ontological category rather than y. In one systematization of the form-sets x might be, in another y. The global relativism just described also affects the form-sets where the answer seems to be clear (the cores of the basis and surplus). This is because global relativism implies that there is not always a clear answer to the question whether some x is an onto-logical category in isolation. The answer depends not just on the x but also essentially on its 'surroundings', on which other form-sets there are. In some surroundings x will be an ontological category, in others not.

§55   Base-sets and axioms

Both local and global relativism are actually very familiar if we con-sider the problem of expressing some theory in an axiomatic frame-work. What axioms are for a theory, base-sets or ontological categories are for the world. If we want to axiomatize a theory, our task is to select some proper subset of the sentences of the theory which is as small as possible and which entails all the sentences of the theory. Reading 'is constructed from' as 'is entailed by' we are thus looking for a base-set of sentences such that all sentences of the theory can be constructed from them. If the sentences of the theory are sufficiently homogeneous there will always be such a set which is a proper subset of the original set. It is clear, however, that there will often be more than one such set. To axiomatize such a theory we could then choose any one of a collection of subsets. There is therefore not always a unique answer to the question 'What are the axioms of the theory we are considering?'—this is local relativism regarding the axioms of a theory. The parallel with global rel-ativism is even more obvious. Clearly it does not make sense to ask for any one sentence whether or not it is an axiom—that depends on its theoretical surroundings, i.e. on the *other* sentences of the theory. In the presence of some sentences it could be an axiom, in the presence of others it cannot be. This appears to be obvious given our contem-porary conception of axioms. There is, however, another conception which has been very prominent during the history of philosophy, and that is the conception of axioms as self-evident truths.[64] We could call this the *absolute* conception of the axiom, as opposed to the *relative* one usual nowadays which treats axioms as part of the framework we use to systematize our theories. Given this absolute conception it *would* make sense to ask whether some sentence considered in isolation (say, one

[64] See Oeing-Hanhoff (1971).

of Euclid's postulates) was indeed an axiom. This leads us to consider an interesting parallel with the conception of ontological categories. In the same way as there are absolute and relative conceptions of axioms, there are such conceptions of ontological categories. On the absolute conception there is a determinate sense in which a certain set of categories rather than any other set constitutes the set of ontological categories, of most fundamental things there are in the world. It is also sensible to ask whether some particular category (say, that of events) is or is not an ontological category. As the preceding argument showed, there is something deeply problematic about the absolute view. In our inquiry after a conception of ontological categories which fulfilled certain central demands, we were forced towards an account which treats ontological categories not as the most fundamental parts of the world but as the most fundamental parts of *our systematization of the world*. Such an account must necessarily be relative. There is usually more than one way of organizing a body of knowledge, nor does it make sense to attribute a certain rôle in the systematization (such as being an axiom or a base-set) to particular elements independently of the other elements. It therefore turns out that our account of ontological categories in terms of base-sets has interesting consequences for our conception of ontological categories in general.

A different parallel—less mathematical but equally instructive—worth considering is that between base-sets and the words of Basic English. Basic English, which was developed by C. K. Ogden in the 1920s was supposed to constitute a curious halfway house between the simplification of English to facilitate its employment as an international language and the construction of an artificial universal auxiliary language.[65] Its main objective was to give a selection of about 850 English words (about 600 nouns, 150 adjectives, 16 verbs, and 100 structural words) from which virtually all others (excluding proper names, loan words and the like) could be defined. The vocabulary of Basic English was thus intended to furnish the speaker with the semantic resources for most communicative situations, as well as providing a minimal list of words to be used in definitions in monolingual dictionaries.

Reading 'definition' as 'construction' it is clear that the vocabulary of Basic English behaves structurally very similarly to our base-sets. Basic English attempts to provide a reduction of the lexical plenitude

---

[65] Ogden (1930).

of English to a minimal subset. Of course such a subset is unlikely to be unique, moreover no word qualifies as a word of Basic English just by itself—this depends on the other English words around. It is easy to imagine variants of English where a 'basic word' had to be a defined one, or where a previously defined one had to be treated as basic. Finally, the interpretation of 'definition' is similarly open-ended as our conception of 'construction'. No system of pre-prepared definitional frameworks is given, but it is up to the intelligence and linguistic creativity of the speaker (or the ingenuitiy of the philosopher in the metaphysical case) to develop a definition or construction of an item not included in the set of basic elements.

4   BASE-SETS AS ONTOLOGICAL CATEGORIES

Let us now summarize the advantages of our account, which considers base-sets as an explication of the notion of an ontological category, over the other accounts discussed so far. At the beginning of the previous chapter we listed some problems for the traditional accounts which can be grouped into two sorts, those relating to the *cut-off point problem* and the *problem of too special categories* on the one hand, and those relating to *issues of containment of categories* on the other. Both kinds of problems disappear once we consider ontological categories as base-sets.

§56   Cut-off point problem and too special categories

As explained above, the division of form-sets into redundant sets and base-sets was specifically introduced to cope with this problem. The conception of form-sets is enhanced by adding a further criterion which selects a proper subset of them. This criterion is based on the idea that some form-sets are constructible from other form-sets and that these form-sets (the redundant sets) are not the ones which are ontologically interesting. The ontologically interesting sets are the base-sets, which provide the basis of the phenomenal plenitude of the world. They determine what kinds of things there are.

The idea of redundant sets explains why certain kinds of things (certain form-sets) are 'too special' to be ontological categories. They are 'too special' because their being there would not make any fundamental difference to what kinds of things (what form-sets) there are in the world. They are one sort of form-sets which (if they are removed) can be immediately recovered from the form-sets which are still there. Elements of redundant sets are like Lego blocks which can be constructed by putting together two other Lego blocks. If you took away all these redundant Lego blocks from my set, I could use a construction of my remaining Lego blocks as a substitute for them. The reduction of my set of Lego blocks would make no qualitative difference, that is no difference regarding the *kind* of structures I could build with them (although it would make a quantitative difference—I would need more blocks to build the same structures).

By distinguishing base-sets and redundant sets we are also able to give an explanation of the difference between semantically anomalous statements and statements which express category-mistakes. The former involve the violation of categories which are parasitic on the existence of base-sets (such as 'building', 'group', 'book' and so on). Category-mistakes proper, on the other hand, violate more fundamental categories; they violate the categories which are responsible for the kinds of things there are in the world.

§57   Sommers' law and hierarchical structure

It should be clear that the construction described in §48 generates a containment structure on the set of form-sets which is in accordance with Sommers' law. Remember that this claims that for any two types either they are disjoint or one properly contains the other. The case that one type is contained in two other types (i.e. the case that the two types overlap) is ruled out. By considering restrictions of the set of data we can construct a containment hierarchy on a collection of types *post festum*. In particular, we can can generate the containment hierarchy which a division into weak form-sets would have generated had it been able to generate a hierarchical structure at all. Furthermore, once we have constructed such a hierarchy, additional incoming information will never destroy it. New data coming in will usually refine the typing we have, but it will never merge old types, so that Sommers' law is satisfied.

We have shown how the set of form-sets can be arranged into a containment hierarchy, a structure systems of ontological categories are generally taken to possess, and one which is in addition supposed to be especially psychologically natural (as argued in § 24). This structure is generated by linking information about the typing of the constituents of states of affairs we currently know with information about a smaller set of states of affairs (which might have been all the states of affairs we knew at an earlier time). The hierarchical structure is perpetuated by refining our typing of constituents of states of affairs as new data come in.

However, we do not equate ontological categories with form-sets in general, but with particular form-sets, namely base-sets. Why can we be assured that the containment structure of this subset of the set of form-sets is also a hierarchy? In order to see this we have to take into account that when constructing very restricted form-sets from base-sets we want to construct a set of objects which can only go into very special states of affairs. We also want our set of base-sets to be small. We would rather want to have one set of base-sets for doing all the constructions, than choose a new one for every form-set to be constructed. Since our construction procedures are increasing rather than decreasing, we choose form-sets which can go into many different states of affairs and then restrict them by construction into those which can only go into a very limited number of states of affairs. Now it is clear that the higher up a form-set is located in the containment hierarchy, the more states of affairs its members can be intersubstituted in. Therefore the most plausible choice of base-sets are those form-sets which come from the top part of the hierarchy. This explains why the ontological categories (the base-sets) are arranged in a tree structure. It is no coincidence that 'the only ontologically interesting ones are near the top of the tree'[66] in the categorical hierarchy: they are the only form-sets which are sufficiently unspecific to serve as a small basis for constructing all the other form-sets.

Note also that since a form-set which is *contained* in another form-set rigidly *depends* on this form-set, the containment hierarchy also induces an ordering by generality. Categories higher up the hierarchy will be more general than those further down, and non-ontological categories (redundant sets) can also easily be shown to be less general than the base-sets they were constructed from.

---

[66] Keil (1979: 141).

We have therefore established two main points. First, there is a clear difference between ontological and non-ontological categories; the boundary between them is not just vague. Ontological categories are form-sets which can be used to construct all other form-sets, whereas non-ontological categories are those which are constructed. Secondly, due to the increasing nature of the constructive process, some form-sets are more plausible candidates for base-sets than others. The higher up the containment hierarchy of form-sets something is, the greater its plausibility as a base-set. The tree structure of systems of ontological categories can therefore be explained by the fact that the most plausible base-sets are a top part of the hierarchy of form-sets.

§58 Flexibility of the base-set account

Let us also note that identifying ontological categories with base-sets has the advantage that the extension of the concept remains flexible. We would not want our definition of 'ontological category' to result in a fixed list which determines once and for all what the ontological categories are. We *do* want it to tell us why we regard ontological categories as ontological categories, i.e. by which criteria we pick them out. But because of global and local relativism there will still be the further problem whether this or that class fulfils the criterion. Whether something is an ontological category (a base-set) depends firstly on which other form-sets there are, and secondly on the way in which these form-sets are systematized relative to the notion of ontological construction. This, however, is a problem for ontology and not for the metaontological account we are sketching here.

Further controversy surrounds the notion of ontological construction, as even a cursory look at the history of ontology shows. It is usually a controversial matter whether one kind of thing can be constructed from ('reduced to') other kinds of things. But again this is unproblematic for us. The metaontological inquiry we pursue is supposed to deliver a satisfactory account of ontological categories. In order to do this it provides us with a number of criteria for checking whether something is indeed such a category. As we have seen, these criteria crucially involve the notion of ontological construction. What follows from the fact that certain constructional relations hold between base-sets is a question metaontology will have to answer. But whether such relations hold in particular cases is not for metaontology to determine. In the same way a metaethical theory advocating a specific account of moral norms need not say whether the specific norm z is really a moral norm and not a norm of some other kind: metaethics should provide us with the criteria for answering this question, but it cannot also be expected to say whether these criteria are satisfied by this or that norm. What is important is that we have a yardstick which allows us to distinguish ontological categories from other categories and thus ensures that we are dealing with a well-defined concept. But questions which arise in measuring a particular category by that yardstick are for ontology, not for metaontology, to answer.

§59 Ontological categories without states of affairs

The account of ontological categories described in this chapter was presented within the framework of a theory taking states of affairs as a basic primitive. The reason for this is that, on the one hand, I think there are good arguments for according a central place to states of affairs in our philosophical theorizing (as described in the preceding chapter), and on the other hand that there are important and somewhat surprising implications of theories based on states of affairs which have not yet been sufficiently discussed (these will be described in the following chapter). I am aware, however, that, as with most philosophical accounts, neither the assumption of the existence of states of affairs nor indeed the stronger thesis of their status as a fundamental primitive can be regarded as uncontroversial. Nevertheless, even philosophers not wanting to assume that they live in a world of states of affairs will need a workable account of ontological categories. My account is flexible enough to be compatible with a variety of philosophical approaches; it does not depend on assuming that states of affairs are a fundamental primitive. This section will describe how the theory of ontological categories described above can be formulated independent of the framework of states of affairs I have been working in.

The first ingredient we need for a successful account of ontological categories are collections of objects. These collections do not have to be form-sets as described in § 38, indeed they do not have to be sets at all. Any sort of collection will do for our purposes, there is no need that they conform to the specific axioms of set theory. We can also be rather liberal about how these collections are formed. They might be constructed around a particular prototype of paradigm object, as maximal collections of mutually resembling objects, they might be constructed by grouping together objects which are referred to by expressions of the same syntactic class in a particular language, or yet in some other way.

The second ingredient is the notion of construction of one collection from others. As noted in § 49 it is not possible to formulate a general definition covering all construction operations, given the considerable structural differences between the individual operations which can be used in constructions. All we need at this point is the possibility of constructing collections from collections in such a way that the constructed collections display the same essential properties as some unconstructed collections. These unconstructed collections then become dispensable, there is no further need to refer to them anymore, as all we can do with them can now also be done with the collections just constructed. The process of construction has not reduced the number of collections (by constructing a collection with the same essential properties as an unconstructed one we do not make the unconstructed one disappear), but has systematized it. We now know which collections are dispensable (because they can be constructed from others) and which are not (because we cannot produce any substitutes for them). Ontological categories are then identified with the subset of collections of objects the members of which can construct all others, using some particular constructional operations.

We should first of all note that this generalized 'constructivist' or 'axiomatic'[67] account of ontological categories (like the one described in terms of form-sets and base-sets) deals with both the cut-off point problem and the hierarchical ordering of ontological categories. The distinction between ontological and non-ontological categories is not vague, not a matter of degrees. Whether some collections can construct all others is a yes-or-no matter. This account therefore provides us with a clear conception of what an ontological category is which also allows us to distinguish it from other kinds of collections.

Secondly, this generalized account which is just based on the two notions of a collection of objects and a construction operation making collections from collections shares the relativistic implications described

---

[67] See the comparison of ontological categories and axioms described in § 55.

in §§ 50 and 54. Local relativism is entailed because there is usually more than one subset of a set of collections which can construct all the remaining collections. Therefore the set of ontological categories is generally not unique; there will often be several subsets which are equally good candidates for systematizing the set of collections.

Global relativism holds because truths about constructibility crucially depend on the presence of objects which can be used as the basis of construction. To construct a particular collection certain other collections must be there to act as the raw material the constructive operation can work on. Now as long as we assume that which collections of objects there are in the world is not a necessary truth, that some kinds of objects present in our world might not exist in another possible world and vice versa, a collection can be constructible in one world but not in another one. This global relativism cuts deeper than the local variety. The point here is not just that the set of ontological categories is generally dependent on our choices concerning how we want to systematize the variety of objects present in the world. Assume we had somehow got round this local relativism, perhaps because we could show that *de facto* only one set of collections could act as a basis for a plausible reduction of the remaining collections, or because all the possible subsets had a non-empty intersection and we decided to identify the ontological categories with this intersection. It would then still not be possible to claim that the fact that a certain collection of objects constituted an ontological category was a fact about *these objects* in particular and was a reflection of their nature or essence. This is because the collection achieves its status as an ontological category only because of the presence of precisely those other collections which in fact exist. In the company of other collections, in another possible world, a particular collection might not be necessary to construct all of the remaining collections, indeed it might be constructible itself. Being an ontological category is therefore not a property which is stable across possible worlds.

It should therefore be evident that the present constructivist account of ontological categories can be divorced from the framework of a theory of states of affairs in which it is formulated and still retains its most characteristic properties: its ability to deal with the cut-off point problem and the hierarchical organization of ontological categories and its locally and globally relativistic conclusions. For this reason it should be of interest to metaphysicians independently of their position regarding the existence and status of states of affairs.

Those metaphysicians attracted by states of affairs as a basic primitive, however, should be aware that theories based on these have rather surprising implications regarding what is generally taken to be a set of key distinctions between ontological categories, namely the distinctions between individuals, properties, and relations. These implications will be the subject-matter of the following chapter.

V

Individuals and properties in an ontology of states of affairs

The account presented in the preceding chapter defends the thesis that our knowledge of ontological categories should be explicated in terms of two other things: knowledge of *combination* (about what can form states of affairs with what), and knowledge of *construction* (which kinds of things could be put together from which other kinds of things).

It is interesting to note that certain traditional ontological distinctions can be made on the basis of this account, while others cannot. For example, the realms of the abstract and the concrete will come out as two different ontological categories (supposing that there is no satisfactory way of reducing the one to the other). But what we would suppose to be the rather straightforward ontological distinction between individuals and properties cannot be made, insofar as the two cannot even be distinguished on the level of form-sets. This leaves open two different possibilities:

- although the distinction cannot be made in a purely combinatorial way, there are other kinds of information which can be regarded as structural and which, when taken into account, allow us to draw the distinction.

- the distinction must be drawn in a purely non-structural way.

As we argued at the end of § 35, taking the complex principle epistemologically seriously means that all the information available for identifying the candidates for ontological categories (the form-sets) is combinatorial and thus structural. As we will see in a moment, there are certain prominent ontological distinctions which cannot be drawn in this combinatorial way. It might therefore be worthwhile to consider other possibly relevant non-combinatorial information which can also be regarded as structural. We will particularly be interested in the question whether information regarding the *inferential relations* between the different objects will be of any use here.

We follow Carnap in equating structural information with *relation-descriptions* and non-structural information with *property-descriptions*.[1] Relation-descriptions tell us about certain relations objects stand in, while property-descriptions (unsurprisingly) tell us about their properties. Combinatorial information is structural because it is about the way the different parts of states of affairs are related in 'fitting together' to form complexes. Logical information is structural because it is about entailment relations between the complexes.[2]

If structural (i.e. combinatorial and logical) information is not sufficient for drawing the distinction, the remaining possibility is that it has to be drawn non-structurally (and is thus quite different from the purely structural distinctions). In the case of the distinction between individuals and properties we consider non-structural ways of distinguishing them to be those which do not just make reference to constituents of states of affairs and the relations between them, but to some further kind of object. For example, one relatively popular way of trying to distinguish them is by considering their relation to space and time (individuals are taken to be those objects each of which is at one place at a time, whereas properties can be at more than one place at a time). Alternatively we may distinguish them by appealing to the mental act of judgement: individuals correspond to the things the judgement is about, properties to what it says about them. Similarly one might try to refer to grammatically well-formed sentences and claim that their subjects pick out individuals, the predicates properties.[3]

---

[1] Carnap (1928: 11–12). Carnap claims that relation-descriptions and thus structural descriptions are the *only* descriptions science deals with.

[2] In the following the use of the adjective 'structural' is therefore to be treated as nothing more than shorthand for 'pertaining to the relations between the objects in question'. I do not claim that any two different relations must differ structurally (in the sense of 'structurally' usually opposed to 'materially'), or that no two non-relational characteristics can differ structurally. There is a particularly obvious counterexample to the first claim. The relations 'having a greater weight than' and 'having a greater height than' are different relations, but share the same structure. Their difference must be explained materially, with reference the the 'weight' and 'height' components involved. A bit more contentious is to argue that the non-relational characteristics 'weighing one kilogram' and 'weighing two kilograms' differ structurally but not materially (this will depend on whether the 'numerical' components can be regarded as sufficiently structural).

[3] Ramsey (1990: 8–9) claims that unlike the above 'psychological' or 'physical' criteria the only promising way of getting at the distinction between individuals and properties is via their structural (which he calls 'logical') properties. Of course in the end he famously concludes that this does not work either and hence that the distinction is illusory.

Given that we do usually make a distinction between individuals and properties it is clear that some of the above accounts (or something like them) must be what motivates us in making this distinction. However, there seems to be a sense in which the purely structural distinctions are the more fundamental ones and therefore more important. It is thus necessary to have a look at the distinction between individuals and properties to find out what kind of distinction we are actually dealing with here. We will first try to show that the distinction between individuals and properties cannot be drawn in a purely combinatorial way.

1 TYPINGS AND THEIR TRANSFORMATIONS

§60 The problem

Let us look at an uncontroversial example of objects from form-sets belonging to the different types of individuals, properties, relations and so on. I take it that it is as uncontroversial as anything can be in ontology that we consider a particular like the Tower of London as belonging to the form-set or type of *individuals*, something like 'being red' as a *first order (monadic) property* of individuals and something like 'being a colour' as a *second order (monadic) property of first order monadic properties*. We do this because of the way these three parts of states of affairs can make up states of affairs. The individual and the first order property can go together to make up a state of affairs (the one picked out by the sentence 'The Tower is red') as can the first order property and the second order property ('Red is a colour'). However, the individual and the second order property cannot go together to form a state of affairs. We assume that these facts are encoded in our typing the three objects in the way we do, i.e. that our calling the one individual, the other first order monadic property and so on just expresses these combinatorial possibilities.

But this is not the only way in which we can type the objects. Suppose we consider 'being red' as an individual (let us call it 'Red' for that purpose) and *both* 'being the Tower' and 'being a colour' as first order properties (let us call them 'to tower' and 'to colour'). In this case the objects fit together to produce the very same states of affairs as those above. The state of affairs corresponding to the one denoted by 'The

Tower is red' (and which is now denoted by 'Red towers') consists still of an individual and a first order (monadic) property, although their rôles are reversed. There is also an equivalent to the state of affairs denoted by 'Red is a colour' (now 'Red colours'), but now this has exactly the same form as the previous one, rather than being made up of a first order and a second order property. Equally there could not be a state of affairs consisting of 'to tower' and 'to colour' since things forming a state of affairs cannot be at the same level (excluding this possibility was achieved in the first typing by the fact that they were not located at *neighbouring* levels).

There are still further ways of typing the above objects. For example we can consider both 'being the Tower' and 'being a colour' as individuals (and call them 'Tower' and 'Colour') and have 'being red' again as a first order property. Or we could 'lift' the two last examples of typings by moving everything to the next higher type; individuals would become first order properties, first order properties second order properties. Finally we could reverse our initial typing which made use of three levels so that now 'being a colour' is an individual ('Colour'), 'being red' a first order property, and 'being the Tower' a second order property. As the reader is invited to check, all these typings allow for the same states of affairs to occur and are thus equally acceptable.

Perhaps we should pause here and be somewhat more explicit about how we can be so sure that the above typings really all are alternatives in that they make the same states of affairs possible.

§61   Data and conventions

First of all let us note that there are such things as *ontological data*. These are information about what can form states of affairs with what, for example that 'red' and 'Tower' go together in a state of affairs which is denoted by the sentence 'The Tower is red'. To be a bit more concise let us write t, r, and c for 'Tower', 'being red', and 'being a colour' independent of the ontological type assigned to them in a particular typing. We will call the collection of these the *basis* of our data. We will employ the notation introduced in § 46 to describe which members of the basis can go together to form states of affairs. If some elements can do this, we express this by prefixing a list of them with the predicate **C** (recall that this means that some permutation of the string—some way of putting the elements together—is a state of affairs). Thus the ontological data D we have about t, r, and c is that $\mathbf{C}(tr)$, $\mathbf{C}(cr)$ and $\neg\mathbf{C}(tc)$, $\neg\mathbf{C}(tt)$, $\neg\mathbf{C}(rr)$, $\neg\mathbf{C}(cc)$. These data act as a constraint on the typing we want to construct: they are what the typing is to be a theory of.

There is also another kind of constraint involved which I will call the *type-form conventions*. The conventions which were in play in the above typings said that types are indexed by an ascending, uninterrupted sequence of ordinal numbers beginning with zero and that members of these types can only go together in states of affairs if they are all located in two directly neighbouring types. Also, all members of a certain type can be intersubstituted in all states of affairs in which they appear. This is just the picture of types found in the Russellian simple theory of types. In fact it is presumably more restrictive than we want our theory of types to be. For example this account will have problems with accounting for objects which are applicable to other objects at more than two levels ('is a property' is applicable to first order properties, to second order properties and so forth). There are also difficulties with relations which take arguments from different levels ('instantiates' takes one object from level n and one from a directly adjacent level). But of course all we will have to say below will equally apply to *less* restrictive type-form conventions.

The task of constructing a typing for a particular set of objects means finding a way of remaining faithful to the ontological data within the type-form conventions in play. Of course it can happen that a certain set of ontological data cannot be typed at all given a set of type-form conventions. For example if your data are $\mathbf{C}(ab)$, $\mathbf{C}(bc)$, and $\mathbf{C}(ca)$ there is clearly no way of typing this in the stratified way just suggested. If you put a at one level, b must go into the level directly above or below. Now c must go directly above or below *that* level, so that in every case the resulting typing cannot remain faithful to all the ontological data. But of course if such a thing happens this just shows that your type-form conventions (determining the structure of your type theory) are unable to deal with the data given. These data cannot be captured in the framework, so we had better choose a different framework.

Of course this was not the case with the examples discussed above. There it is straightforward to check that all of the above typings were in accordance with the ontological data. But we have also seen that there can be more than one way of achieving such accordance. For example if our data demand that two objects cannot go together in a state of affairs (as e.g. for t and c above) we have different ways of accounting for this. We can put them 'types apart' or, to achieve the same effect, put them in the same type. The important point is that this can happen even if we have agreed on one system of type-form conventions. It is clear that such a system is purely conventional (hence the name). We could have selected a set of conventions which postulated that elements from the same type can go together, or that only members of types with the same parity can go together, or any other such regulation. But even after settling for a framework in which to give an account of our ontological data the form of the resulting typing is still radically underdetermined. Above we have given five substantially different alternative typings for a set of data on the basis of one set of type-form conventions. In some there are three levels of types, in others only two; in some there are individuals, in others there are not; and in particular each element could turn up at any level, as an individual, a first order property, or a second order property.

Of course the data restrict to some extent the number of possible typings relative to some type-form conventions. For example, typings where t was an individual, c a first order property, and r a second order property or where t and r are individuals and c a first order property cannot faithfully represent the data since on the above type-form conventions they would entail that $\mathbf{C}(tc)$ and $\neg\mathbf{C}(rt)$. However, the restriction is not restrictive enough to guarantee uniqueness.

§62 A graph-theoretic perspective

There is the possibility of giving a two-dimensional account of the notions of ontological data and their typings by invoking some simple graph theory. Take the members of the basis to be the vertices and say that whenever we have an entry of the form $\mathbf{C}(st)$ in the data, the vertices s and t are linked by an edge. We then introduce an extra non-graph-theoretic construction to represent a typing of a graph. We consider a typing of a graph to be a function which assigns to every vertex some member of the infinite sequence $\langle 0, 1, 2, \ldots \rangle$ of natural numbers in such a way that vertices s, t are mapped to numbers i, j such that $|i - j| = 1$ iff s and t are linked by an edge.

Intuitively, what a typing of a graph does is to slice it up into slices numbered $0, 1, 2, \ldots$ in such a way that vertices connected by an edge are assigned to directly neighbouring slices. Figure V.1 shows what the intuitive way of typing the graph described by the above data looks like.

It is now easy to see that the above alternative typings were achieved by three kinds of transformations of the typings of the graphs, that is by changing the ways in which the vertices are divided into slices. These transformations are:

- LIFTING which increases the ordinal assigned to each type and thus lifts all types one level up.

- MIRRORING which takes some vertex a (which is not connected to any object at a higher level) at level n and moves all the vertices which are connected to a by a path at lower levels to higher levels: those at $n - 1$ go to $n + 1$, those at $n - 2$ to $n + 2$ and so on (this is *upwards* mirroring) or, alternatively, it takes some vertex a (which is not connected to any object at a lower level) at level n and moves all the vertices at higher levels to lower levels: those at $n + 1$ go to $n - 1$, those at $n + 2$ to $n - 2$ and so on (*downwards* mirroring). Upwards mirroring can be applied to all typings, downwards mirroring only if there is 'enough space' below: if a is at level n and the highest vertex in the path is at level m then we can mirror downwards if $(m - n) \leq n$.

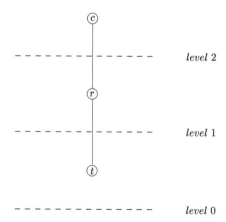

Fig. V.1 An intuitive typing

The second graph from the left in Figure V.2 is the first graph mirrored upwards, the third the first one mirrored downwards. The fourth graph *c—d—e* can only be MIRRORED upwards, but not downwards.

Finally there is

– FOLDING which 'folds' the graph downwards (upwards) at some vertex located at level *n* so that some or all of the vertices which are connected by an upward (downward) path to that vertex and which are *m* levels above (below) it are *m* levels below (above) it in the transformation.

The result of applying LIFTING to typing 1 once can be seen in Figure V.3. LIFTING typing 1 up two levels and then MIRRORING it downwards reverses it (Figure V.4). The result of FOLDING downwards at *r* is depicted in Figure V.5.

We get a general *applicability result* for these transformations of the following form: *If a graph can be typed in a stratified way according to the*

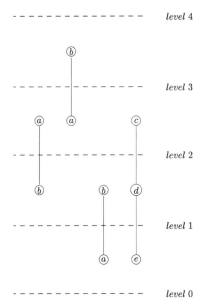

Fig. V.2 MIRRORING a typing

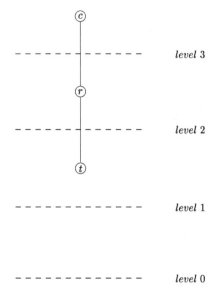

Fig. V.3 LIFTING typing 1

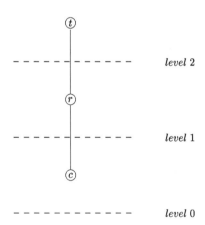

Fig. V.4 Reversing typing 1

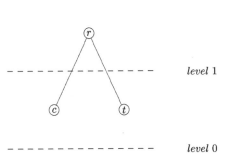

Fig. V.5 FOLDING typing 1

above conventions at all, all applications of LIFTING, MIRRORING, *and* FOLDING *preserve accordance with the data.*

This is immediately obvious in the case of LIFTING and MIRROR-ING. To see that it holds for FOLDING as well, consider that if we fold downwards (upwards) at some level n all vertices at level $n + 1$ $(n - 1)$ go to $n - 1$ $(n + 1)$, those at $n + 2$ $(n - 2)$ go to $n - 2$ $(n + 2)$ and so forth, while the edges between them are preserved. FOLDING thus keeps each vertex always in the company of its direct level-neighbours.

§63 Ontological import of transformations

It is debatable to what extent all three kinds of transformations result in genuinely alternative typings. LIFTING seems to be the least prob-lematic in this respect. Even though we might say that a typing which dispensed with individuals altogether by regarding all (former) individ-uals as first order properties, all (former) first order properties as second order properties and so on presents a genuine alternative to the typing with individuals, iterating this lifting further does not make much of a difference, in particular since all the levels below the level at which the first items occur are empty. It does not seem to be sensible to say that the crucial difference between two typings is that in the first one the items of the lowest level are at level 26, while in the other they are at level 27 and that this has any ontological import. We would rather be tempted to say that the individuals in a typing are *whatever* inhabits the low-est level, in which case LIFTING would not constitute an ontologically relevant transformation at all.

This is essentially what Russell claims in the *Principia*:

> In practice, we never need to know the absolute types of our variables, but only their *relative* types. That is to say, if we prove any proposition on the assumption that one of our variables is an individual, and another is a function of order n, the proof will still hold if, in place of an individual, we take a function of order m, and in place of our function of order n we take a function of order $n + m$, with corresponding changes for any other variables that may be involved.[4]

Transformations lifting expressions to higher types are well-known in Montague grammar as well as in other forms of categorial grammar. They help to connect expressions which live in different categories (such as sentence negation, predicate negation, and subject negation) but which really belong to the same grammatical kind (they are all instances of negation). Montague himself introduced the following lifting rule:

> The type of any expression of type a may be lifted to type $((a, b), b)$, for arbitrary b.[5]

This implies for example that some expression belonging to Montague's type e of names can be lifted to type $((e, t), t)$, which is the type of monadic second order properties. It also licenses the general lifting of expressions from type n to type $n + 2$.[6]

MIRRORING is more problematic since it allows us (together with LIFTING) to reverse a typing, making individuals of a typing into properties of the highest order, and vice versa, as well as reversing all the levels in between. Gaskin, however, considers reversing to be ontologically harmless:

> Let us try to imagine a world-view which systematically reverses the order in the Fregean hierarchy of his zeroth- and first-level expressions, by systematically reallocating the expressions which he locates in the zeroth level to the second level, and then renumbering the levels accordingly. It is at least clear that under this transformation the valencies of different types of expressions would not be affected. Proper names such as 'Socrates', now located at level 1, would still be constructed with predicates like 'wise', now located at level 0, and their corresponding referents would still engage with one another in the appropriate way, though now with reversed ontological allegiance: that is, the erstwhile basic particulars would constitute the new first level universals, and

---

[4] Whitehead and Russell (1925: I:165). See also 161–2.
[5] van Benthem (1986: 126).
[6] Dowty et al. (1981: 184, 188).

the erstwhile first level universals the new basic particulars. [. . .] Metaphysically speaking, the two purportedly different ways of looking at things would surely just be doublets of one another. In other words, there would be no absolute difference between the rival hierarchies: the only absolute difference would be the *difference of level* (i.e. the different valencies of expression or object) respected by both hierarchies. [. . .] The one view says that the particular Socrates instantiates (among other universals) the universal wisdom, the other that the particular wisdom instantiates (among other universals) the universal Socrates. But the two views are surely just using different notations to calibrate the same facts.[7]

Note, furthermore, that we can only reverse typings got from finite sets of data and those got from infinite sets which can be typed using only a finite number of types. A hierarchy which is infinite in one direction can obviously not be reversed in the above way, nor could a finite hierarchy which is considered to be extensible à la Dedekind. If we assume that the hierarchy has a largest element but that we can also extend it into one in which the largest element is greater by one (i.e. by adding higher order properties) then this gives us a substitute for directionality in the finite case. We cannot reverse the hierarchy since the 'real' top of the hierarchy is the part which can always be extended.

MIRRORING like the one getting us from the first graph on the left to the second graph in Figure V.2 is in fact legitimized by Montague's lifting rule which makes it possible to reverse the rôles of function and argument.[8] This rule says that instead of applying the expression referring to the monadic property b (which is of type (e, t)) to that referring to the individual a (which is of type e) we can also, after lifting a's type to that of a monadic second order property (i.e. $((e, t)t)$) apply a to b's (e, t). In both cases this evaluates to t. We therefore get the same joining behaviour, but in one case b is below a, in the other a below b.

FOLDING seems to be the most problematic transformation. After all it implies that elements of levels with the same parity can suddenly be at the same level, or that in certain cases elements at level n can be moved to level $n + 2$ or $n - 2$. FOLDING goes even further than the transformations Gaskin is willing to countenance since for him the '*differences* of level in the hierarchy [. . .] are absolute'.[9] If we accept FOLDING this will no longer be true. It is not just not clear which

---

[7] Gaskin (1998: 29–30).   [8] van Benthem (1986: 126).
[9] Gaskin (1998: 27), see also 30–1.

objects are located at which level, but also how many levels there are (in the above example applying FOLDING could reduce a typing with three levels to one with only two).

Some justification for a transformation like FOLDING could come from the linguistic study of coordinating expressions such as 'and', 'or', 'but' etc. It is quite attractive to regard for example 'and' as a coordinator linking two expressions of the same linguistic type, as in *Peter and Paul went to Paris* (where it links two names) or *Kate is short and John is tall* (where it links two sentences). But this idea does not harmonize well with cases containing singular indefinites, such as 'a student' or 'some scholar'. According to the traditional Fregean analysis these are quantifier expressions and their denotata therefore items at level 2. But if we do not want to interpret the coordinating expression in such sentences as *Bella and some of the men got a first* as linking expressions of different types, we need a transformation which either moves the denotatum of 'Bella' two levels up, or that of 'some of the men' two levels down. FOLDING does just this. Note further that while the idea of regarding singular indefinites as denoting items at level 0 ('regarding them as referring expressions') which is made possible by FOLDING might shock some philosophers as a reactionary move back to pre-Fregean times, the idea has actually been successfully employed by linguists in the study of indefinites.[10] It would therefore be premature to dismiss FOLDING as an admissible transformation unless it can be shown to lead to inconsistencies in typings.

§64   The flexibility result

The three transformations together give us the following *flexibility result*: *A typing of the graph according to the above conventions where some object* a *is at level* n *can by successive applications of the three transformations be made into another typing which is also in accordance with the data but where* a *is located at level* m, *for any* m. A proof of this can be found in § 98 in the Appendix.

The flexiblity result shows that by applying the above transformations given some ontological data and the above type-form conventions, we can put any particular object in any type we choose, provided we fudge

[10] Hoeksema (1988: 23).

around with the other assignments in the required way. Clearly that does not mean that this can be done for *all* objects simultaneously and that thus all typings are adequate. Rather, if we put some object in some type first, faithfulness to the data will imply that we are restricted in where to put the other objects. Nevertheless, for each particular object we can put it into whichever type we like.

§65   Expansions: adding more of the same

Of course it is important to find out whether the above results are only produced by worlds with three elements or whether they can be generalized. Let us look at a world with four elements $c, s, t,$ and r which are supposed to be the type-neutral equivalents of 'a cup of tea', 'being 63°C', 'being a temperature between 30°C and 70°C', and 'being a temperature-range', that is something we would intuitively regard as a set consisting of one individual, a first order monadic property, a second order monadic property, and a third order monadic property. Our Data will contain $\mathbf{C}(cs)$, $\mathbf{C}(ts)$, $\mathbf{C}(rt)$, while all other pairwise combinations of members of the basis will be prefixed by $\neg\mathbf{C}$. The intuitive picture is given in Figure V.6.

If we consider a typing of the data in accordance with the above type-form conventions it is clear that LIFTING will preserve accordance with the data. We can also reverse the typing by regarding temperature-ranges as individuals, 'being a temperature between 30°C and 70°C' as a first order property of such ranges, 'being 63°C' as a second order property of this and 'being a cup of tea' as a third order property of temperatures. This would then just be the reverse of the 'intuitive' typing 2 suggested below (Figure V.7).

Similarly we could apply FOLDING to let the temperature of 63°C come out as a first order property, 'being a cup of tea' and 'being a temperature between 30°C and 70°C' as second order properties of this, and 'being a temperature-range' as a third order property of the latter (Figure V.8).

It thus turns out that the typing remains just as underdetermined even if we consider worlds with more than three elements. Nevertheless, we note that in the above case we encounter a phenomenon we did not get in the case with three elements: now there can be elements at level n such that they cannot go together with both elements at level $n+1$ and

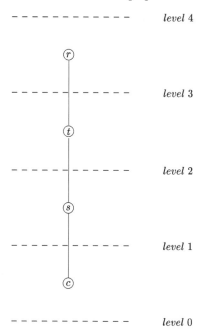

Fig. V.6 Typing 2

with elements at level $n - 1$, *although there are elements at both levels.* (For example, in the above case after FOLDING 'being a cup of tea' could go together with the object directly below it (the temperature of 63°C) but not with the only thing on the level above it ('being a temperature-range').) While this might seem odd, it is not ruled out by the type-form conventions given above, as these only specified that no two elements on the same level could go together and that only elements at two directly adjacent levels could go together. This does not imply that elements must be able to go together with all other elements at adjacent levels. In fact we would not want our type-form conventions to demand this. We suppose that these give necessary but not sufficient conditions for 'fitting': *only if* they are obeyed do two objects 'fit', but not *whenever* they are obeyed. For example, if we want our theory of types to be able to come to terms with individuals of different kinds we would not want to claim that 'likes Cadbury's chocolate' fits together with 'the moon',

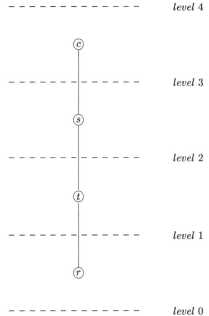

Fig. V.7 Reversing typing 2

although the first is a monadic first order property and the second an individual.

In fact this is exactly the distinction Stenius draws in terms of logically homogeneous and logically unhomogeneous spaces.[11] In a logically homogeneous space we know that if something is an individual and something else a monadic first order property the two can go together in a state of affairs, whereas in an unhomogeneous space this is not the case. We will not want to adopt type-form conventions which *force* the space we are dealing with to be homogeneous. Any set of data of reasonable complexity is very likely to give rise to an unhomogeneous space. If our type-form conventions were so restricted as to forbid this, we would no longer be able to type these data.

Given that the above result seems to generalize in this way it is then apparent that for any set of data which consists only of pairs of elements

[11] Stenius (1960: 71–9).

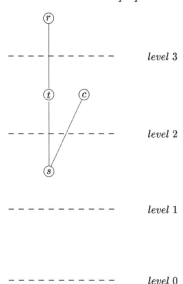

Fig. V.8 FOLDING typing 2

(as is the case for the above data) and which can be typed given the above type-form conventions, all three transformations preserve accordance with the data. This would then imply that in a world where all elements are monadic, nothing is essentially of any specific type.[12]

§66   Expansions: the polyadic case

The next thing we want to check is what happens in the polyadic case. We thus consider some data such that the strings marked by C or $\neg C$ can contain more than two elements.

Consider the fact denoted by 'Peter is married to Clare' and abbreviate its constituents (i.e. the elements in our world) by p, c, and m. Our ontological data D will then look as follows: $\neg C(pc)$, $\neg C(pm)$, $\neg C(cm)$, $C(mpc)$, $\neg C(mpp)$, $\neg C(mcc)$, $\neg C(mmp)$, $\neg C(mmc)$, $\neg C(mmm)$, $\neg C(ppp)$, and $\neg C(ccc)$. Intuitively we will type p and c as individuals and m as a first order dyadic property. Now suppose we reverse this typing and let m be an individual ('Marriedto') and p and c first order dyadic properties ('peters', 'clares'). Then the fact that Peter

[12] See Denyer (1998: 623).

is married to Clare ('Marriedto peters clares') consists of one individual and two first order dyadic properties. Note that the property 'peters' differs from 'married to' in that, although both are dyadic and first order, 'married to' requires two individuals to form a state of affairs, while 'peters' requires one individual and one first order dyadic property (in our case this is 'clares'). Again this might appear odd, but it is not in conflict with the type-form conventions. They do not imply that no two elements of the same type can form part of a state of affairs (otherwise even the 'intuitive' typing of the above data would not be correct since 'Peter' and 'Clare' are both of the same type). They only specify that no collection *purely from one type* could go together.

Clearly this reverse of the original typing is in accordance with the data. It is also possible to extend our graph-theoretic account to deal with elements of data with more than two members. We continue to treat elements with two members in the usual way. For each $C(s_1, \ldots, s_n)$ for $n > 2$ we connect the vertices in such a way that each s_n is connected with exactly two others s_j, s_k. We call the resulting structure a *cluster*. To distinguish clusters from the connections described above we will draw the edges in clusters as lines of a different kind, as shown in Figure V.9.

Given that our type-form conventions stipulate that only objects at directly adjacent types can go together, every cluster will be wholly located within two distinct levels. We then note that clusters behave relative to LIFTING and MIRRORING exactly as the usual graphs do. For example we can reverse typing 3 by applying LIFTING and MIR-RORING (Figure V.10).

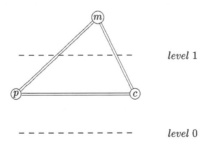

level 1

level 0

Fig. V.9 Typing 3

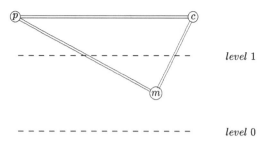

Fig. V.10 Reversing typing 3

Clusters can be FOLDED in a similar way to ordinary typings. To see how this works consider a slightly more complex example.

Consider a world with five elements c, g, s, t, and f which are supposed to be the type-neutral equivalents of 'being the converse of', 'being greater than', 'being smaller than', the number three, and the number five. Our data will contain $\mathbf{C}(cgs)$, $\mathbf{C}(gtf)$, $\mathbf{C}(stf)$, while all other pairwise combinations of members of the basis will be prefixed by $\neg\mathbf{C}$. Intuitively of course the numbers three and five are taken to be individuals, 'being smaller than' and 'being greater than' dyadic properties of these, and 'being the converse of' a dyadic property of properties. The typing representing this is given in Figure V.11.[13] FOLDING this downwards along the vertices g and s results in the typing shown in Figure V.12.

It is then easy to check that the above applicability and flexibility results generalize to the polyadic case. Neither adding more elements nor the introduction of polyadic elements makes the underdetermination of typings by data disappear. We can always apply the above transformations to some typing to end up with something which is also in accordance with the data, but which takes the elements to belong to quite different types from the original typing.

§67 Tightening the type-form conventions?

Let us now look at two ways of ruling out some of the transformations on typings so as to avoid the flexibility result. Both rely on tightening

[13] We use different styles of edges to tell apart the three different clusters involved.

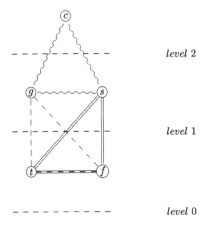

Fig. V.11 Typing 4

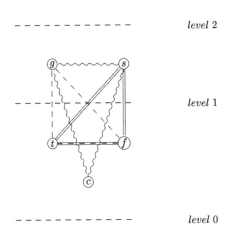

Fig. V.12 FOLDING typing 4

the type-form conventions to ensure that in the case of certain transformations the transformed typing is no longer in harmony with the
conventions. We will look at two ways of enforcing an asymmetry in
the relation between the levels in a typing.

§68 Rigidity

Suppose we enlarge the above example involving Peter, Clare, and 'married to' by adding the monadic property 'sleeps'. We thus enlarge our data by $C(sc)$ and $C(sp)$ (while all other combinations containing S will be prefixed by $\neg C$). The intuitive typing of the result will look like the one given in Figure V.13. If we then reverse typing 4 we end up with two individuals ('Marriedto' and 'Sleeps') and two first order properties, 'peters' and 'clares', as in Figure V.14.

It might now be argued that applying the transformation in this case shows that we have destroyed a property which we intuitively expect of typings. We usually think that objects can go together with a *fixed number* of other objects at the level directly below (a predicate either takes one name, or two, or three, and so on) while the cardinality of sets of objects they can go together with which involve objects from the level directly above is *flexible* (a name can go with one monadic

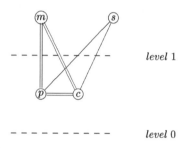

Fig. V.13 Typing 5

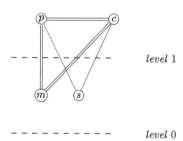

Fig. V.14 Reversing typing 5

predicate, or with one dyadic predicate and another name, or with one triadic predicate and two other names etc.)[14]

But in the above case the first order properties can go together with a flexible number of individuals: 'peters' can take just 'Sleeps' or 'Marriedto' together with 'clares'. The first order properties would thus have to be regarded as multigrade properties which can have a variable number of arguments.

The type-form conventions given above do not enforce this asymmetry of 'upwards flexibility' and 'downwards rigidity'. Of course we can enlarge them by adding the following conditions (we will use $\phi, \psi, \ldots$ as variables ranging over strings).

If a typing assigns s_i to level n and there is some $\phi = (s_i, s_j, \ldots, s_n)$ and $\mathbf{C}\phi$ and

all the members of ϕ apart from s_i are assigned to level $n - 1$ then there is no ψ containing s_i which is of a different cardinality than ϕ and $\mathbf{C}\psi$.

or

all the members of ϕ apart from s_i are assigned to level $n + 1$ then there are ψ containing s_i which are of a different cardinality than ϕ and $\mathbf{C}\psi$.

As is now easy to check, if we enlarge our type-form conventions by this then the transformations of LIFTING and MIRRORING together (which allow us to reverse) and FOLDING will generate typings of the graph which are no longer in harmony with the new type-form conventions in cases containing at least one dyadic and one monadic property (LIFTING on its own, however, remains still possible). Thus the most problematic sources of underdetermination are eliminated.

But of course now the question is whether we want to adopt these strengthened type-form conventions which are obviously more complicated than the ones we employed at the beginning. We already considered these to be too restrictive and might therefore be wary to accept anything which confines us even more. The greatest problem with the above strengthened conventions is undoubtedly that they rule out multigrade predicates and properties. And indeed there are some who think that properties essentially have fixed adicities:

It is naturally an essential part of understanding—that is, 'grasping the sense of'—a relational expression for instance, that you should know that it requires completing by *two* proper names. Similarly it would be natural to think that it

---

[14] This point has been made by Carruthers (1983: 53–5) and Gaskin (1998: 27–8).

must belong to the essence of the relation itself—conceived of as the *reference* of the relational expression—that it should hold between two objects, rather than holding of one or between three.[15]

However, while it is perfectly possible to give a precise semantics for multigrade predicates[16] it is far from obvious that we can get by with reducing all supposedly multigrade predicates by changing them to fixed-adicity predicates holding of some sort of 'plurality'.[17] If we cannot, then, of course, we would not want our type-form conventions to forbid the existence of something we obviously need.

§69 Cardinality

The different levels in the set-theoretic hierarchy are related to one another by cardinality constraints. If there are n objects at some level m, there are exactly 2^n objects at level $m + 1$. One might want to transfer this cardinality constraint to ontology and incorporate it into the type-form conventions.[18] The idea would be to demand that a typing is adequate only if the cardinalities of objects at two neighbouring levels m and $m + 1$ are related to one another as n and 2^n.

The motivation for such a demand is obvious in the case of such positions as set-theoretic nominalism, which conceives of all properties as sets of individuals. It is clear that according to such an account there cannot be *more* properties of individuals than sets of individuals. But equally once we accept the set-builder we accept all the sets which can be recursively constructed from the urelements (the individuals in our case). So if properties are really nothing more than sets of individuals, in a world with n individuals there will be 2^n first order properties, 2^{2^n} second order properties and so on, all the way up the set-theoretic hierarchy.

For an intensionalist who claims that for every extension there is a corresponding property, but who does not want to identify properties with extensions (since he fears there might not be enough extensions to go round to account for all the properties), 2^n is obviously only the lower limit: there might conceivably be even more first order properties.

[15] Carruthers (1983: 54).
[16] See e.g. Taylor and Hazen (1992).
[17] Oliver and Smiley (2001).
[18] This consideration was suggested to me by Peter Simons.

The opposite position would be held by someone who wants to differentiate properties by extensions, but who insists that all properties must be instantiated. In this case 2^n would be the upper limit: there could not be more first order properties, but there might be less, since the properties corresponding to some extensions might not be instantiated.

Once we incorporate the cardinality constraint into our type-form conventions it is evident that none of the above three transformations are allowed any more. Even the unproblematic LIFTING is ruled out. It is easy to see why this is so. Suppose we have some typing which satisfies the cardinality constraint which we LIFT by two levels. The first two levels will now be empty so that the first objects will not be encountered until level 2. But given that level 0 has cardinality 0, level 1 should have cardinality $2^0 = 1$, which it does not, since it is empty as well. Therefore the typing transformed by LIFTING no longer satisfies the type-form conventions incorporating the cardinality constraint.

It is similarly obvious that both MIRRORING and FOLDING are ruled out as well. Both transformations affect the number of objects at a given level: MIRRORING by permuting the cardinalities at different levels, FOLDING by increasing the cardinality of one level at the expense of another. Each of these necessarily disturbs the rigid structure imposed by the cardinality constraint.

The asymmetry introduced via the cardinality constraint into the type-form conventions allows us to determine in all cases in which we can construct a typing at all whether some level in the typing is or is not above another one. For example, if our ontological data consist of information about eleven objects, eight of which are grouped together in one level, while the remaining three are in another one, it is clear that the second level must be the most fundamental level, with the first level directly above it.

But such determinacy comes with a price. The price in our case is the impossibility of typing vast ranges of ontological data in a way that obeys the type-form conventions which incorporate the cardinality constraint. Data such as those represented in typings 1, 2, and 3 above could no longer be typed with the strengthened type-form conventions. Given that these data are in no obvious way deviant, we should be able to type them with the resources at hand. If our conventions do not allow us to do this, so much the worse for the conventions.

But in fact this is not the only problem with the cardinality constraint. Much more problematic is the fact that the picture of individuals and properties contained in it is highly implausible from an epistemological point of view. If we consider properties as regularities by which we structure information about the individuals we encounter there should not be more properties than individuals, but considerably less. And if the existence of *predicates* of different levels is anything to go by, the picture we get is not that of the bucket or cone familiar from set theory, but rather that of a funnel turned upside-down. It is easy to think of examples of first order predicates, second order predicates are a bit harder to come by, while the amount of third order predicates is really very small. Predicates of even higher order are rarely encountered in natural languages. All of this is of course as it should be. There is a great epistemological demand for systematizing similarities between individuals, which is done by the first order predicates. There is less need for regularities between regularities, while we need hardly ever to refer to regularities between regularities of regularities. If there is anything like a cardinality constraint at work in the way we actually type objects in natural language, it seems to be the opposite of the constraint proposed above.

There is of course also the possibility of regarding both individuals and properties as abstractions from something else. This is the position favoured by the present inquiry, where both are regarded as abstractions from states of affairs. In this case the cardinality of the sets of individuals and properties will be smaller than that of the set of states of affairs, but otherwise there will be no systematic correlation between the sizes of the two.

It thus turns out that the cardinality constraint only really makes sense in the context of set-theoretic nominalism. But apart from the fact that this theory is riddled with an enormous number of problems, if we already accept it, assuming that there are individuals and the set-builder and that properties reduce to set-theoretic constructions from individuals, it is not clear why we bother with attempts like the above to construct a purely structural account of ontological categories. If set-theoretic nominalism is the form of a satisfactory ontological theory, then all the questions regarding the ontological categories and their relations we want to settle by the above investigations are already answered.

We have now seen that neither the appeal to rigidity nor that to cardinality presented a satisfactory way of tightening the type-form conventions. The problem of underdetermination remains.

§70 Proto-typings

Although we have shown that the typing of the ontological data in the above way is underdetermined, there is a weaker sense of systematizing them in which this underdetermination does not arise. We will call this a *proto-typing* of a set of ontological data. The nice thing about proto-typings is that they are unique: given any set of data there is only one proto-typing in accordance with it. A proto-typing consists of two parts, a partition on the set of elements and a set of rules.

The partition divides the elements into strong substitution types: two elements belong to the same strong substitution type if they can be interchanged in each ontological datum without changing it from a collection of elements which can form a complex to one which cannot, or vice versa. Strong substitution types are exclusive. The set of rules tells us which members of types can be combined in states of affairs. It is then possible to show that for every set of ontological data there is only one proto-typing which is in accordance with the data. The proof of this is given in § 99 in the Appendix.

The problem, however, is that a proto-typing is not a typing. Suppose we construct the proto-typing of the items c, s, t, r discussed in § 65. We then get four types, $\tau_1 = \{c\}$, $\tau_2 = \{s\}$, $\tau_3 = \{t\}$ and $\tau_4 = \{r\}$; the rules will say that two items, coming from either τ_1 and τ_2, or τ_2 and τ_3, or τ_3 and τ_4 can form a state of affairs together. But this proto-typing, although a sort of typing, no less underdetermines the different typings we can construct if we want to give a typing in accordance with the above type-form conventions than the ontological data on their own.

Thus the underdetermination remains. Given this underdetermination of typings, we see that if we say that an object belongs to a certain type we have certainly not mentioned any essential property of the object. It is even doubtful whether we have said anything important about the object at all, since by making amendments elsewhere, everything could be in any type. The only important information will be contained in the proto-typing (since this will reflect the initial ontological data), but not in whether a particular object is assigned to this or that type in a particular typing. It is thus evident that whether something is an individual, a property or a relation is not something which can be decided just on the basis of the combinatorial information about what goes together with what. But then the complex principle seems to imply that this combinatorial information is all we have in drawing ontological distinctions. At this point it is instructive to have a look at Frege's distinction between saturated and unsaturated entities. What Frege is doing there is precisely trying to establish a structural distinction between individuals and properties. Ultimately this is unsuccessful, but it is unsuccessful in an interesting sense. We will show that Frege's method can only succeed if it violates the complex principle. Why this is so and what lessons to learn from it will be the subject of the next part of this chapter.

2 FREGE'S DISTINCTION BETWEEN INDIVIDUALS AND PROPERTIES

§71 Saturation and complexes

That Frege embraced a version of the complex principle seems to be implied by the fact that he regarded the notion of the complete thought (a complex, which has obvious close connections with the notion of a state of affairs) to be prior to the distinction between saturated and unsaturated entities and thus between concepts/properties and objects/individuals.[19]

The notion of a complex outlined above provides us with a good way of spelling out the concepts of saturation, saturatedness, and unsaturatedness, some of the 'most important yet most obscure concepts employed by Frege'.[20] How to give a precise account of these concepts is still a matter of some controversy.[21] However, the theory of complexes seems to present a rather natural framework in which many important aspects of saturation can be captured.

We will regard strings as the items which are said to be saturated or unsaturated. We will call a string ϕ *saturated* just in case $C\phi$ and

---

[19] See Hylton (1984: 382), Linsky (1992: 268).
[20] Simons (1981: 73).
[21] See e.g. Simons (1981).

unsaturated if $\neg \mathbf{C}\phi$. Justification for this can be got from the following passage:

I am concerned to show that the argument does not belong with a function, but goes together with the function to make up a complete whole; for a function by itself must be called incomplete, in need of supplementation, or 'unsaturated'.[22]

The 'complete whole' is what we take to be a complex. Something unsaturated is something which is not a complex but which is such that 'supplementing' it by some item makes it a complex. For example, $\neg \mathbf{C}(\neg)$ but $\mathbf{C}(\neg, p)$. In the words of Frege:

The thought does not, by its make-up, stand in any need of completion; it is self-sufficient. Negation on the other hand needs to be completed by a thought. The two components, if we choose to employ this expression, are quite different in kind and contribute quite differently toward the formation of the whole. One completes, the other is completed.[23]

The two concepts of saturatedness and unsaturatedness are connected in the idea of *saturating* one item by another. We will say that a string ϕ can *saturate* another string ψ ($S(\phi, \psi)$) if $\neg \mathbf{C}\psi$ and there is a (possibly empty) finite collection of strings $\omega_1, \ldots, \omega_n$ such that $\mathbf{C}(\phi^\frown\psi^\frown\omega_1^\frown \ldots ^\frown \omega_n)$. Saturation is thus represented as a dyadic property of strings. The motivation behind this definition is the fact that if ϕ can saturate ψ this does not mean that the result of this is saturated (this is the point of introducing the ωs). For example a two-place function can be saturated by a name, but the result of this is not saturated: it needs a further name to do this.

Also note that Frege remarks the following regarding saturation:

not all parts of the thought can be complete; at least one must be 'unsaturated' or predicative; otherwise they would not hold together.[24]

The unity of the whole comes about through the fact that the thought saturates the unsaturated part or, as we can also say, completes the part needing completion. And it is natural to suppose that, for logic in general, combination into a whole always comes about by saturation of something unsaturated.[25]

This property is obviously possessed by S: if $S(\phi, \psi)$, ψ must always be unsaturated.

[22] Frege (1962b: 19–20), McGuinness (1984: 140).
[23] Frege (1966a: 68), McGuinness (1984: 386).
[24] Frege (1962a: 78), McGuinness (1984: 193).
[25] Frege (1966b: 72–3), McGuinness (1984: 390).

§72   Defining the Frege hierarchy

We are now able to see how Frege uses the above concept of saturation in order to give an account of the difference between individuals and properties.

1. A string ϕ belongs to the type τ_0 of *individuals* if $\mathbf{C}\phi$.[26]
2. A string ϕ belongs to the type τ_0^1 of *monadic first order properties* if its type description is $(\tau_0|\mathbf{C})$.

The idea here is that if you take something which is saturated and saturate a monadic first order property by it, the result is again saturated. To use an example of Frege's on the level of language:[27] 'being the capital of x' is a monadic first order *predicate* since if you join it with the name 'the German empire' (which is saturated) you get another saturated thing out, i.e. another name, namely one name of Berlin.

Similarly if we take the individual 'Frege' and join it to the monadic first order property 'had a beard' we get another individual out, namely the state of affairs that Frege had a beard.

3. A string ϕ is a *dyadic first order property* if it belongs to τ_0^2, the type description of which is $(\tau_0|(\tau_0|\mathbf{C}))$.

A dyadic first order property is such that if you saturate it with an individual, you get a monadic first order property.

4. A string ϕ is a *monadic second order property of monadic properties* if it belongs to τ_1^1, the type description of which is $((\tau_0|\mathbf{C})|\mathbf{C})$.

A monadic second order property of monadic properties is such that if you saturate it with a monadic first order property, you get an individual. In this way individuals and properties of different orders and adicities within the Frege hierarchy can be defined. However, we might also want to make generalizations, speaking about several items of the hierarchy at the same time.

---

[26] This explication of the Frege hierarchy does not distinguish between types on the level of language and types 'out there' in the world. For the sake of simplicity talk here is framed in terms of the latter; note, however, that the definitions will work equally well if we write 'name' or 'sentence' for 'individual' and 'predicate' for 'property'. Frege himself took the notions of being saturated and being unsaturated to be equally applicable to both senses and references. See Frege (1966a: 68), Simons (1981: 74).

[27] Frege (1962b: 27), McGuinness (1984: 147).

We then say that a string ϕ is a first order property (of arbitrary adicity) if the type description of its type is of the form $(\sigma_1 \sigma_2)$, where σ_1 is a (possibly empty) finite sequence of the form $\tau_0 | \tau_0 \ldots | \tau_0 |$ and σ_2 is the sequence $(\tau_0 | \mathbf{C})$.[28] Thus a first order property is something which takes some finite number n of individuals and returns a first order monadic property (depending on n, its adicity will be $n + 1$). In a similar way second and higher order properties of arbitrary adicities can be defined.

Analogously we say that a string ϕ is a monadic property (of arbitrary order) if the type description of its type is of the form $(\sigma_1 \sigma_2)$, where σ_1 is a finite sequence of the form $(\tau_0 | \mathbf{C}) | (\tau_0 | \mathbf{C}) \ldots | (\tau_0 | \mathbf{C}) |$ and σ_2 is $\mathbf{C}$. A monadic property is something which takes either an individual or a property and returns an individual. In a similar way dyadic, triadic, etc. properties of arbitrary orders will be defined.

Frege thus manages to give a purely structural account of the difference between individuals and properties. The only notions appealed to are formulated in terms of saturation which is in turn entirely reducible to talk about $\mathbf{C}$.

§73   Extending the Frege hierarchy

Nevertheless, the above account of the Frege hierarchy is not entirely satisfactory. Individuals and states of affairs are regarded as items of the same kind, namely as being of type τ_0. No distinction is drawn between names and sentences (on the side of language) and objects/individuals and truth-values/states of affairs (on the side of the world). For Frege this is of course perfectly acceptable, given his bicategorial account of saturated and unsaturated entities, where properties are the only unsaturated entities, while everything else is saturated.[29]

Nevertheless, this equation of individuals and states of affairs might give the impression that we did not manage to define the whole Frege hierarchy, but rather some strange variant containing only properties and 'individuals', but where these 'individuals' were both states of affairs as well as constituents of states of affairs. But individuals and states of affairs seem to be sufficiently distinct for us to want to distinguish them in terms of the types they belong to. Unfortunately the framework given above lacks the expressive power to do just this.

[28] For the sake of simplicity we assume that bracketing has been taken care of.
[29] Compare Meixner (1997: 302).

However, the resources we already have can be exploited to draw the distinction we want to draw, both for language and for the world, at least if we have the concept of a state of affairs where Frege has that of a truth-value. [30] The difference we are going to exploit is that one kind of complex is made up of other items, while the other is not. Admittedly this is more straightforward when talking about the world. States of affairs are made up of different items which are not all states of affairs themselves, while individuals are not made up of any items in a comparable way. We could argue that the same is true of names and sentences, but in this case we have to hold a rather restricted view of names which assumes that all names are syntactically simple, so that definite descriptions for example could not function as names. But let us accept this restriction for the moment.

We will then want to say that

1′. A string ϕ is an *individual* if $\mathbf{C}\phi$ and it is not the result of saturating some string by another string.

Thus an individual is a saturated entity which is not the result of saturating any entity with another entity.

Similarly we define that

2′. A string ϕ is a *state of affairs* if $\mathbf{C}\phi$ and it is not an individual.

Our further definition of the extended Frege hierarchy will then proceed by splitting the type $\mathbf{C}$ into two according to the above definitions, namely into the type $\mathbf{I}$ for individuals and $\mathbf{S}$ for states of affairs.

This extension of the Frege hierarchy provides us with considerably greater expressive power than we had on the account described in § 72. Many categorially important distinctions (for example that between monadic first order properties of individuals and unary operators on states of affairs) which we can now draw would have been represented by the same expression in the old system (in this case by $(\tau_0|\mathbf{C})$).

Unfortunately the Fregean way of achieving this greater expressive power is far from philosophically satisfying, as we will see in the next section. Frege regards both individuals and states of affairs as saturated items which are then told apart by further criteria, while everything else

---

[30] As done in Meixner (1997: 229).

is considered as unsaturated. However, we will see that Frege's conception of individuals as saturated is very problematic and not in harmony with the complex principle. It then turns out that if this criticism is accepted, a Fregean theory can no longer distinguish between individuals and properties.

3 CRITICISM OF THE FREGEAN ACCOUNT OF SATURATION

A central point in the Fregean theory of saturation is the definition in terms of saturated and unsaturated entities of the distinction between names and objects on the one hand and predicates and properties on the other. This way of drawing the distinction has also been advocated by Strawson, who claims that

a subject-expression is one which, in a sense, presents a fact in its own right and is to that extent complete. A predicate-expression is one which in no sense presents a fact in its own right and is to that extent incomplete. [...] The predicate-expression, on the new criterion is one that can be completed only by explicit coupling with another. [...] We find an additional depth in Frege's metaphor of saturated and unsaturated constituents.[31]

This approach has been severely criticized in the past, most notably by taking up some thoughts of Ramsey's on the problem of universals. We will have a look at this criticism and inquire into the effects it has on the formulation of the Frege hierarchy. First of all, however, we should give an account of the different ways in which Frege himself spells out the distinction between saturated and unsaturated entities.

§74 Analyses of unsaturatedness

Frege gives at least five different, though related, analyses of the notion of unsaturatedness.

1.   Unsaturated entities are in need of supplementation (*ergänzungs-bedürftig*), incomplete (*unvollständig*) and contain empty places.

---

[31] Strawson (1964: 187–8).

An object is anything that is not a function, so that an expression for it does not contain an empty place.[32]

The concept is predicative, it is in need of supplementation, in the same way in which the predicative part of a sentence always demands a linguistic subject and is incomplete without it.[33]

2. Unsaturated entities are not self-sufficient (*unselbständig*).

It is clear that the concept cannot exist in the self-sufficient way the object does, but it can only occur in combinations. It can be said that it can be distinguished within them but not extracted from them.[34]

3. Unsaturated items depend for their existence on other items.

The concept is unsaturated, that is, it demands something which it can subsume under it, so that it cannot exist on its own.[35]

4. Unsaturated items are functional.

I call the function unsaturated or in need of supplementation since the expression for it has to be supplemented by the expression for an argument to have a determinate meaning.[36]

The idea here is that a functional item is 'almost an x', i.e. it becomes an x if you add a missing piece. For example the verb 'swims' is functional since it becomes a sentence as soon as we append a name to its left.[37]

5. Unsaturated items are the things held fixed in substitutions.

Suppose that a simple or complex symbol occurs in one or more places in an expression [...]. If we imagine this symbol as replaceable by another (the same one each time) at one or more of its occurrences, then the part of the expression that shows itself invariant under such replacement is called the function; and the replaceable part, the argument of the function.[38]

---

[32] Frege (1962b: 27), McGuinness (1984: 147).
[33] Frege (1969d: 246). See also Frege (1962a: 78), McGuinness (1984: 193).
[34] Frege (1967: 270). See also Frege (1966a: 68), McGuinness (1984: 386).
[35] Frege (1976: 164).
[36] Frege (1969b: 246).
[37] This interpretation is e.g. defended by Simons (1981: 87).
[38] Frege (1993: 16), Geach and Black (1980: 13).

§75   Ramsey's criticism

Ramsey criticized attempts to define the difference between particulars and universals in terms of subject and predicate by claiming that the two can switch rôles while preserving the meaning of the sentence involved. This implies that the grammatical distinction between subject and predicate cannot be taken as indicating an ontological distinction. Ramsey claims that

> there is no sense in the word individual and quality; all we are talking about is two different types of objects, such that two objects, one of each type, could be the sole constituents of an atomic fact. The two types being in every way symmetrically related, nothing can be meant by calling one type the type of individuals and the other that of qualities, and these two words are devoid of connotation. [39]

His example is that if we could identify particular and universal as object and subject, the sentence 'Socrates is wise' would tell us that Socrates, being the subject, is a particular, while 'is wise', being the predicate, is a universal which Socrates instantiates. But we can reformulate the sentence into 'Wisdom is a characteristic of Socrates' which arguably has the very same meaning as 'Socrates is wise'. Now the rôles of subject and predicate are reversed so that Wisdom is the particular and Socrates (or Socratesness or at least 'being a characteristic of Socrates') is the universal it exemplifies.

This argument may be attacked in a number of ways, most notably by arguing that the two versions of the sentence do not really say the same thing. Note, however, that Ramsey is not just criticizing attempts at getting ontological distinctions from grammatical ones. If this were all he was trying to do, his argument would be far less interesting than it actually is. Ramsey's argument shows something fairly fundamental about the possibility of distinguishing individuals and properties (particulars and universals) in terms of saturatedness and thus in a purely structural manner. What it shows is that the distinction between saturated and unsaturated entities is *completely symmetric.*[40] Every reason Frege proposes for individuals being saturated and properties being unsaturated can equally be taken as a reason for the opposite. But if this is the case,

[39] Ramsey (1990: 28).   [40] Sahlin (1990: 195).

drawing a distinction between individuals and properties in terms of saturation will be a hopeless enterprise.

Let us see how this affects the different ways in which Frege spells out saturation. If we take predicates as in need of supplementation, as incomplete, as something with an empty place, the name will surely have all these properties as well. The predicate is in need of supplementation *to form a sentence*—so is the name. It is not a complete sentence on its own—neither is the name. It contains a 'loose end' or empty place something has to be attached to to produce a sentence—this is also true of the name.[41]

If we spell out unsaturatedness in terms of lack of self-sufficiency or dependence upon items which can be subsumed under it then it is far from clear whether this does not also work the other way round. Individuals do not depend on things falling under them, but they cannot exist without something which is true of them: they depend on something under which they can be subsumed and are thus by these criteria as unsaturated as properties. In fact they might be even more so: although there are properties which do not subsume anything under them, an individual which is not subsumed under anything at all seems to be an impossibility.[42]

The final two readings of unsaturatedness, in terms of functionality and substitution come closest to the interpretation we have been advancing so far. But clearly any analysis which treats a predicate as functional because it is 'almost a sentence' could equally well treat names as functional, since if we add a predicate to a name, we get a sentence.

---

[41] It might be argued that the way in which a predicate has an empty place differs fundamentally from the way in which a name can be said to have an empty place (see Carruthers (1983: 53–5)). A predicate will always have a fixed number of empty places (determined by its adicity) while *the very same name* can be represented as having a different number of empty places: if we think of it in terms of the possibility of putting it together with a monadic predicate, it has one empty place; if we think of it in terms of putting it together with a dyadic predicate and another name it will have *two* empty places; and so on. Nevertheless, this phenomenon seems to be replicable in the case of predicates as well. For example, we can describe a predicate as dyadic (having two empty places) because it takes two names a, b, or alternatively as monadic because it takes the *concatenation ab* of two names. Moreover, even if we do not grant this, the fact that names and predicates have empty places *in different ways* still means that they have empty places so that both (and not just the predicates) can be taken to be incomplete sentences.

[42] Kleemeier (1990: 209).

This symmetry is even more clear in the case of substitution. If we take the name as fixed and the predicate as replaceable, the name will come out as the unsaturated element and the function as saturated. In fact the respective passage from Frege seems to suggest that what is the function and what argument depends crucially on us, i.e. on what we 'imagine as replaceable'.

§76 Morals to draw

None of this shows that the distinction between saturated and unsaturated entities is flawed. We can still claim with Frege that 'concepts and objects [unsaturated and saturated entities] are fundamentally different and cannot be substituted for one another'.[43] The important point is that the line between the saturated and the unsaturated should be drawn elsewhere, in such a way that individuals and properties are located on the same side of the divide. In accordance with Ramsey's criticism we should claim that *only complexes* (that is in our case states of affairs) *should be considered as saturated* and everything else as unsaturated. Frege is also right in assuming that elements making up complexes can be complexes themselves (and thus saturated); we just do not want to say that *names* are such elements. Regarding saturation, names and predicates should be considered as completely on a par.

It has been argued that such a view would cause problems; two unsaturated entities, one might claim, cannot make one saturated one.

In the case of an object falling under a first-level concept we have the completion [. . .] of an incomplete (unsaturated) function by a complete (saturated) object. In the case of second-level concepts, such as quantifiers, the only way to deploy these metaphors is to characterize the application of function to argument as the completion of an incomplete thing with another incomplete thing, or the saturation of an unsaturated thing with another unsaturated thing. It is as though putting one unsaturated sponge together with another would produce a saturated pair of sponges. The metaphors have gone entirely limp; they cast no light whatever. [. . .] The unsaturated predicative part holds together with other parts which are saturated. But in the case of propositions involving quantification all the relevant parts may be incomplete. One kind of incompleteness must be capable of completing another kind of incompleteness. Here, however, the metaphors do no work whatever.[44]

---

[43] Frege (1969b: 130).
[44] Linsky (1992: 265). See also Gaskin (1998: 28).

Perhaps it would be more useful to read Frege's metaphoric notions in terms in which he intended them to be understood, rather than cashing them out with examples from one's own bathroom. Frege took the notions of saturated and unsaturated entities from the chemistry of his time.[45] Both were closely connected with the concept of valence.[46] It was assumed that

each [chemical] element has a certain number of 'units of affinity', which may be entirely, or only in part, engaged when it enters into combination with other elements [. . .]. Compounds in which all the units of affinity of the contained elements are engaged are said to be *saturated*, while those in which the affinities of contained elements are not all engaged by other elements are said to be *unsaturated*.[47]

In fact the term *ungesättigt* is still applied in modern chemistry to hydrocarbons where the carbon atoms are not bound to the maximal number of hydrogen atoms. On this understanding of unsaturatedness it is possible that two unsaturated items should give one saturated item. If, for example, we take two carbon atoms which are bound to three hydrogen atoms each (and are thus unsaturated) and join the two remaining 'loose ends' of the carbon atoms together, we get something which is saturated, namely an ethane (C_2H_6) molecule.

On our account of complexes it is of course perfectly possible to have two strings ϕ, ψ such that neither is a complex while $\mathbf{C}\phi^\frown\psi$. In fact there are numerous cases of this even outside chemistry, for example expressions which do not make up a sentence on their own but manage to do so together, or two sets of tiles such that neither can tile the plane, but the two sets together can.

It is therefore not problematic to consider names and predicates as equally unsaturated since we can make good sense of two unsaturated objects saturating one another. But now it becomes apparent that the Fregean identification of types has to deviate from the complex principle at a crucial point in order to generate the required asymmetry between names and predicates. Frege is not just taking the complexes (states of affairs) as epistemologically given but also assumes that we can discern complexes within complexes (that is individuals within states of affairs). We are therefore supposed to have immediate epistemological access to

[45] Majer (1996), Martin (1983: 250–1).   [46] See Palmer (1959: 6), (1965).
[47] Everitt (1910: 41).

the parts of states of affairs, rather than assuming that these parts are identified (if not brought about) via a primitive overlapping relation on them, as discussed in § 43 and as suggested by the complex principle. If this assumption is abandoned, there seems to be no way for the Fregean account to distinguish between individuals and properties.

The reason Frege did not realize this difficulty is that he held two different views of complexes, sometimes the one and sometimes the other.[48] One is occasionally called the *unity-model*, the other the *constituent-model*.[49]

The unity-model says that the structure of a complex is an unstructured entity which gets its structure only by splitting it up. This is the model supported by the epistemological reading of the complex principle. As Frege puts it:

Instead of constructing the judgement from an individual as a subject together with a previously generated concept as a predicate, we proceed in the opposite way by splitting up the content of the judgement and thereby generate the concept.[50]

I thus do not start from concepts and use them to construct thoughts or judgements, but I generate the parts of a thought by splitting up the thought itself.[51]

The constituent-model, on the other hand, takes the complex to be made up of constituents in an atomistic fashion. According to this view, the complex is already internally structured.

But even the act of grasping a thought is not [. . .] an act of setting its parts in order, for the thought was already true, and so was already there with its parts in order, before it was grasped.[52]

There is an obvious tension between the two models which would lead to an inconsistency in the conception of a complex unless we argued that somehow the models are not models of quite the same kind of complex (for example one could adopt the unity-model on the epistemological level and the constituent-model on the ontological level).

This tension is essentially the same as that between the function-argument and the part-whole view of complexes,[53] which is in turn closely

[48] Bell (1996: 595).
[49] Kleemeier (1990: 29–37).
[50] Frege (1969c: 18).
[51] Frege (1969d: 273).
[52] Frege (1966a: 371), McGuinness (1984: 382).
[53] Bell (1996: 594–5).

related to that between decomposition and analysis. On the function-argument view, splitting up the complex is something done by us when we are presented with the complex which we take to be the value. There is usually more than one way of doing this. We can regard the 'complex' of the number six as the value of $4 + 2$ or 2×3 or $15 - 9$ and so on. On the second view, however, the complex is taken to be put together from a determinate number of building-blocks. They are not the result of our analysis but are literally present in the complex.[54]

It is clear from our discussion of the complex principle that states of affairs should be understood according to the unity/function-argument model. But as we have seen, Frege needs to appeal to the constituent/part-whole model as well, because he has to identify individuals as those parts of states of affairs which are complexes themselves. Therefore Frege's attempt to give a purely structural analysis of the distinction between individuals and properties is not successful.

4 ADDING LOGIC

As we saw in the preceding sections, there is no successful way of drawing a distinction like that between individuals and properties in a purely combinatorial manner. But we mentioned at the beginning of this chapter that combinatorial information is not the only information which can be regarded as structural. It might be the case that although the distinction between individuals and properties cannot be drawn in purely combinatorial terms it suddenly comes into play once we take logical relations into account as well. This is the possibility we are going to investigate in the present part.

The ontological data we have considered above provide us with purely combinatorial information, that is with information about what can go together with what. As such the data need not be about parts of states of affairs at all: they could describe any collections of objects where it made sense to speak of some objects 'fitting into' some other objects. Our data could for example describe which atoms can go with which

---

[54] Bell (1996: 596) for example dissolves the tension by arguing that *senses of propositions* should be distinguished from *thoughts*: while the former have a part-whole structure, the latter have a function-argument structure (and thus no 'determinate, intrinsic' structure).

other atoms to make up a molecule, or which tiles of some given set can be used to tile a plane, or which nuts fit into which bolts. It is therefore not so surprising that we could systematize these data in lots of different ways and that they do not automatically fall into the slots of the simple theory of types in a unique way. One kind of object is not inherently above another one, nor is there an inherent 'up' in the hierarchy of levels: these are just results of our theoretical systematization of the data.

We might think that the hierarchy only emerges in a determined (or at least less underdetermined) way once we regard the objects the composition of which is encoded in the combinatorial data (the states of affairs) as fit for applying a logic to, that is as *propositional*. The idea would thus be that the simple theory of types is embedded in our conception of inference: it shows up only once we consider not merely what goes together with what but also what *follows* from what. This would then distinguish the objects we are considering from atoms, tiles, nuts, and bolts: it does not make sense to say that a molecule or a collection of tiles entails another molecule or tile, while it *does* make sense to say this about propositional objects and this is what generates the hierarchy of types. If we take this additional feature into account a great part of the above underdetermination might disappear.

§77 Quantificational reasoning

Quantificational reasoning seems to be what we want to look out for when considering entailment relations. Here is a simple example of how taking quantification into account could rule out the transformations discussed above. There are different ways in which to interpret quantifiers, but one that has been rather influential is to regard them as higher level properties. In particular, quantifiers over objects at level n are regarded as level $n + 2$ objects. (For example, we can regard the first order existential quantifier as a property of a property of individuals, namely as the the property of being non-empty.) Now if we have objects at a given level n, there does not seem to be anything to keep us from quantifying over these, thus introducing level $n + 2$ objects into our hierarchy. Therefore the hierarchy will be potentially infinite. Now if we have this picture, it no longer seems to be possible to reverse a typing, since we can now identify a top end of the hierarchy: this is the end where new levels can be added to the hierarchy.

Hugh Mellor has argued (in his exegesis of Ramsey) that we should identify the place of individuals in the hierarchy via quantification: they are exactly what our first order quantifiers range over.[55] Similarly first order properties could be identified as those objects second order quantifiers range over, and so on. This will rule out some of the transformations. For example, typing 1 depicted in Figure V.1 will support the claim that there is exactly one object the first order quantifiers range over (namely t), while neither the lifted (Figure V.3) nor the folded typing (Figure V.5) do this.

However, neither of these two approaches attempting to remove the underdetermination by recourse to logic is really satisfactory. Consider first the idea that reversing a typing conflicted with the introduction of higher order quantifiers. This is only the case if we assume that the quantifier is always two levels higher than the objects it ranges over. But in fact this is an additional assumption not implied by the way in which quantifiers (understood as higher order properties) enter into states of affairs. Clearly all that is demanded is that the quantifier is located at a level directly adjacent to that of the properties of the objects it quantifies over. But this can also be the case if it is on the very same level as these objects. Thus we could apply FOLDING and for example say that quantifiers over individuals are also a particular kind of individual (since they can form states of affairs with properties of individuals). But then it is clear that the demand for adding quantifiers of ever higher orders does not enforce the hierarchy to be open-ended in one direction. If our current highest level is m and we want to quantify over objects at level $m - 1$ we can introduce a level $m + 1$, but we could equally place the quantifier at level $m - 1$.

Similarly the proposal inspired by Mellor's exegesis of Ramsey does not seem to help in providing us with a non-circular structural characterization of individuals. It presupposes that we have a prior way of checking whether some quantifier is first or higher order. But this cannot just be based on taking them to be located at particular levels in the hierarchy for, as we have seen, their position will be affected by transformations as well. Any other way of determining their order, however, will just reintroduce the distinction between individuals and properties through the back door.

[55] Craig (1998: VIII: 48), Mellor (1990: xx).

§78 Distinguishing objects through their logics

A rather sophisticated argument for a purely structural distinction between objects at different levels has been developed by Nicholas Denyer.[56] He argues that a structural difference between objects at different levels is implied by the different metalogical properties of logics quantifying over them. Denyer considers first order logic, which quantifies over objects at level 0, pure second order logic, which quantifies over objects at level 1,[57] and standard second order logic, which quantifies over both. First order logic is compact, complete, and the Löwenheim-Skolem theorem holds for it. Standard second order logic has none of these properties. Pure second order logic has a property which neither of the other two has: logical truth is decidable in it.

If this works it is surely a most elegant way of removing the underdetermination of typings by appealing to logic. We will then for example be able to say that the objects which *really* belong to the zeroth level are those such that the logic quantifying over them has a particular set of properties, while other levels are distinguished by the specific metalogical properties of the logics quantifying over *them*.

But unfortunately several caveats have to be added here. The metalogical properties of a logic depend crucially on the semantics relative to which we determine these properties. The metalogical distinctions between first and second order logic appealed to certainly hold if we give second order logic a standard semantics. But if we take a Henkin or a many-sorted semantics (or first order semantics, as the second is sometimes called), the differences disappear: second order logic is now compact, complete, and the Löwenheim-Skolem theorem holds for it.[58]

Henkin semantics and many-sorted semantics differ from the standard semantics in important ways. In Henkin semantics the analogues of properties are regarded as subsets of the powerset of the domain (and thus as set-theoretical constructions from the individuals). But as compared to standard semantics not all the members of this powerset are included in the semantics (unless we have a full Henkin model, which is then in turn equivalent to a standard model). Many-sorted semantics,

---

[56] Denyer (1998).

[57] For the formal details of pure second order logic see Denyer (1992).

[58] Shapiro (1991: 88–95); see pp. 70–4 for a survey of these different kinds of semantics.

on the other hand, takes the denotation of predicates to be objects in some distinct and disjoint sets in the model (and therefore *not* as constructed from the individuals). Because of this many-sorted semantics needs a primitive predication function which connects the individuals with the properties (standard and Henkin semantics could just use set-membership for this purpose). Henkin and many-sorted semantics are very closely related—for any model of the one sort there is an equivalent model of the other sort.[59] However, in the context of our inquiry there are important differences which are brought out by distinguishing the two.

The standard semantics for second order logic seems to be attractive because it is a natural continuation of that of first order logic, whereas Henkin or many-sorted semantics deviate from this standard. But such a unity can also be achieved by using a many-sorted semantics for first *and* for second order logic. In such a uniform semantics the metalogical differences just mentioned will disappear.

Let us first consider a simple variant of first order logic which we will call **L1** and which has the peculiarity that it contains the primitive predication predicate ε.[60] Thus instead of formulae like Fa we will have $\varepsilon(F, a)$; instead of Gab, $\varepsilon(G, a, b)$; and instead of $(\exists x)(Fx)$, $(\exists x)(\varepsilon(F, x))$. Instead of the non-well-formed formulae aF, aGb, Gb and the like we will have $\varepsilon(a, F)$, $\varepsilon(a, G, b)$ and $\varepsilon(G, b)$, which will be well-formed but false.

To see how this works consider that the semantics for this first order language is very similar to the standard semantics for standard first order logic. It consists of a domain $D = \{\mathbf{a}, \mathbf{b}, \ldots\}$ of objects and an interpretation function I. I assigns an $\mathbf{x} \in D$ to each name of our language, a subset of D to each monadic predicate letter, a set of ordered pairs from D to each dyadic predicate letter and a set of n-tuples from D to each n-adic predicate letter. We shall denote the referents of the names and predicate letters given in this way by underlining them.

A sentence of the form $\varepsilon(F, a)$ is then true in a model of the above kind if $\underline{a} \in \underline{F}$, $\varepsilon(G, a, b)$ is true if $\langle \underline{a}, \underline{b} \rangle \in \underline{G}$. $(\exists x)(\varepsilon(F, x))$ is true if there is at least one $\mathbf{x} \in D$ such that $\mathbf{x} \in \underline{F}$. It is then clear

---

[59] Shapiro (1991: 88).
[60] Compare the Δ predicate introduced in Bealer (1982: 82).

that $\varepsilon(a, F)$, $\varepsilon(a, G, b)$ and $\varepsilon(G, b)$ are all false since they denote the non-obtaining facts that $\underline{F} \in \underline{a}$, $\langle \underline{G}, \underline{b} \rangle \in \underline{a}$ and $\underline{b} \in \underline{G}$.

We thus interpret the predication predicate ε simply as set-membership. In this way the semantics for **L1** does not need any more resources than standard first order logic. Its point is just to make the predication expressed implicitly in standard first order language by concatenation explicit by assigning a special syntactic element to it.[61]

We now introduce a first order language **L2** which is syntactically just like **L1** but which does not have a standard semantics like **L1** but a many-sorted semantics. A model of **L2** will consist of a domain D which is the union of infinitely many sets $D_0, D_1, \ldots$, an asymmetric dyadic relation P between n-tuples from D_0 and one member from D_n (where $n \geq 1$) and the interpretation function I which assigns a member of D_0 to each name, a member of D_1 to each monadic predicate and so on. A sentence $\varepsilon(F, a)$ will then be true if $P(\underline{F}, \langle \underline{a} \rangle)$, $\varepsilon(G, a, b)$ if $P(\underline{G}, \langle \underline{a}, \underline{b} \rangle)$ and $(\exists x)(\varepsilon(F, x))$ if there is at least one member of D_0 such that the singleton containing that member stands in the relation P to $\underline{F}$.

This semantics introduces the special relation P as the interpretation of the ε predicate, rather than using $\in$ to fulfil this rôle. This is usually only done in giving many-sorted semantics for *second* order languages[62] but there is no good reason why it should not be done for first order languages as well. It allows us to give a uniform semantics for first order, pure second order, and standard second order languages, simply by postulating that in the first case our quantifiers range only over members of D_0, in the second case over members of any set *other* than D_0, and in the third case over members of any D_n whatsoever.

Given that for the third case it can be shown that the system is compact, complete, and the Löwenheim-Skolem theorem holds for it, these results also hold for the first and the second case, where we quantify not over members from *all D_n*, but only over some. But in this case the argument for the difference between individuals and predicates from the different metatheoretical properties of the logics quantifying over them hinges on our adopting the standard semantics in all three cases, rather than the many-sorted semantics. We will thus need an

---

[61] Shapiro (1991: 77).   [62] Shapiro (1991: 75).

argument why the standard semantics is inherently preferable to many-sorted semantics.

The obvious thing to say here seems to be that Henkin models do not allow our quantifiers to range over really *all* properties. In assigning a denotation to for example a dyadic predicate-letter in a Henkin model we might not have the entire set of pairs of individuals in the domain to choose from, but only a limited subset of this. This limitation is essential for the metatheoretical properties of the logic. If it is lifted we get a full Henkin model (or, equivalently a full many-sorted model) which will allow us to prove the same metalogical results as the standard model.[63] We might now argue that if we formalize our talk about 'all properties' of a certain sort we should choose a semantics in which this is faithfully represented, rather than one which understands our 'all' as an 'all of some particular kind'.

§79   Blind logic

But let us suppose we accept this criticism. In this case the metalogical distinctions are reinstated. But even so they do not give us the required distinction between individuals and properties. The fundamental problem is that, as we have seen, metalogical distinctions only make sense once we have a semantics. But all usual semantics, including the ones discussed above, already *presuppose* the distinction we want to draw between individuals and properties, since they assign structurally different objects to names and to predicate letters (objects to the former and sets of objects to the latter in the standard case, objects from different sets in the many-sorted case). Therefore the metatheoretical differences appealed to are actually the result of the distinction between individuals and properties drawn at the level of semantics, rather than a guide to such a distinction.

In all of the above systems the properties of the predication function (regardless of whether we took it to be set-theoretical membership or a primitive relation) provided us with an obvious way of identifying the individuals in the semantics. There were always some items in the semantics which could not occupy the first position in the predication function, the ones which could not have any members nor could be

---

[63] Shapiro (1991: 89).

predicated of anything. These, of course, were the individuals. This identification relies on the fact that the predication function is asymmetric: if a can be predicated of b (b is a member of a) b cannot be predicated of a (a cannot also be a member of b) and must therefore be an individual. But the fact that there is such a predication function present is not a fact of logical necessity. In fact we can devise a logic, a *blind logic*, as one might call it, which can do everything which the above logics can, but the semantics of which does not contain a predication function but only a weaker symmetric substitute, called *application*. In this logic individuals and properties cannot any longer be distinguished in the above way.

Let us look at a toy example of such a blind logic. The alphabet of our language will consist of the seven names t, j, p, f, l, n, o, the multigrade symmetric application predicate A,[64] the propositional connectives $\neg$ and $\wedge$, a way of expressing quantification, and the necessary punctuation conventions. The names will be divided into three types, $\tau_1 = \{t, j, p\}$, $\tau_2 = \{f, l\}$, and $\tau_3 = \{n, o\}$. An atomic sentence is well-formed if it has one of the two following forms:

$$A(\tau_1, \tau_2)$$
$$A(\tau_1, \tau_1, \tau_3)$$

Thus writing down the application predicate followed by a list of names, one from the first type and one from the second gives a well-formed formula. So does writing down the application predicate, two names from the first type and one from the third. If $A(\tau_i, \ldots, \tau_k)$ is well-formed, so is every permutation of the τs. If ϕ, ψ are wffs, so are $\neg\phi$ and $\phi \wedge \psi$. Furthermore, if ϕ is well-formed, replacing one name belonging to τ_i in it by an x and prefixing the result with an $\exists x_{\tau_i}$ is also well-formed.

A model of this language consists of three sets $D_1 = \{T, J, P\}$, $D_2 = \{F, L\}$, and $D_3 = \{N, O\}$, a set S of multisets of elements of D_1–D_3 and an interpretation function I which assigns an object from some D_i to every name and an element from S to every atomic sentence. A sentence of the form $A(u, v)$ will be true if $[\underline{u}, \underline{v}]$ is in S, where the referents of names are again denoted by <u>underlining</u> the names. $\neg\phi$

---

[64] A multigrade predicate P is symmetric just in case if $P(a, \ldots, n)$ holds, so does $P(\pi(a) \ldots, \pi(n))$, where π is any permutation of the $a, \ldots, n$.

is true if ϕ is not true, $\phi \wedge \psi$ if both ψ and ϕ are. $\exists x_{\tau_i} A(x, u)$ is true if there is some x in the D_i such that $[\underline{x}, \underline{u}]$ is in S.

There is also an intuitive interpretation of this language. In this interpretation T, J, and P stand for three Cambridge Colleges, Trinity, St John's, and Peterhouse, F stands for the property 'being first in the league-table', L for 'is liked by tourists', O for 'is as old as' and N for 'is next to'. So $A(j, l)$ is true if there is an actual state of affairs containing just St John's and 'being liked by tourists' (i.e. if St John's is liked by tourists); $A(t, l) \wedge A(t, j, n)$ is true if both Trinity is first in the league-table and Trinity is next to St John's; and $\exists x_{\tau_2} A(x, p)$ if either Peterhouse is liked by tourists or it is first in the league-table.

Now it should be clear that everything a standard first order theory of the three Colleges, their two properties, and two relations can express can be expressed using this blind logic. However, as opposed to standard systems with standard or many-sorted semantics we cannot draw a distinction between the different items in the model according to the position they occupy in expressions of the form $A(u, v)$, since for example $A(u, v)$ and $A(v, u)$ will be logically equivalent.

Intuitively we would claim that T, J, and P in the model are individuals, F and L first order monadic and N and O first order dyadic properties. This is surely a sensible assumption to make. But there is nothing in the semantics which forces us to go down that road. As we have seen in the previous sections, we could equally regard T, J, and P as first order monadic properties and F, L, N, and O as different kinds of individuals. Or T and J could be taken to be individuals, P as a second order property and F, L, N, and O as first order properties which can take arguments both from level 0 and from level 2.

§80 Ordered application

The reader may have realized already that the expressive equivalence between our theory of the three Colleges formulated in blind logic and in standard first order logic only holds because we took care to include just symmetric relations. Assume we had included some non-symmetric predicates (such as 'admires') or asymmetric predicates (such as 'has more students than'). In this case expressive equivalence would not have been preserved, since clearly we can express that Trinity has more students than St John's in the standard first order language as $M(t, j)$, while the blind logic equivalent $A(m, t, j)$ only tells us that m can go together with t and j in a state of affairs, but not in which direction it does.

In order to get full expressive equivalence with standard first order logic we therefore have to add to our logic some device for expressing this 'direction' or 'ordering' of elements. We do this by introducing a second application predicate A' which only occurs in the scope of A. For example if we add the two names a, m to the above language (standing for the predicates 'admires' and 'has more students than') which belong to a type τ_4, we would amend the above rules for forming atomic sentences by adding

$$A(\tau_4, A'(\tau_1, \tau_1))$$

We had multisets of objects to serve as the denotata of formulae containing the A predicate and will use multisets of objects and ordered sets of objects from the Ds as referents of formulae which also contain the ordered A' predicate. The ordered sets correspond to the 'ordered' part of the formula which is in the scope of the A'. We thus expand our set S to S' so that it contains not just multisets of objects from the Ds but also multisets of objects and ordered sets of objects from the Ds and say that a formula of the form $A(u, A'(v, w))$ is true iff $[\underline{u}, \langle \underline{v}, \underline{w} \rangle]$ is in S'. We can then for example express sentences like 'St John's admires Trinity but not the other way round' as $A(a, A'(j, t)) \wedge \neg A(a, A'(t, j))$, something which obviously could not be done in a language containing A alone. It is then clear that a language containing the two application predicates has the same expressive power as standard first order predicate calculus.

§81 Ordered states of affairs and natural language

The problem of distinguishing a state of affairs like 'Albert loves Becca' from its converse is obviously not just relevant for the formal language we have been discussing, but is equally acute for natural languages. Different languages have different ways of tackling this problem. In English the fact that 'Albert' comes before 'Becca' in 'Albert loves Becca' indicates that Albert is the lover and Becca the beloved, rather than the other way round. The two states of affairs are thus distinguished by *word order*.

The second linguistic mechanism by which this can be achieved is *case marking*. To indicate that Domitilla sees Polybius in Latin we put Domitilla's name in the nominative case and Polybius' in the accusative: 'Domitilla Polybium videt'. In the case of triadic relations like 'x gives y to z' we also employ the dative, as in 'Domitilla Polybio librum dat'.

The two methods are each on their own able to fulfil the task of distinguishing different 'directions' of relations. Once a case marking system is in place we do not need to appeal to word order for the same purpose, or vice versa. In Latin the word order is quite flexible, though not completely arbitrary. There are, however, examples of languages employing case markers such as the native American polysynthetic language Mohawk where sometimes every permutation of the words of a sentence is a sentence as well.[65]

Whether a language employs word order or case marking seems to be a quite fundamental difference which is decided by how very general parameters are set.[66] The formal languages of logic have always gone for employing word order, rather than case markers. The above syntactic device can be seen as incorporating some elements of such case marking, since the order of application (like the case marking) applies only to certain parts of the sentence, not to the entirety of its constituents.

§82   Distinctions which can be drawn

We have now seen that neither ordered nor partially ordered application gives us a way of structurally distinguishing individuals and properties. Let us therefore look at the distinction between the objects in the domain which *can* be drawn in terms of the two application predicates A and A'. The criteria of well-formedness tell us which objects can go together to form states of affairs. For example, from the fact that $A(\tau_1, \tau_1, \tau_3)$ is well-formed we know that one object of the kind denoted by names of type τ_3 and two objects of the kind denoted by names of type τ_1 can be assembled into a state of affairs. This is essentially the same information which is formulated in the type descriptions introduced in § 47 and in the graph-theoretic model developed in §§ 62–6. In the type descriptions the above would have been formulated

---

[65] Baker (2001: 88–9).
[66] For the notion of a hierarchy of parameters and the rôle of the polysynthesis parameter see Baker (2001: ch. 6).

as $\tau_2 : (\tau_1|(\tau_1|\mathbf{C})$; in the graph-theoretic model each collection of vertices consisting of one member of τ_3 and two members of τ_1 would be part of a cluster of three elements.

This information is not sufficient, however, for achieving a structural distinction between individuals and properties. We cannot argue that in a state of affairs described by a formula of the form $A(\tau_1, \tau_1, \tau_3)$ τ_3 is a dyadic property since it takes two other objects to form a state of affairs, because this is also true of the τ_1 (this is essentially the point made in § 66). We are in the strange situation that we can structurally establish whether some state of affairs contains an n-adic constituent but not which constituent this is.

This situation is not changed in any significant way by introducing the ordered application predicate A'. In denoting the state of affairs that John loves Kate it is not essential that 'John' and 'Kate' are within the scope of the A' predicate. The same state of affairs can equally well be denoted by $A(j, A'(l, k))$ or $A(k, A'(l, j))$ and so on. It is essential that order is introduced at some point, but not that it is introduced at any particular point.

On the basis of all the combinatorial and logical information which we can bring in to decide this matter there is no way of settling the issue. From a purely structural point of view (which, as we have argued earlier, is the only acceptable point of view in ontological contexts) there is no fact of the matter and therefore no distinction between the ontological categories of individuals and properties.

§83   Structural ontological distinctions

Let us now summarize what the resulting picture of an ontological theory based on purely structural distinctions looks like. At the fundamental level there will be different types of objects (different formsets) which are distinguished by the way in which they form states of affairs with other objects. These types can be arranged in a hierarchical order by establishing a containment structure on the set of types in the way described in § 48. None of the types in our ontology will be constructively redundant, i.e. all will be base-sets. For no type of objects is it possible to construct another type having exactly the same essential properties from the remaining types.

This picture of an ontological theory is in close harmony with many of the structural features of the examples of ontological systems described in chapter I. It caters for the existence of a hierarchical structure, for the existence of minimal categories, for the fact that hierarchies of ontological categories are upwards closed, and for Sommers' law. It furthermore incorporates central components of the most successful accounts of ontological categories discussed in chapter II, in particular the notion of intersubstitutability present in the accounts of Ryle and Sommers, but also the idea of the importance of the notion of an essential property for the constitution of ontological categories present in the Frege-Dummett account.

At the same time our approach will be particularly attractive to anyone inclined more towards a 'factualist' than to a 'thingist' view of ontology. Such an inclination is clearly present in Wittgenstein; it can to a certain extent be encountered in the works of Frege and Dummett and has found its most forceful recent advocate in David Armstrong.[67]

In my account this approach is merged with a holist conception of ontological inquiry. Such a conception, characterized by the adoption of some form of the complex principle, has until now been prominent mainly in epistemology[68] and most recently in logic.[69] This holist perspective towards ontological distinctions has been little explored and leads to some new and rather unusual views of ontology. These views should at least find some support in the fact that the theory they are derived from manages to give a rather more satisfactory account of ontological categories than that presented in the traditional attempts at clarifying this subject-matter.

Some of the more unusual features of our account of ontological categories have already been discussed. Particularly important among these is the relativism introduced by our reference to the notion of base-sets.[70] On this account 'being an ontological category' is no longer an *essential* feature of a collection of objects but rather a *relative* feature. It depends

[67] Meixner (1997) is another example of recent work based on such factualist inclinations.

[68] In Carnap's *Aufbau*, where elementary experiences are regarded as the primitive complexes, as well as in belief dynamics, where this rôle is played by beliefs or sets of beliefs.

[69] See Koslow (1992), Martin and Pollard (1996a; b), Gärdenfors (1988: ch. 6).

[70] See §§ 50, 54.

on whether or not there are other sets such that the particular set we have in mind can be constructed from them. The picture of an ontological category we get is therefore not so much that of a fundamental property of objects, but rather a fundamental concept in our systematization of and theorizing about objects.

An even more apparent divergence from the traditional picture of ontological categories is implied by the argument set forth earlier in this chapter. We came to the rather surprising conclusion that what appear to be the most structural ontological distinctions, namely those between individuals and properties and between properties of different adicities and orders, are not in fact determined by purely structural information about states of affairs at all. The transition from the structural theory of different form-sets in terms of their type descriptions to traditional ontological distinctions like those between individuals and properties is not straightforward. It is instructive to compare this transition to the relation between grammatical categories identified in categorial grammar and the categories of traditional grammar. It is not always the case that talk in terms of the former can be translated into talk about the latter in a unique way. Consider the simple example of the primitive category n in categorial grammar. In the system presented by Ajdukiewicz this can be regarded as standing for the traditional grammatical category of proper noun as well as for that of common noun:[71] categorial grammar does not distinguish between the two. This leads to certain problems, so it has been suggested that one should treat n as standing for proper nouns and use the functor which takes a proper noun, such as 'Peter', and returns a proposition, such as 'Peter walks', to stand for common nouns. Unfortunately this just shifts the bulge under the carpet elsewhere: now the functor $n|s$ includes both common nouns and verbs. Gardies argues that our intuitions 'do not allow us to group together a common noun such as "man" and a verb in the third person singular such as "walks"'[72] as belonging to the same grammatical category. Given this persistent mismatch between categorial and traditional grammatical categories, of course something will have to give way—our 'traditional' intuitions or our structuralist picture. The same is true in

---

[71] Gardies (1985: 77–8).   [72] Gardies (1985: 81).

ontology, and I have argued that it is some of the received conceptions about ontological categories which should give way.

We have seen that the move from type descriptions to the sort of typing where different levels and different adicities are distinguished is far from automatic. There are usually several ways of accommodating the information present in the type descriptions, and which one of these we choose (and therefore whether we regard something as an individual or as a second order property, as an object of order two or of order three) depends on *our* interests, on the structural features *we* want to highlight in the theory of ontological data our typing constitutes, rather than on any systematic relation between the type descriptions and the typings themselves.

It might help at this point to recall the graph-theoretic formulation of the ontological data introduced in § 62. There we represented the fact that two objects could enter into a state of affairs together by connecting the vertices representing them with an edge. Since we wanted to be able to talk about relational states of affairs as well, we had to enlarge the graph-theoretic picture in § 66 by introducing clusters linking more than two vertices. In § 80 we considered a possibility of representing the difference between symmetric and non-symmetric states of affairs by including not just ordered but also partially ordered sentences. We can translate this into our graph-theoretic picture by introducing *directed edges*. When representing sentences containing ordered application such as $A(l, A'(a, b))$ in a graph-theoretic framework we will then link the vertices corresponding to the names joined by A' (i.e. a and b in the above case) not by ordinary, but by directed edges. The result in this case would be a cluster containing three edges, one of which is directed.

We would then end up with a set of vertices representing the constituents of states of affairs which are linked in different ways—by directed and by undirected edges, pairwise or in clusters. This graph-theoretic picture will represent our ontological data. Now any typing of these data consists of 'slicing up' the graph in accordance with different rules, so that vertices belonging to one type end up in a common slice. But as we saw above, even for conditions imposed on this slicing procedure which were more likely to be too restrictive than too liberal, there were different, equally acceptable ways of accomplishing the slicing. How to slice is not forced on us in any unique way by the structure of the ontological data.

It therefore appears that the distinctions between individuals and properties and between properties of different adicities and orders are as 'material' (as opposed to 'structural') as the distinction between for example abstract and concrete objects. The purely structural ontological theory will tell us that these are two different types, simply because they cannot go together in certain ways (e.g. an abstract property such as 'is prime' cannot go together with a concrete individual). But whether to identify these two different types with the traditional ontological types of the abstract and the concrete or with something else is not determined by the structural ontological theory—doing one or the other is rather a way of interpreting the theory. The same is the case with the distinctions between individuals and properties and between properties of different adicities and orders. Our structural ontological theory will tell us that there are these different types which behave in characteristic ways. But whether to understand some object as an individual or as a property, whether to sort types into different levels à la Russell, whether to regard something as an object with a fixed or a flexible adicity is not fixed by the structural theory. The answer to such questions will only be settled by inspecting the result of interpreting and systematizing the structural ontological theory derived from the data. There will be better or worse ways of doing this, but certainly none of them can claim any *systematic* priority.

It might be argued that the technical apparatus employed in the construction of our account of ontological categories does not cohere well with the results just argued for. Given that we employ sets in our theory of form-sets and base-sets and rely on a parthood relation between states of affairs, how can we say that the distinction between individuals and properties is ontologically suspect? Are not sets just abstract *individuals* and relations special kinds of *properties*? Let us note that we did not assume that the individual–property distinction was either nonexistent or fundamentally misguided, so that it should disappear like other relics of bygone ages. We draw distinctions between individuals and properties all the time, and seem to be rather successful in doing so. In fact the distinction is so widespread that it even turns up in the languages of quantificational logic, languages which usually take great pride in expressing the underlying logical, rather than grammatical form of a sentence.

What we have been arguing is that the distinction between individuals and properties of different adicities and orders cannot be as fundamental as it appears. On a satisfactory account of ontological theories like the one we sketched above it does not come out as an ontological distinction, nor is it a distinction which could be drawn in a similarly fundamental way, for example by recourse to logic. But of course this does not imply that we should not continue talking in terms of individuals and properties, but rather that we should not attach any ontological significance to such talk. Wherever the distinction between individuals and properties of different adicities and orders comes from, it is certainly not one which should trouble us at the ontological level.

VI

Philosophical implications

In this final chapter I shall do three things. First of all I will give a synoptic overview of the account of ontological categories developed in the preceding three chapters. Rather than recapitulating the arguments set out earlier I will identify the four main assumptions the account rests on and discuss their justification. I will then describe how the four assumptions can be put together to yield a satisfactory account of ontological categories.

The second main part of this chapter will elucidate the three main consequences of our account, relativism, holism, and a particular understanding of the individual–property distinction.

The chapter concludes with a third part which describes a variety of philosophical projects which have made similar assumptions to the ones postulated in my account. These include Wittgenstein's ontology and theory of logic, structuralist logic, trope theory, and situation semantics. These accounts are not intended to be self-contained expositions of these projects, or even evaluations of them. I include them in the hope that they will put some features of my account into sharper focus and will also help to locate it more generally in the philosophical discussion within metaphysics, logic, philosophy of language, and semantics.

1 MAIN ASSUMPTIONS
AND THEIR INTERACTION

§84 Main assumptions

My account of ontological categories rests on four main assumptions.

[FACTUALISM]   We take states of affairs to be the fundamental primitive and base our account of ontological categories on them.

[NEUTRALITY]   We make no assumptions about the internal constitution of states of affairs, although we assume that they are structured in some way.

[CONNECTION]   We assume that states of affairs stand in different relations, in particular that some of them overlap and that they can imply one another.

[STRUCTURALISM]   All the information about states of affairs we consider is structural, i.e. it is derived from relations between states of affairs. In particular all information about constituents of states of affairs must be so derived, that is, it must be conceived of as an abstraction from relations between states of affairs.

Our aim is to develop an account of the constituents of states of affairs (and thus of different form-sets) which is in agreement with the neutrality assumption and which defines these constituents in a structuralist manner on the basis of relations between states of affairs. The four assumptions employed in order to achieve this differ in the amount of argumentational support they require. *Factualism* certainly needs the most detailed explication and defence; it has been discussed at length in chapter IV.

Factualism is also the assumption which establishes the most obvious parallel with the ontology of the *Tractatus*. This then radically new ontological position is succinctly captured in its second proposition, claiming that 'The world is the totality of facts, not of things'. Brian Skyrms notes that

Wittgenstein's truly daring idea was that the ontology of the subject (nominalism) and the ontology of the predicate (platonism) were both equally wrong and one-sided; and that they should give way to the ontology of the assertion. We may conceive of the world not as a world of individuals or as a world of properties and relations, but as a world of facts—with individuals and relations being equally abstractions from the facts. John would be an abstraction from all facts-about-john; Red an abstraction from being-red-facts; etc.[1]

Wittgenstein's 'truly daring idea' is of course the same as the factualism defended in this thesis. Unlike in the case of Wittgenstein, where it largely takes the form of an unargued for assumption, I tried to show

---

[1] Skyrms (1981: 199).

above that factualism can be given support from the way we know the world, from the way we form theories of the world, and from the way we get to know the meaning of sentences representing the world. These arguments suggested that epistemically, theoretically, and semantically speaking, the fact or state of affairs is 'where the action is'.[2]

We should also note at this point that the adoption of factualism manages to circumvent Bradley's notorious regress problem, that is the problem of how the constituents of a relational fact hang together without the need of a further relation relating the terms to the first relation and so on *ad infinitum*.[3] Our account takes states of affairs as primitive and constructs their constituents by abstraction. The unity of a state of affairs is thus presupposed at the outset, since the adoption of the complex principle entails that we do not conceive of the states of affairs as dependent on their constituents, but rather consider their constituents to be dependent on them. If we assume that the constituents of a state of affairs are there first and are only subsequently unified into a complex the problem of how this unification is to proceed and why it does not necessitate ever higher orders of unifiers is indeed likely to arise. But if we assume that the dependence relation holds the other way round the problem disappears, since there is nothing to unify: the constituents of the states of affairs only exist (or at least are only known) as already unified in a complex.

If we derive our support for factualism from the complex principle, the *neutrality* assumption mentioned in § 37 will not be particularly controversial. If states of affairs are prior to their constituents in some way, then it is sensible to refrain from making any assumptions about the particular structure of states of affairs from the outset. We will rather want to develop an account of these constituents on the basis of information about the primitives.

Note that even somebody who thinks with Armstrong that states of affairs are made up from 'particulars, properties, relations and, in the case of higher-order states of affairs, lower-order states of affairs'[4] will not consider the neutrality assumption to be false, but merely pointless. For him, we somehow already have a direct grasp of the constitution of states of affairs. To pretend with the neutrality assumption that we do not could only have two consequences, neither of which is particularly

---

[2] Skyrms (1981: 204).   [3] See Olson (1987: ch. 3).   [4] Armstrong (1997: 1).

interesting: either we find a way of establishing the above structuring of states of affairs in spite of the neutrality assumption, and thus gain a more longwinded route to a familiar fact, or we do not, in which case we just see how central our immediate perception of the constituents of states of affairs really is.

As we remarked above, however, Armstrong's assumption makes the relation between sentences and states of affairs suspiciously cosy and is introduced without any supporting argument. I therefore think that it is important and theoretically rewarding to inquire how far we can get without the assumption.

Our neutrality assumption has a parallel in Wittgenstein's treatment of objects. He assumes that concatenations of these make up states of affairs. Unlike Armstrong, however, Wittgenstein does not argue that objects already come in different flavours, that some are individuals, some properties, some relations, and so on. As we will see in more detail below, it is plausible to assume that Wittgenstein regarded all objects as having the same ontological status.

Assuming that states of affairs are *connected* in different ways is rather uncontroversial as well. All that is required is that the meanings of 'has a part in common with' and 'implies' can be stretched sufficiently to cover not just their familiar relata (material objects and sentences) but also states of affairs. Taking the overlapping relation to be the sharing of parts, it seems easy to make sense of the first, and to do so in a sense which is not obviously syntax-dependent, as was argued in § 43. States of affairs involving the Chancellor of Cambridge University and states of affairs involving the Duke of Edinburgh will overlap in Prince Philip, although none of the sentences picking them out might share any constituents. The step from implications between sentences to implications between states of affairs seems to be even easier to make. Assuming states of affairs as the denotata of sentences, we can easily stretch the meaning of a relation assumed to hold between representations (the sentences) to hold between the states of affairs themselves. This is also supported by the fact that we do not want our implication relation to depend on contingent representational features of the sentence, but rather on what particular classes of sentences (sometimes also called propositions) which somehow 'all say the same thing' have in common.[5]

---

[5] For a detailed ontological inquiry where both relations between states of affairs play a major rôle see Meixner (1997).

Our *structuralist* assumption which was introduced at the beginning of the last chapter finally is a good example of a framework assumption.[6] It underlies our whole project and is therefore difficult to justify within the confines of our theory. It is apparent, however, that as we do make distinctions between different kinds of constituents of states of affairs, the only way to account for these distinctions in the presence of the neutrality assumption is by giving some structuralist explication of them.

Nothing like the structuralist or connection assumption is to be found in Wittgenstein's ontology. Nevertheless it is the combination of these with the factualist and neutrality assumptions which is responsible for a great part of the interest of the present inquiry. The genesis of ontological categories in a factualist framework has never been explored in a structuralist manner. Part of the point of the preceding chapters was to show that even if we do not make Armstrong's assumption, and opt instead for starting with a neutral picture of the composition of states of affairs, there is enough information present in the relations between them to allow us to abstract an interesting and philosophically satisfactory theory of ontological categories from this.

§85 Putting the assumptions to work

Having identified our main assumptions in constructing a satisfactory account of ontological categories, we will of course want to see how they can be put to work in getting us from a set of states of affairs to a system of ontological categories. This part will give a condensed description of how our main assumptions enable us to define the entities we want to take as an explication of the notion of an ontological category.

We start our construction with a collection of states of affairs. These constitute the raw data which will be systematized in our ontological theory. Like many other objects, states of affairs can be similar to one another. In the case of medium-sized dry goods this similarity is usually spelt out in terms of properties shared by different objects: two objects will be similar if they have a property in common, and the degree of similarity will increase with the number of properties shared. In the case of states of affairs similarity will be taken as the sharing of constituents: the

[6] For a different metaphysical theory based on a similar structuralist assumption see Dipert (1997).

state of affairs that John is tall is similar to the state of affairs that John is male, that Kate loves John is similar to that Albert loves Kate, and so on. Given that we recognize such similarities between states of affairs, it is tempting to use this similarity relation to give us a conception of constituents of states of affairs. Our neutrality assumption implies that we cannot just assume that states of affairs consist of individuals, properties, and relations, nor can we just claim that any component in an expression denoting a state of affairs denotes a constituent of that state of affairs. Many such constituents are just generated by the framework of representation and do not denote anything at all. Even if we can eventually tell some story which allows us to get at just the representing part of the representation, it would surely be naive to consider this as a guide to the structure of the represented state of affairs (as naive as going from facts about a Gödel number to facts about the formula represented).

We utilize Carnap's procedure for going from a similarity relation between primitives to objects which can go proxy for the constituents of these primitives. The proxy objects are of course just Carnap's familiar similarity circles, that is sets of states of affairs such that a) each pair of states of affairs in them is similar and b) they are the greatest such sets, i.e. no state of affairs outside is similar to each one inside. These sets of states of affairs are then assumed to play the rôle of constituents of states of affairs. At this point we have to make recourse to an additional assumption which we did not list together with the main assumptions above. It is the following

[INFORMATION]   For any two constituents we know whether they fit together to form a state of affairs.[7]

This assumption claims that information about a particular kind of relation between states of affairs (to which we are restricting ourselves, as fixed by the structuralist assumption) is indeed available. It is another framework assumption, and this makes it impossible to argue for it

---

[7] Note that a stronger form of this would read 'For any *set* of constituents . . .'. This is problematic, since the set may be very large. Our weaker form will be sufficient, however, since if some set of constituents fits together, two will fit together 'directly', then another constituent will fit into this larger constituent and so forth, so that knowledge of the whole set fitting together can be reduced to knowledge of different pairs of constituents fitting together.

within the system. Our theory of ontological categories is supposed to be a systematization of just this knowledge about how constituents of states of affairs go together to make up new ones. Unless the information assumption (or something very much like it) is accepted, the structuralist theory of ontology I am envisaging will simply not get off the ground.

Similar assumptions are plausible in other contexts. For example, we would want to agree that for any two words in his native language a competent speaker will know whether there is a grammatical sentence containing those two words in direct succession. Similarly, it seems that for any two pieces of a jigsaw, any competent player knows whether they fit together. Of course one might want to quibble and object that in some cases questions of grammaticality are unclear. Similarly it might be the case that we thought two words could not occur adjacent in a grammatical sentence when in fact there is a slightly *recherché* example where this could happen. This would not mean that we are not competent speakers of the language. But then it should be borne in mind that the 'for any' in the above condition is only in place to neaten up the structure of our systems of ontological categories, by avoiding overlapping categories.[8] If we are willing to accept a degree of messiness here, we could weaken the information assumption so that it only applies to a large number of cases.

We should also note that the kind of knowledge referred to in the information assumption is implicit or tacit knowledge; it is knowledge we generally do not know that we possess. A theory of ontological categories is a systematization of this implicit knowledge of ontological fit, in the same way in which a grammatical theory systematizes our implicit knowledge of which syntactic structures are well-formed.[9]

Now assuming that we know when constituents of states of affairs fit together, we can sort them into types according to their joining behaviour. The underlying idea is simply that constituents which can

---

[8] See § 57.

[9] A further parallel between implicit ontological and grammatical knowledge might be that the former is as much a reflection of our biological make-up as the latter. Although there is currently not enough evidence for spelling this out in a sufficiently precise manner it does not strike me as wildly implausible conjecturing to assume that our brain structure might have a decisive influence not only on how we structure our language, but also how we structure our most general representations of the world. Some interesting research on this matter may be found in Hurford (2003).

be plugged in for one another in states of affairs without destroying the coherence of the whole will be put into the same type. These sets then constitute our form-sets. As such, form-sets seem to be rather attractive candidates for ontological categories. They explain why philosophers have given accounts of ontological categories in terms of substitution patterns, they collect together objects which are in a very general sense of the same kind, and they are picked out in a way in which grammatical categories often are (thus explaining some relations between these two kinds of categories).

But unfortunately, as we have argued at length above, form-sets do not fit the rôle of ontological categories closely enough. The advantages of form-sets cannot be denied, but not all of them can be ontological categories. Many of them are far too specific, being generated by the fact that they are only intersubstitutable in a very small class of states of affairs and have thus nothing of the generality usually ascribed to ontological categories. The answer to this problem lies of course in observing that certain form-sets can be constructed from others. If we have this notion of construction in place, the entire plethora of form-sets can be shrunk to a proper subset (the set of base-sets) out of which the remainder can be constructed. This smaller set of form-sets can then with all justification be regarded as more fundamental than the big set. This does not mean, however, that redundant sets are somehow not part of the subject-matter of ontology and thus not something which should play a rôle in our ontological discussion. Ontological categories are an essential part of the subject-matter of ontology, but they do not exhaust it: the investigation of the joining behaviour of redundant form-sets and their possible systematization by base-sets is every bit as important as the discussion of the base-sets themselves.

The content of the base-sets is all we need in order to reconstruct the ontological plenitude of the world. No kind of thing is lost if we restrict ourselves to the set of base-sets. At the same time our organization of the different kinds of things is unified, since it becomes clear how they can all be derived from a smaller subset. Ontological categories therefore have the same privileged place amongst kinds of things as axioms have amongst propositions; indeed we might want to regard them as a sort of axioms of kinds of objects.

This construction of ontological categories fulfils the key demands we have formulated earlier: it solves the cut-off point problem and the problem of too specific categories, and it lets categories come out as sets of objects which can be arranged in a non-overlapping hierarchy.

2   MAIN IMPLICATIONS OF OUR ACCOUNT

We just sketched how, given the above four main assumptions as well as the information assumption, it is possible to formulate a definition of 'ontological category' which escapes the problems encountered by the traditional attempts and furthermore possesses a number of desirable structural features. We will use the remainder of this chapter to bring out the general philosophical implications of the conception of ontological categories I have defended.

§86   Relativism

There are three main conclusions to draw. The first is a

- *relativist view of ontological categories.* Ontological categories turn out not to be the fundamental kinds of things there are in the world, but fundamental ways in which we *systematize* the world.

This is a direct consequence of the local relativism regarding ontological categories defended in § 50. There is no inherently best choice between the sets of form-sets, which makes one a better basis than another. Adopting a system of ontological categories is not solely a consequence of the most basic way things are in the world, but will also incorporate our decision to systematize how things are in the world in one form or another: this will provide the reason for choosing one set of form-sets as a basis rather than another one.

It is important to notice that this relativism does not extend to the form-sets themselves. What form-sets there are is settled by the world, rather than by our decision to organize the world in a certain way, simply due to the fact that objects go together to form states of affairs in a certain way. But as we saw above, a list of form-sets is not yet an ontological theory. A list of form-sets contains all sorts of kinds of things, even those which are far too special to fall within the precinct of ontology, which is after all supposed to be a theory of the most general kinds of things there are in the world. Relativism comes into play when we begin to *systematize* the list of form-sets into a theory of base-sets, that is into an ontological theory. This kind of relativism is benign; while there is a problem with relativism in the case of the ways of being, for they must be one way or another, there is none in the case of ways of systematizing: there is no necessity that there should be a unique or even a best way amongst the most fundamental ways of systematizing information about the world.

The comparison of a system of ontological categories with the axiomatization of a theory might be helpful once more. While the answer to the question whether proposition A or $\neg A$ is a *truth* of Euclidean geometry does not depend on us but is settled by something else (although it is surprisingly difficult to specify exactly what this 'something else' is), the answer to the question whether proposition A rather than B is an *axiom* of Euclidean geometry is not settled by this something else, whatever it may be. Assuming that A and B are both true, it is settled by us and by our desire to systematize the truths of Euclidean geometry in a certain way.

It therefore turns out that we have to say goodbye to the conception of ontological categories as a unique and objective fundamental set of objects which encompass the most general kind of things there are. In the same way in which we do not regard axioms as self-evident truths any more, but as truths which play a certain rôle in a particular systematization of some body of knowledge, ontological categories have to be regarded as kinds of things which play a certain rôle in our systematization of the phenomenological plenitude of the world.

§87 Holism

Our second conclusion is a

- *holist conception of ontological categories*. Whether a set of objects constitutes an ontological category, and whether some object belongs to a particular form-set does not depend on the nature of the object or objects considered, but on what *other* objects there are.

Let us consider the first point first, that whether a set of objects constitutes an ontological category depends on what other objects there are. The relativist view of ontological categories entailed that certain form-sets could come out as base-sets (and thus as ontological categories) or as redundant sets, depending on the systematization of the set of form-sets. But remember that in § 50 we mentioned the possibility that some form-sets might belong to the intersection of all bases, and could thus not be constructed from any other form-sets (we called the set of these form-sets the core of the basis). We might now be tempted to assume that these form-sets, which come out as base-sets on *any* systematization of the set of form-sets, could be regarded as being essentially ontological categories. But in fact this is not the case. Whether a form-set belongs to the core of the basis depends on what *other* form-sets there are. Relative to one world (one set of form-sets) a particular form-set might be in the core, but relative to another world it might not be. This is the thesis of global relativism regarding ontological categories we argued for in § 54. But this of course means that it cannot be due to the nature or essence of the objects in the form-set that it belongs to the core. We therefore see a holist picture emerging. The place of a set of objects in the set of form-sets is determined by the objects themselves together with the other form-sets there are, since these are responsible for the joining behaviour the objects show, which in turn determines what form-set they belong to. Whether some set of objects constitutes an ontological category is thus fixed by the whole world, rather than by individual objects in isolation.

The above holism also implies that whether some object belongs to a particular form-set depends on what other objects are around. Here it is helpful to make a comparison with *semantic* holism. This claims that we cannot look into a word to see what it means, but that we must look at its relations with other words. We have to adopt a behaviourist approach towards meaning: meaning is not something to be found deep down in the nature of a word, but something arising from the interrelationships between many different words.

Our *categorial* holism incorporates an exactly parallel view. We cannot tell the form-set something belongs to by merely looking at *it*— we have to see how it behaves relative to other objects in the formation of states of affairs.[10] But of course how something relates to other objects depends on what other objects there are. Therefore the form-set an object belongs to can change if the collection of other objects present in the world changes. That two objects have the same joining-behaviour

---

[10] Compare Black (1966: 10): 'It might seem to follow that acquaintance with even a single object would imply acquaintance with all. For to know such an object is to know the possibilities and impossibilities of its combinations with *all* other objects—and so in some sense to know them also.'

(and thus belong to the same form-set) might just be a product of their present environment: relative to some other environment they might not be in the same form-set.

At this point we might be tempted to assume that the difference in joining behaviour an object shows in different worlds (that is in the presence of different collections of objects it can form states of affairs with) is somehow determined by the object's inner nature or essence. As we saw in § 37, this would be one way of accounting for it, but not the only one. Since I do not know how to settle the matter I made the structuralist assumption of restricting myself to information about this joining behaviour only in order to set up our theory. We now realize that the conclusions arrived at in this way actually contradict an explanation of joining behaviour in terms of essences. Since the joining behaviour and thus a form-set an object belongs to varies from world to world (depending on the other objects there are in the world), and since essences are supposed to be invariant across world-shifts, essences cannot be what is behind the joining behaviour of constituents of states of affairs. Note that a 'brain-based' explanation of joining behaviour would do better here. Its assumption is that the limits of conceivability are to some extent hard-wired into our brain, so that certain representations could not be combined. But since the existence of alien objects in a different world would presumably entail that the neuronal representation of these objects is different from any representations we have at present, facts about which representation can 'go together' will be different in the other world too. And this is just as it should be, given that the joining behaviour of objects is not assumed to be stable across worlds.

The anti-essentialist conclusion just arrived at contradicts the usual ontological position that it is a necessary part of the nature of an object to belong to a particular ontological category. Membership in the ontological categories an object belongs to, it is argued, is one of the properties an object cannot lose without ceasing to be *that* object. Individuals are essentially individuals, properties essentially properties, abstract objects essentially abstract objects, and without their category memberships they would cease being what they are. But on our account of ontological categories ontology systematizes information about how objects can go together to form states of affairs. Thus whether some set of objects is an ontological category and whether some object belongs to a particular form-set is fixed by the whole world. Both can change if new objects with new joining behaviour are introduced into the world: a form-set which is not constructible may become constructible, an object might now belong to a different form-set since its joining behaviour is changed due to the presence of the new objects. But none of this will mean that the nature or essence of the old objects is changed thereby.

We will therefore have to give up the idea that information about ontological categories supplies us with information about the essences of objects.[11] It provides us with a unified account of how objects in this world fit together into states of affairs. But since what things there are in the world is a contingent matter, claims about ontological categories cannot have the modal force attributed to them when it is claimed that they provide us with information about the essential properties of things.

This conclusion is quite radical and contradicts the usual understanding of ontological categories. We might also consider it to be obscure. How could it possibly be the case that objects switched the ontological categories they belong to in different worlds? What could it *mean* to say that an individual like this apple might have been a property, or the number 2 an event?

It is therefore easy to imagine a critic crying for the application of *modus tollens*: since basing our theory on a primitive fitting relation between constituents of states of affairs will not let category-membership come out as an essential property, and, moreover, the holist conclusion implied is obscure, he argues, we should dump a theory based on such a primitive

I have two things to reply to say in this. First, regarding the charge of obscurity it might once again be helpful to draw a parallel with grammar. As I remarked at various points in the discussion the account of ontological categories defended here is quite close to that of grammatical categories developed in modern linguistics, for example in categorial grammar. Let us therefore imagine a language called Exotic, spoken by a small tribe where a particular group of words which belong to the category of nouns in English belong to the category of verbs. Let us say that all the nouns denoting inanimate natural phenomena, such as 'mountain', 'tree', or 'river', in Exotic are grammatically indistinguishable from

---

[11] It is important to note that I do not deny the existence of essential properties, they even have a place in my own account (see § 52). What I deny is that the ontological category an object belongs to is one of its essential properties.

the words English uses to express such activities as to run, to speak, or to fight. A cultural explanation for this phenomenon might be that the tribe believes that inanimate natural phenomena are really emanations of one goddess of nature, who, proteus-like, can appear in many forms: over there she mountains, here she trees, and in between she rivers. Now a perfectly straightforward way of describing this situation is that a relatively small group of words which are nouns in English (i.e. belong to a different grammatical category from 'to run', 'to speak' etc.) are verbs in Exotic (i.e. they belong to the same grammatical category as 'to run', 'to speak' etc.). Between languages they have switched categories.

The very same phenomenon could happen in the case of different worlds. Some objects which belong to different form-sets relative to one collection of objects or world might belong to a different one relative to another world, or vice versa. Whether we use the same term to refer to the different collections of form-sets across worlds (whether we call the category containing the expressions for 'mountain', 'tree', 'to run', 'to speak' etc. in Exotic verbs) is purely a question of convenience. We might want to say that some nouns of English are verbs of Exotic, or that some of our events are numbers in a different world, or we might refrain from giving trans-world (or trans-language) names to categories, and simply say that things belonging to a common category in one world/language belong to two distinct ones in another one. In either case it seems to be perfectly clear what we mean by saying that objects can change their category membership.

Secondly, regarding the demand for *modus tollens* because of the view of essential properties my account entails, there is exactly one condition under which I would agree to go down that route: if the defender of essences is able to come up with a satisfactory theory of ontological categories based on the notion of essence as a primitive. As I have argued in § 27, all the attempts at doing this which can be found in the literature are fundamentally flawed and I think the feat cannot be done. Until I see an account which actually achieves this, I claim that the essentialist's justification for appealing to *modus tollens* at this point is not sufficient.

Let us conclude this section by some brief comparative remarks. The reader might have noted that the holism just discussed is not in harmony with the ontology of the *Tractatus*. First of all it does not sit comfortably with Wittgenstein's claim that the form of an object (its possibility of occurring in different states of affairs) must lie in the object itself.[12] If

---

[12] Wittgenstein (1989: 2.0141, 2.012).

all this means is that relative to a world any 'given object enters into a perfectly determinate number of facts'[13] the tension disappears. But if we interpret it as a claim that the form of an object can somehow be ascertained by considering the object on its own, without the necessity of taking into account what else there is in the world, this claim will contradict the complex principle which forms the basis of our account.

A more important deviation from Wittgenstein results from the fact that the above discussion of holism relies on assuming that *there might have been different objects than there are in fact* in arguing that not even the members of the core of the basis are essentially ontological categories, and that even membership in a particular form-set is dependent on what other objects there are. Wittgenstein explicitly rules out this possibility. His objects are the 'substance of the world'[14] and exist equally in all possible worlds. It is then clear that while statements about the forms of objects (such as whether a particular form-set is an ontological category, or whether it is the set of dyadic relations) may still be relative, what form a particular object has is settled in a unique way by what objects there are, and how these combine to form states of affairs. For Wittgenstein only local, but not global relativism would be an issue. If the same objects are present in all possible worlds, it is not only necessary for an object to belong to *some* form-set or other,[15] it is also necessary that it belongs to the set it indeed belongs to. While I agree that every object necessarily has some form, I do not accept the stronger conclusion that it necessarily has to have the form it has, simply because I do not see why there could not have been other objects than there are in fact. In this case it will be contingent that something belongs to a particular form-set, since this is a direct consequence of the sorts of things there are in the world, and *this* in turn is a contingent matter.

§88   Individuals and properties

Our third and final conclusion is

- *the unfoundedness of the individual–property distinction*. Individuals and properties cannot be told apart in a purely structural way by looking at the way in which the different constituents of a state of affairs can be

[13] Palmieri (1960: 75).
[14] Wittgenstein (1989: 2.021, 2.024).
[15] Wittgenstein (1989: 2.011).

combined. The distinction must arise from another source and, given our argument that structurally established distinctions are the most fundamental ones, cannot be as basic as is usually assumed.

This conclusion was argued for at length in chapter V. The point there was that there are certain supposedly fundamental distinctions (such as those between individuals, properties, and relations) which cannot be made even on the level of form-sets if we employ a structuralist approach. Relativism does not just come into play in passing from form-sets to base-sets or ontological categories, but already on the level of form-sets. Note, however, that we are not just making the obvious point that what form-sets we end up with depends on the amount of data we have about objects 'fitting together' in states of affairs. Rather the point is that given any amount of data, the form-sets we generate will never neatly slice up the objects into individuals, properties, and relations.

Chapter V established that the individual–property distinction (and its close relations, the distinctions between particular and universal, subject and predicate, and function and argument) cannot be established in a purely combinatorial or purely logical manner (or, for that matter, by any combination of the two). Of course showing the *general* ontological untenability of the distinction demands that we examine all possible ways of defining the distinction and show each of them to be wanting. We obviously have not done this in the course of our investigations; in fact there is a general problem with the feasibility of such a procedure, as it presupposes some way of enumerating all the possible ways in which the individual–property distinction can be drawn.

Even a cursory inspection of the relevant literature shows the variety of procedures which have been employed in attempting to establish a viable distinction between individuals and properties. These include *linguistic* approaches in the spirit of the Fregean distinction between saturated and unsaturated expressions and the corresponding saturated and unsaturated entities, *logical* approaches which are based on the observation that in our language predicates but not names are closed under logical operations,[16] those trying to establish the distinction via the assumed asymmetry of the *instantiation relation*,[17] those arguing that properties but not individuals have individual essences or *quiddities*,[18]

---

[16] Strawson (1970), (1974); Dummett (1981: 64), Geach (1968), Anscombe (1965).
[17] Bigelow and Pargetter (1990: 38–41).
[18] Armstrong (1990: 55).

those claiming that individuals but not properties can take a variable *number of arguments*,[19] as well as the popular definition of properties as objects which can be *at different places at the same time*.[20]

The main difficulty of the linguistic approaches lies in attributing any modal force to a distinction between two kinds of entities established by reference to saturated and unsaturated entities. That particular formal and natural languages make a distinction between functional and non-functional expressions may be a matter of convenience. Perhaps the same expressive capacities could be achieved without recourse to this device (for example by having unsaturated entities saturate one another, as described in §76). In this case the function–argument distinction could hardly be taken as indicative of a fundamental ontological divide.

There might be a way of strengthening this linguistic approach by appeal to neurobiology. Recent research suggests that there might be a neural correlate of the function–argument distinction, grounded on the fact that the processing of objects and of properties proceeds via different neural pathways.[21] I think this is a very interesting avenue to explore and would, if successful, lead to a strengthening of the modal force we could attribute to the individual–predicate distinction: it could be claimed that it is not just necessary relative to the language we speak but also necessary relative to the brain we use to process information about the world. Nevertheless, this would at best serve as a demonstration that the individual–property distinction is *cognitively fundamental* and this is, I fear, very much weaker than what ontologists fond of this distinction would like to claim.

The logical approach is faced with a similar difficulty as the linguistic one. It has to argue that it is not just a matter of fact that in our language we negate predicates but do not negate names, but that there is some modal force behind this: that negating names would in some sense lead to inconsistency or other grave problems, so that the distinction thus violated could be regarded as sufficiently important. Unfortunately this stronger claim is far from obvious.[22]

---

[19] See MacBride (1999: 489).

[20] For a thorough discussion of this see MacBride (1998).

[21] See Hurford (2003), as well as the various responses on pp. 283–316 of the same journal.

[22] See Zemach (1981) for further discussion of this point.

The arguments based on the instantiation relation and quiddities of properties strike me as not particularly strong because it seems very hard to motivate them independently of their use in establishing the individual–property distinction. Anyone attracted by a monistic account in which the distinction did not hold would not be concerned about the instantiation relation being symmetric or individuals and properties being on a par regarding their possession or lack of quiddities.

The approach based on the number of arguments individuals and properties take and that referring to the possible multiple spatial location of properties appear to be more substantial, although I do not regard them as wholly successful. My reservation about the first are noted in §68, those concerning the second in § 35.

I consider the structuralist procedure for establishing the individual – property distinction to be the most elegant and parsimonious approach of all of those just mentioned. It is one which uses the fewest resources (only the notions of combinability into states of affairs and implication) and which can therefore claim to be the most general possible way of drawing the distinction. Given the failure of this approach described in the preceding chapter we conclude that there is indeed some justification in regarding the individual–property distinction as unfounded.

It might be argued that there is a problem in denying the fundamental status of the distinction between individuals and properties as constituents of states of affairs while actually appealing to relations (the similarity relation between states of affairs, the 'fitting' relation between constituents of states of affairs) and their relata (states of affairs, their constituents conceived of as sets of states of affairs) in our argument to that effect. Are we not thereby making ontological presuppositions about the existence of states of affairs, sets of them, and relations between them on the metalevel? And are we not in particular helping ourselves to a distinction we regard as philosophically suspect—that between properties (relations) and their relata (states of affairs, sets)?

On the first point I plead guilty as charged. No theory can proceed without primitives, and the proposed metaontological theory of ontological categories is no exception. This fact becomes problematic only if one of the primitives appealed to is actually the very thing we want to explicate within the theory, but by another name. But this is not the case with my approach. Neither the notion of a state of affairs, nor that of a similarity relation between them, nor that of a set of states of affairs and a 'fitting' relation between such sets contains, openly or covertly, the concept of an ontological category. Of course all of these belong to ontological categories themselves—but then everything does, so this can hardly be a complaint against the primitives of the theory.

Regarding the second charge (that of helping myself to philosophically suspect entities on the metalevel) note that I do not deny that we somehow draw a distinction between individuals and properties (so much is evident from our everyday classification of phenomena), but I deny that this distinction is in any way ontologically fundamental. Therefore my claim, that the ontologically fundamental classification of constituents of states of affairs should proceed not in terms of the notions of individuals and properties but of their joining behaviour, does not entail any suspicion against the *constituents*, but against a particular *systematization* of them. Similarly, if I refer to relations and relata on the metalevel, this does not entail that I accord the distinction any fundamental status even on the metalevel. None of the features of states of affairs, sets, and relations between them my account appeals to implies in any way that some of them are to be conceived of as individuals, others as properties. It may be the case that the ontologically fundamental manner of systematizing these metalevel entities should *not* be formulated in terms of individuals and properties, but I can nevertheless use these terms to construct an intelligible metatheory. It is of course true that we cannot formulate what the more fundamental systematization of states of affairs and relations between them is within the framework of our theory (that is in terms of joining behaviour of constituents of states of affairs). But then we do not expect a metalinguistic theory of some truth-predicate in an object-language to be simultaneously a theory of its own metalevel truth-predicate.

§89   The significance of ontological categories

The preceding three conclusions lead to a reassessment of the significance of the notion of an ontological category in metaphysics as well as in philosophy more generally. That this notion is important and should be accorded a central place in philosophical theorizing is still widely claimed. For example, we read in a recent introduction to ontology that 'it is a central aim of ontology as an exact science to construct a plausible system of ontological categories'.[23] Such claims are usually justified by the alleged special status of ontological categories:

[23] Meixner (2004: 166).

Everything which is subsumed under an ontological category is so subsumed with conceptual necessity, and what is not subsumed is equally not so subsumed with conceptual necessity. If for example x is an individual then it is conceptually or logically necessary that x is an individual, and if it is not, then it is conceptually necessary that it is not an individual. Assignments to ontological categories are never a contingent matter.[24]

Unfortunately such claims, and the one just given is no exception, are rarely backed up by any precise specification of what an ontological category is. Authors usually introduce the notion with a couple of examples and then just *assume*, rather than argue for, claims like the above, which, if the arguments given in the preceding chapters are successful, do not appear to be true.

In the preceding chapters I have tried to construct such a precise account of the notion of an ontological category which agrees with the central claims usually made about ontological categories in the literature: that they are the most general kinds of things, that they are hierarchically organized, that they do not overlap, that certain categories are too special to be ontological categories. It should be comforting news for all ontologists that these specifications *can* actually all be integrated into one account, and that the notion is therefore not straightforwardly inconsistent. The less comforting news is that the notion of ontological category which emerges when taking the initial specifications into account is not as central or philosophically important as ontologists usually assumed. Relativity asserts that which set of ontological categories we choose is primarily a matter of convenience, in the same way as specific axiomatizations of propositional logic or Newtonian mechanics are more convenient to use than others. Holism furthermore entails that the frequently postulated link between category membership and essence does not hold. What ontological category a thing belongs to is not dependent on its inner nature, but dependent on what other things there are in the world and this, we claimed, is a contingent matter. It therefore turns out that while which ontological categories we employ is still a very interesting question from a cognitive point of view, as it tells us much about how we human beings systematize fundamental information about the world, it does not carry much philosophical weight. Constructing a system of ontological categories cannot be 'the

[24] Meixner (2004: 20).

central aim of ontology as an exact science'.[25] Ontological categories are certainly not something ontologists should ignore when inquiring into the nature of being, but they are equally not the basis of ontology, or the fixed point around which the enterprise of metaphysics ought to revolve. Important as axioms are, given their fundamental arbitrariness the theorems are what we should be really interested in, and this holds regardless of whether we are dealing with axioms of geometry or with the axioms of things.

3 COMPARISONS: PARALLELS AND DIFFERENCES

I would like to conclude the present chapter by comparing the assumptions underlying my account of ontological categories with those made by various philosophical projects which might be regarded as closely related. I hope that by clarifying these intra-philosophical connections selected claims of my theory will be brought out more clearly.

§90 Objects and logical form

It is interesting to compare our conclusion regarding the unfoundedness of the distinction between individuals and properties with the conception of 'objects' Wittgenstein defends in the *Tractatus*. Different commentators have argued that the Wittgensteinian conception of 'objects', a concatenation of which makes up states of affairs, subsumes both individuals as well as properties and relations under them.[26] Indeed this interpretation seems to be backed up well by textual evidence both from the *Tractatus* and from supplementary material. In a 1915 entry in the *Notebooks* Wittgenstein writes that 'relations, properties etc. are objects

---

[25] Of course I have no argument that it is not possible to construct an account of ontological categories which incorporates the features I have incorporated, *as well as* their alleged special modal status. I would be very interested to see it. In the absence of such an account, however, I regard it as fair to say the usual claims about the central metaphysical and philosophical status of ontological categories have to be revised.

[26] Most famously Stenius (1960: 63). Anscombe (1963: 109) and Copi (1958: 160–5) disagree.

as well'.[27] In a comment on proposition 2.01 of the *Tractatus* Wittgenstein is reputed to have said

Objects etc. is here used for such things as a colour, a point in visual space etc. [...] 'Objects' also includes relations; a proposition is not two things connected by a relation. 'Thing' and 'relation' are on the same level. The objects hang as it were in a chain.[28]

Ontologically speaking, all the constituents of states of affairs are on a par, none of them are essentially saturated or unsaturated, all are just distinguished by their logical form.[29] This is of course exactly the thesis we argued for in chapter V.

It is particularly instructive to consider Wittgenstein's treatment of elementary propositions in this context. Elementary propositions are truth-functionally simple; they do not imply any other elementary propositions.[30] They are a concatenation of names.[31] It is tempting to equate elementary propositions with atomic formulae of predicate calculus, such as Fa or Rab, but this would be quite wrong. The form of an atomic formula can be specified very precisely, for example by saying that Fa consists of the concatenation of a monadic predicate with one name. In the case of elementary propositions, however, something like this cannot be done. Although we know that they consist of names, and nothing else, since 'we are unable to give the number of names with different meanings, we are unable to give the composition of elementary propositions'.[32] Since elementary propositions picture states of affairs, the same must apply for the structure of states of affairs. We should not claim that *they* are made up of a relation and a fixed number of individuals. In fact it would be completely arbitrary to ascribe any specific form to them.[33] Wittgenstein explicitly disagrees with Russell's assumption that states of affairs are made up of a relation linking a fixed number of individuals.[34] The logical form of an elementary proposition and thus the membership of the constituents of states of affairs in

[27] Wittgenstein (1961: 16.6.15).
[28] Lee (1980: 120).
[29] Compare Lokhorst (1988: 36–8), Fahrnkopf (1988), Kennick (1991), Fahrnkopf (1994).
[30] Wittgenstein (1989: 5.134).
[31] Wittgenstein (1989: 4.22).
[32] Wittgenstein (1989: 5.55).
[33] Wittgenstein (1989: 5.554).
[34] Wittgenstein (1989: 5.553).

particular form-sets cannot be determined *a priori*.[35] We need information about the world which can only come from experience, that is information about which parts of states of affairs can be combined—we need ontological data. In the same way we cannot determine *a priori* what most general grammatical form an arbitrary sentence of natural language would have. In order to do this we have to look at the atomic constituents of natural languages and see how they can be combined into well-formed sentences. Only this kind of *a posteriori* knowledge will give us any clue as to whether some grammatical sentences might involve a 27-place relation in an essential way.

This harmonizes well with our results from chapters IV and V. First of all, the knowledge about the ontological structure of states of affairs (which form-sets their constituents belong to) is derived from knowledge of the combinability relation (symbolized by the monadic predicate C of strings), and thus from knowledge which is obviously derived from experience. Secondly, there is no unique route from the information about form-sets to the familiar ontological notions of individuals and properties of specific adicities and orders. The ascription of a particular form to a state of affairs *in these terms* depends to a crucial extent on *our* interests, on the kind of features *we* want to bring out in systematizing information about its structural properties.[36] This would also explain why the 'false concept' Wittgenstein attributes to Russell, Ramsey, and himself is indeed false. This is the concept that

one awaits a logical analysis of facts, as if for a chemical analysis of compounds. An analysis by which one really finds a 7-place relation, like an element that actually has a specific weight of 7.[37]

We cannot *really* find a 7-place relation in a fact. There is information about form-sets which can be *systematized* by employing the notion of a 7-place relation, but as we saw in chapter V, no information about form-sets whatever *forces* us to adopt such a systematization.

[35] See Griffin (1964: 142–3).
[36] Compare Griffin (1964: 146): 'The forms [of objects] which, according to the 6.3's, we can intuit *a priori* are obviously fairly general ones; and the forms which, according to the 5.55's, we definitively cannot know *a priori* are the most specific ones: for example, whether there are dyadic, triadic, etc. relations.'
[37] Black (1966: 208).

§91   Structuralist logic

Of course nothing of the above argument entails that we cannot draw
the individual–property distinction in some non-fundamental way. Indeed, given that people usually do draw the distinction, and seem to do
so in a non-arbitrary way there is presumably some explanation for this.
I doubt, however, that it is in any way ontologically fundamental. The
distinction seems to me to be more like that between active and passive:
a matter of difference in presentation, rather than a matter of difference
in existence. Hardly anybody will claim that there are different *actions*
involved in whatever corresponds to 'Albert chases Becca' and 'Becca is
chased by Albert' out there in the world.

But if the individual–property distinction is to be regarded as a quirk
of language (or at least not as ontologically fundamental) it should not
be incorporated into the syntax and semantics of logic, at least if logic
is supposed to be an expressive framework of the greatest ontological
neutrality. That it is possible to formulate a logic with the same expressive power as classical logic which does not explicitly or implicitly make
the individual-property distinction has been argued in §§ 79–80. There
we adapted the classical model-theoretic semantics of first order logic in
a way which treated names and predicates completely alike. While this
was convenient for expository purposes, it appears to me that a much
better framework for developing a *neutral logic* of the kind I have in
mind is Arnold Koslow's system of *structuralist logic*.[38] This system can
in many respects be regarded as the natural logical framework to sup-
plement our structuralist conception of ontological categories.

The most apparent difference between the structuralist and standard
theories of logic is their treatment of syntax. In standard logical theory
the syntax of an expression tells us about its logical behaviour. If we
know that a formula has the conjunction symbol as its main connective,
we know that it implies both its immediate subformulae. If a formula is
of the form 'p or q' this means that it implies at least either p or q. In
structuralist logic we proceed in the opposite way. We consider a set of
objects and a primitive implication relation (which is characterized by
a specific set of axioms) between these objects. We then use the information about which objects stand in the implication relation to infer

---

[38] For a thorough discussion of structuralist logic see Koslow (1992); the *Reader's
Digest* version is in Koslow (1999).

their internal structure, i.e. to find out which of them are conjunctions, disjunctions, hypotheticals, universal generalizations, and so forth.

In such a setting we do not assume anything about the nature of these objects, they might be more or less anything. We therefore do not make any particular assumptions about their internal structure and about their constituents: they might have a structure similar to that of propositions, or a different one, or no structure at all; they might be composed of individuals and properties, of names and predicates, or of something entirely different.[39]

Note how the whole outlook of structuralist logic ties in very well with the theory of ontological categories we described above. Of course the neutrality regarding the nature of the objects linked by the implication relation is one of the most central features of structuralist logic. Nevertheless in the present context it proves to be quite fruitful to identify them with states of affairs. States of affairs can be regarded as the relata of implication relations with at least the same right as propositions, and indeed a number of interesting ontological points can be made by employing this identification.[40] Structuralist logic can therefore be understood to cohere nicely with the factualist assumption endorsed by us. The parallels with the assumptions of connection and structuralism are also obvious: the idea is to develop all the logical information about the primitives from information about the way they are related by the implication relation. This information is the only source of information appealed to to find out about the logical structure of the primitives—no other resources (in particular no syntactic considerations) are allowed or required. Furthermore, this logical structure is not something which is supposed to be knowable prior to the knowledge of the implication relations between them; this is a case of the epistemic reading of the complex principle regarding logical structure.

The only case where structuralist logic clashes with the fundamental assumptions of our theory of ontological categories is in the case of the neutrality assumption. It is a surprising and rather unsatisfactory feature of structuralist logic that its neutrality assumption regarding the relata of

---

[39] Koslow (1992: 3) argues that the structuralist approach 'does not presuppose that the elements upon which the operators act are distinguished by any special syntactic or semantic features'. In fact they do not have to be syntactical objects at all (6).

[40] See e.g. Meixner (1997: 5–7).

the implication relation is not matched by a similar neutrality regarding the *constituents* of these objects (as our neutrality assumption regarding states of affairs would have it). This is apparent in the structuralist treatment of quantification. One ought to think that if absolutely any kind of object can play the rôle of the relata of the implication relation (given that there is a relation between them for which the axioms of the implication relation hold) it is not sensible to assume any one internal structure for these objects, in particular nothing as specific as a predicate-name structure. But this is exactly what structuralist logic does. Of course the need to appeal to the internal structure of the relata of the implication relation does not arise in the case of propositional logic. When considering propositional inferences we never need to refer to the constituents of an atomic proposition: we can take these as primitive and do not have to have any view whatsoever about their structure. This is different in the quantificational case, however. In order to make sense of quantificational inferences we have to look *inside* the atomic propositions to make out the constituents our quantifiers range over. We usually make out two kinds of constituents, those we take to be referring to individuals and others which we take to be referring to properties and relations.

This is also the line adopted by Koslow. He deals with quantification not in ordinary implication structures containing objects and an implication relation between them, but in 'extended' implication structures which contain a further set of objects and functions from infinite sequences of these to the original objects.[41] These functions are explicitly conceived by him as substitutes for predicates. If we adopt the above conclusion about the unfoundedness of the individual–property distinction, however, this way of proceeding deprives the structuralist account of much of its appeal. The objects linked by the implication relation are no longer considered as primitive, but are assumed to involve predicates with particular adicities.[42] But this division of atomic propositions into names and predicates, or that of atomic facts into individuals and properties is not something which can itself be given a structural justification, but rather an assumption made from the outset.

---

[41] Koslow (1992: 181).

[42] Koslow (1992: 182) uses the concept of 'support' to model this.

A much more satisfactory account of quantificational reasoning within a structuralist framework would therefore be one which does not make any assumptions about the fundamental make-up of the constituents of the objects linked by the implication relation. To present this in detail would require a treatment of a length and technical detail which would not fit harmoniously with the rest of these investigations. We will therefore just sketch what such an account might look like in its barest outlines.

Since states of affairs are regarded as primitive objects we cannot develop an account of their constituents, which we need for quantificational logic, by 'taking them apart' in some way. We will rather regard the constituents of states of affairs as particular *sets* of states of affairs. We do this in the quasi-analytical way described in § 44. The procedure employed there is that of identifying constituents of some primitive objects in terms of a symmetric and reflexive similarity relation between these objects by equating them with sets ('similarity circles') fulfilling two conditions. First of all each pair of objects in the set must be an instance of the similarity relation. Secondly it must be the greatest such set, that is there must be no member in the set which stands in the relation to every object outside the set.

Transferring this idea to the issue at hand we see that the implication structure we have to consider to model quantificational reasoning consists of a set S of objects, an implication relation, and a relation 'has a part in common with' on the set. We consider a set of subsets $a, b, c, \ldots$ of S, which is the set of similarity circles under the parthood-relation. These similarity circles go proxy for the constituents of states of affairs and we define the fact that some $s \in S$ has the *constituent* a to mean that s is a member of a.

There might be some cases where some s has just a, b, and c as constituents, whereas another $s' \in S$ has a, b, and d. In this case we will call s', which is the result of replacing c by d in s, a *variation* of s.

Now suppose there is some s which has a as a constituent and is such that for any $i \neq a$ which is the constituent of some $s \in S$, replacing a by i always results in an object s' which is implied by s. In this case s behaves very much like a universal generalization. For what makes a sentence like $(\forall x)(Px)$ a universal generalization (at least on the substitutional interpretation) is that any result of replacing the x by a name results in a sentence which is implied by $(\forall x)(Px)$.

We thus use the idea of replacing constituents of states of affairs by others to define quantification. Universal quantifications are whatever[43] implies *all* the variations of some state of affairs relative to some constituent, an existential quantification what implies what is implied by *all* the variations of some state of affairs relative to some constituent.

Of course this account cuts a great number of corners and needs a much more detailed technical treatment to deliver a satisfactory theory of quantification. Let us just note for the moment how the structuralist conception of logic harmonizes with a structuralist account of ontology as the one defended above which does not distinguish between individuals and properties. The notion of quantification we just sketched will be essentially neutral between first and higher order quantification since the concept of a variation of some primitive object relative to some of its constituents is defined for all kinds of constituents, be they individuals, first order properties or relations, or higher order properties or relations. It seems to be worthwhile to explore further the relation of the logic so obtained to standard quantification theory. On the one hand it has some higher order features (since it quantifies equally over all types of constituents), on the other hand it is close to first order (since the constituents quantified over are all of the same type).

§92 Quantification

An interesting parallel to explore at this point is the conception of quantification incorporated in the *Tractatus*. It is usually assumed that its logic is some sort of higher order logic. A formal reconstruction of parts of the *Tractatus* claims that

the quantified logic we have extracted from it is a complete higher-order logic, more comprehensive than standard first-order logic because it treats predicates as names [. . .][44]

Skyrms remarks that its semantics differs from that of standard higher order logic. In this

---

[43] This is not quite correct. Following Koslow it has to be the *implicationally weakest* object to do this, i.e. if something else also implies *all* the variations of some state of affairs relative to some constituent, this something will imply the universal quantification.

[44] Lokhorst (1988: 67–8).

properties and relations are taken as *parasitic* on objects. What properties and relations exist in a model depend on what objects do. In Tractarian Nominalism however, we regard the relational quantifiers as ranging over real physical relations whose existence is every bit as contingent as that of physical objects—and consequently the relations which exist in a world may only correspond to some subset of the 'natural' domain [of the powerset of objects] and it is basically this fact which makes second order logic *complete* for the Tractarian Nominalist. [. . .] The natural logic for a Tractarian Nominalist is second-order quantification.[45]

But arguing that the *Tractatus* incorporates a logic of *any* specific order seems to misunderstand the rôle of Tractarian objects. To talk about the order of a quantifier only makes sense if the item we are quantifying into is itself built up from items of different orders, such as individuals, properties, and relations. But this is of course exactly what the ontology of the *Tractatus* denies. Apart from their different logical form (or, as we would say, apart from their different type-descriptions) all constituents of states of affairs are on a par. Where there are no relations, there can be no 'relational quantifiers'. All this is captured well in our substitutional treatment of quantification in a structuralist framework. There is only one sort of quantifier in place which treats all constituents of states of affairs alike.

If we want to describe the logic of the *Tractatus* in a traditional way at all, it is presumably most adequate to regard it as a many-sorted *first* order system rather than as a complete second order one.[46] It is straightforward to see what this semantics would look like. Atomic sentences of the language we consider would obviously be concatenations of names like abc . . .. It would consist of a number of sets $D_1, \ldots, D_n$, containing the Wittgensteinian objects sorted according to their joining behaviour and a set E of ordered sets from the D_i, formed in accordance with the joining behaviour of the objects. We denote the objects the names stand for by underlining them. A sentence abc of our language is then true iff the ordered set $\langle \underline{a}, \underline{b}, \underline{c} \rangle$ is in E. To be arranged in a string thus functions as the semantic equivalent of being concatenated in a sentence. The treatment of quantification is straightforward: $(\exists x)axc$ is true if there is some ordered $\langle a, \ldots, c \rangle$ in E where some element from some D_i occupies the place of the dots. The parallels of this kind of semantics with the many-sorted one described in § 78 are obvious, so

<hr>

[45] Skyrms (1981: 203–4).   [46] Cheung (2000: 256).

that it is clear that the system just described is complete, compact, and that the Löwenheim-Skolem property holds for it.

§93   Logical constants and ontological form

There are some interesting connections of our account with Wittgenstein's conception of logical constants and logical form which I shall discuss in this section. To see what these are we first have to differentiate the notions of the *logical* and the *ontological form* of a state of affairs. These are quite distinct; the logical form of a state of affairs is connected with what states of affairs it *implies*, its ontological form with the *joining behaviour* of its constituents in forming states of affairs with other constituents. The two are frequently confused,[47] but on our account it is evident that they are constructed in different ways. The logical form of a state of affairs is constituted by its *implication relations* with other states of affairs. Its ontological form, on the other hand, is constituted by the 'fitting relation' between its constituents (which are in turn constructed as sets of states of affairs) and constituents of other states of affairs.

We sometimes find authors describing the form of particular states of affairs as for example $Fa \wedge Gb$ or $Ga \wedge Fb$ and so forth.[48] What this sort of notation (which describes the form of states of affairs by formulae of predicate calculus) intends to bring out is exactly the presence of these two types of form. The logical form encodes the way in which the state of affairs implies others: the conjunctive state of affairs $Fa \wedge Gb$ is a conjunction of the two states of affairs Fa and Gb. The ontological form, on the other hand, encodes how the parts of Fa and Gb hang together. Fa consists of the monadic property F and the individual a put together, Gb of the monadic property G and the individual b. There is, however, a certain danger in describing the form of states of affairs by formal languages in this way, since it tends to obscure the very distinction we want to make. In sentences of natural language the two forms are still clearly distinguished: there is the implication behav-

---

[47] See e.g. Black (1966: 14): 'To say proposition and depicted fact have the same logical form comes to saying: to every sensible combination of some of the names with other names in elementary propositions there corresponds a possible combination in an atomic fact of the objects for which names severally deputize—and vice versa, the powers of combination of the names exactly matching the powers of combination of their object partners.'

[48] Lewis(1986b: 92) See also Armstrong (1997: 107–8, 229, also 121).

iour of a sentence, and this tells us about its logical form, and there is the way its parts go together, and this tells us about its grammatical form. One of the main motivations for constructing formal languages was obviously to bridge this gulf between the logical and grammatical form of sentences. Translating a natural language sentence into a formal language gives us a sentence the implication behaviour of which is manifested directly in its grammatical form. Making the move back from language to the world, we might therefore be tempted to assume that the 'grammatical' (i.e. ontological) form of the state of affairs which is the denotation of the sentence is also to be equated with its implication behaviour. As we just argued, however, this is a temptation to be resisted, since we are dealing here with two quite distinct forms of states of affairs.

Note at this point that it is characteristic of the structuralist conception of logic and ontology inherent in our account to consider both the logical and the ontological form of a state of affairs as *extrinsic*, not as something which is 'directly perceived' or 'literally manifested' in the state of affairs, but rather something which is 'manifested only discursively in a system of possibilities',[49] and which is derived from considering the relations between that state of affairs and others.

There are now two important features of logical and ontological form which have to be brought out clearly. The first is that *ascriptions of neither form are referential*. This means that in the same way as there is no denotation of 'and' in the denotation of the state of affairs that a is F and b is G, there are no individuals, properties, and relations in states of affairs either.

The non-referentiality of logical form is of course a familiar Wittgensteinian position. Wittgenstein claims that his 'fundamental idea is that the logical constants do not represent. That the *logic* of facts cannot be represented.'[50] For Wittgenstein, the logical constants denote *operations* on elementary propositions, and only the elementary propositions directly represent the world by picturing states of affairs. The logical constants do not stand for any constituents of states of affairs. It is not the case that 'logical compounds of sentences are pictures in the sense that they depict states of affairs which are combinations of simpler states

---

[49] The terms are due to Black (1966: 14–15).

[50] Wittgenstein (1989: 4.0312). A similar remark is also made in the *Notebooks* (Wittgenstein (1961: 25.12.14)).

of affairs and some special entities called "logical constants" much as elementary states of affairs are combinations of "things"".[51]

This feature is also elegantly brought out in the framework of structuralist logic. Given that it is completely syntax-independent, one will not be tempted to assert that the $\wedge$ in the conjunctive proposition $p \wedge q$ refers to some item called conjuction, or that this item is also present in the state of affairs described by the sentence. In structuralist logic one cannot be assured that conjunctions will contain the '$\wedge$'-sign, or indeed any other special sign. Since we make no assumptions about the syntactic structure of the objects linked by the implication relation (indeed they do not even need to have such a structure), there is no syntactic uniformity which could help us to distinguish conjunctions from other logically complex statements. In structuralist logic, all of the internal logical structure of the sentence is 'pushed out' into the implication relations which inferentially connect that statement with other statements. Whether a statement is a conjunction is no fact about the internal make-up of the statement, but a fact about which other statements it entails.

Our account also entails the non-referentiality of the ontological form of a state of affairs. This means that the ascription of a particular ontological form to a state of affairs (for example saying that it has the form Rab) does not entail that there is a dyadic relation and two individuals 'in it', in the same way as we do not want to say that there is a conjunction somewhere 'in' a conjunctive state of affairs. What we do want to say is that there are certain regularities which turn up in this as well as in other states of affairs and which are always encountered in states of affairs in specific configurations. As we saw in the preceding chapter, giving the ontological form by some expression like Rab can be quite misleading, since it tempts us to claim that the R-component is essentially a dyadic relation, the a and b essentially individuals, and so on. The framework we should use for expressing the ontological form of states of affairs is that given in the description of prototypings in § 70. Wittgenstein's theory argues against treating the logical constants as referring to some kind of item out there in the world. The structuralist ontology I have discussed tries to show that similarly 'ontological constants' (such as the notions of individuals, properties, and relations) are not objects in any fixed sense, which make up the fabric of the world, but rather

---

[51] Stenius (1960: 144).

products of the way in which we systematize information about states of affairs.

The second important feature of logical and ontological forms of states of affairs is that they *can be established independently of one another*. This is in clear opposition to Wittgenstein's view. On his account we only get at the ontological form of a state of affairs once all the logical complexity has been removed. This explains the importance of the notion of an elementary proposition in the *Tractatus* ontology. Logically complex propositions are to be broken down into logically elementary ones; and it is only in the case of the elementary propositions that we can study how names are concatenated to form propositions, and thus, switching to the level of the world, how objects can be combined to form states of affairs.

On our account, however, the ontological form of any state of affairs can be determined directly, by considering the joining behaviour of its constituents. In the same way as our *grammatical* analysis of sentences (which studies how the words constituting them go together) is not confined to sentences which have a certain implicational behaviour,[52] our *ontological* analysis of states of affairs (studying how the objects constituting them combine) is not restricted to elementary states of affairs.

Therefore the notion of an implicationally simple state of affairs does not play the rôle in our account which that of an elementary proposition plays in Wittgenstein's, where it constitutes the direct link between language and the world and the route to the ontological form of states of affairs.

Of course it is perfectly possible to introduce the equivalent of elementary propositions into the system of structuralist logic. But this will then lack the primary motivation that the items so defined are somehow less complex than the non-elementary propositions. Such a motivation is only forthcoming if we assume that if S entails T, T is somehow already present in S, so that going from the entailing to the entailed results in some sort of 'breaking down' or reduction of complexity. But it is far from clear why we should understand implication in this way. And taking into account the non-referentiality of logical and ontological form it seems to be more plausible not to make this assumption. In the same way as $\wedge$ is not part of the proposition $p \wedge q$, p and q are not either. They are entailed by $p \wedge q$ but are not *part* of it in any way which makes

---

[52] Namely, according to Wittgenstein, that no elementary proposition implies them (5.134) and that they do not imply any other proposition (4.211).

it more complex than the conjuncts on their own (while according to the mereological conception of parthood the fusion of two individuals is more complex than either individual on its own). But this entails that there is very little motivation for the notion of an elementary proposition. Although there will be propositions entailing no others, they are not in any clear way less complex than other propositions.

For this reason we do not assign great importance to implicationally simple states of affairs (the truthmakers of elementary propositions) either. Logical and ontological forms of states of affairs are determined by considering two different sets of relations between them, namely implication relations and overlapping relations. It is not necessary for a state of affairs to be atomic relative to one relation to enable us to determine its form relative to the other relation. I regard this lack of importance of elementary propositions as a welcome feature. They are a relatively obscure part of the Wittgensteinian ontology, something the existence of which Wittgenstein thought he could prove, while it was apparently impossible to give any examples of them. If an account of logical and ontological form is able to do without them, so much the better for the account.

§94 Factualism and trope theory

It might be useful to compare the factualist basis of our theory of categories to some of the accounts which have been developed within trope theory. Trope theory is not just burdened with an unfortunate name, but is also often used as an umbrella term for grouping together various kinds of actually very different philosophical positions.[53] We can distinguish at least three main varieties: cluster tropism, kernel tropism, and propositional tropism.[54] Cluster tropism denotes the classical trope theory developed by Williams:[55] tropes are understood as particularized properties (such as the peculiar redness of this apple, the unshareable 'loving' relation between Abelard and Heloïse) and individuals and universals are constructed from these. Kernel tropism is less ontologically

---

[53] A good analysis of the varieties of trope theory (which we are going to follow here) is given in Bacon (2002).

[54] Interestingly, all these theories are capable of modelling one another. See Bacon (1988).

[55] Williams (1953).

parsimonious. In addition to particularized properties either primitive individuals or universals are admitted.[56] Propositional tropism finally differs from the previous two accounts in having a different conception of tropes. Here they are no longer regarded as particularized properties ('the redness of this apple') but rather as what would otherwise be called states of affairs ('that this apple is red'). Here tropes can be either regarded as structured according to the familiar conception of the way in which states of affairs are structured, or they can be treated as unanalysed primitives.

A detailed exposition of propositional tropism is given by John Bacon.[57] Tropes for Bacon are things we are acquainted with when we know that London is in England, or that I had an egg for breakfast. The term 'trope', rather than 'state of affairs' is employed to avoid the likely implication that the entities discussed are complexes of individuals, properties, and relations.[58] In this respect Bacon's account and the theory described in the preceding pages are very similar. One major, and relatively fundamental difference, however, is that Bacon introduces two metarelations (concurrence and likeness) between tropes, where I only have one (c-overlapping of states of affairs).[59] For Bacon the tropes

1. Abelard writing *Sic et non*; and

2. Abelard loving Heloïse

concur, whereas this and

3. Eos loving Tithonus

are *alike*. On my account the states of affairs corresponding to 1. and 2. and 2. and 3. are linked by the same relation, namely c-overlapping. Introducing two distinct relations at this level allows Bacon to construct individuals and universals in terms of these two kinds of resemblance,[60] a distinction which cannot be made on the account presented here. Unfortunately Bacon gives no justification for the introduction of

[56] For an example of the first see Armstrong (1989: 114, 136), for the second Mertz (1996).

[57] (1995). The notion is also discussed in Chrudzimski (2002).

[58] Bacon (1995: 1–2).

[59] Bacon (1995: 9). Cluster tropism also introduces two distinct relations, similarity or resemblance (for constructing universals from particularized properties) and compresence (for constructing individuals).

[60] (1995: 26–56).

the two distinct relations (apart from the intratheoretical one of want-ing to account for the distinction between individuals and universals).[61]
While I think it is highly plausible that human epistemic faculties allow us to recognize the same parts in different states of affairs (an assump-tion encoded in the metarelation of c-overlapping) it is not evident to me that there are actually two different ways in which this recognition proceeds, in terms of likeness and concurrence. This seems to be read-ing back intuitions which basically derive from the syntax of predicate calculus into our basic epistemic facilities.[62]

The account sketched in this inquiry might therefore be conceived of as similar to propositional tropism, as long as it is neither assumed that the primitives employed by me have a subject-predicate structure from the start,[63] nor that such a structure is recoverable on the basis of the primitive metarelations the theory employs.[64] Given this proviso my approach is very close to trope theory, being motivated by the same desires for ontological parsimony[65] and epistemological naturalness[66] which drive propositional tropism.

§95   Situation semantics

As we saw above, structuralist logic is a project which is very close to the spirit of our structuralist conception of ontology. It harmonizes with all the assumptions listed at the beginning of the chapter, apart from neutrality. Another field of investigation for which this is true and which

---

[61] Another problem for the Baconian account seems to occur once we consider the tropes 'Socrates is wise' and 'Wisdom socratizes'. If we regard them as distinct we would have to hold (counterintuitively) that they are *neither* alike nor concurring. If we claim they are the same trope this will be concurring with both 'Socrates is a philosopher' and 'Wisdom is a perfection', and will be alike 'Aristotle is wise' and 'Only one man socratized'. This will lead to conflicts with the theory later on, for example with the claim that 'like tropes are ones that are to involve the same property' (1995: 13–14).

[62] Bacon (2002: section 9) admits that the resources postulated by him to enforce a difference between individuals and universals seem to be *ad hoc*.

[63] As done by Chrudzimski (2002: 148).

[64] As it is in Bacon's (1995) theory.

[65] Bacon (2002: section 2).

[66] 'If there is a concept of trope that is intuitively clear and with which are are all familiar, it could only be the concept of a propositional trope.' (Chrudzimski 2002: 154).

has received a great amount of discussion in the recent past is *situation theory*.

Situation theory was developed in the 1980s as an alternative approach for constructing a semantics of natural language expressions which avoids many of the problems arising from recourse to traditional extensional model theory.[67] Its fundamental primitive is the situation,[68] and its fundamental assumption is that situations, rather than truth-values or sets of possible worlds are the referents of sentences. Situations are very similar to states of affairs.[69] They constitute the basic epistemic point of contact of agents with the world and are limited parts of reality which are 'perceived and stand in causal relations to one another'[70] and with which human beings interact.

In taking state-of-affair-like entities as primitive, situation theory shares the factualist assumption inherent in our theory of ontological categories. Situation theory also favours a structuralist theory of the constituents of situations. Situations are considered to be structured, and both 'metaphysically and epistemologically prior' to their constituents.[71] Constituents of situations are defined via the notion of a uniformity between situations.

Barwise and Perry describe the fundamental idea of situation theory in the following way:

Reality consists of situations [. . .]. We are always in situations; we see them, cause them to come about and have attitudes toward them. The Theory of Situations is an abstract theory for talking about situations. We begin by pulling out of real situations the basic building blocks of the theory: individuals, properties and relations, and locations. These are conceived of as invariants or, as we shall call them, *uniformities* across real situations; the same individuals and properties appear again and again in different locations. We put these pieces back together, using the tools of set theory, as *abstract situations*. Some of these abstract situations, the *actual situations*, correspond to the real ones; others do not.[72]

---

[67] Barwise and Perry (1983).

[68] Barwise and Perry (1983: 50).

[69] Our ontological use of the term 'state of affairs' should not be confused with the technical notion of a state of affairs in situation theory which denotes a particular kind of abstract situation (Barwise and Perry 1983: 55).

[70] Barwise and Perry (1983: 58).

[71] Barwise and Perry (1983: 58).

[72] Barwise and Perry (1983: 7–8).

As we already noted, a crucial difference between the situation-theoretic account and the account of ontological categories discussed above is the absence of the neutrality assumption. Barwise and Perry make an immediate transition (which is not backed up by any argument) from the *existence* of uniformities between situations to *identifying* these uniformities with individuals, properties, relations, and locations. They do not consider these to be all the uniformities there are, but take them to be the most fundamental ones. Furthermore, they consider them to be 'the uniformities which arise in the interpretation of the more basic parts of language'.[73] In constructing a semantics it is certainly sensible to have a look at the language first in order to decide subsequently what kinds of resources we might need. It is thus not following the 'lead of language' which seems to be problematic, but rather that it is not clear *a priori* that individuals, properties, relations, and locations really *are* different kinds of uniformities across states of affairs. What this claim amounts to is surely that when we look at constituents of situations which keep coming up in lots of different situations we realize that they come up in different ways or patterns. Some might never occur on their own, others only together with certain other constituents; the presence of some constituents might exclude the presence of others and so forth. What Barwise and Perry would have to do to make the transition from uniformities to individuals, properties, relations, and locations plausible is first of all to give a precise, non-metaphorical account of uniformities. It then remains to show that a certain subset of these uniformities corresponds to individuals, properties, relations, and locations. There may be other interesting uniformities as well, but this provides no real difficulty. Only after we have made the transition from uniformities to the particular kinds of uniformities that individuals, properties, and locations constitute is it legitimate to focus on *these* uniformities in the further development of our semantic theory.

But if the argument from chapter V is successful, exactly this cannot be done. A distinction between individuals, properties, and relations based purely on combinatorial considerations (without taking any semantic information about the constituents into account) is not forthcoming. It seems to me that it is something along these lines that Barwise and Perry are looking for in their identification of constituents of

[73] Barwise and Perry (1983: 50).

situations. It is difficult to be quite sure about this, however, since the matter is hardly ever discussed with much precision in the literature on situation theory.[74] But since situation theory is otherwise very close to our structuralist and factualist account of ontological categories, it seems worthwhile and desirable to develop a situation-theoretic account of the constituents of situations which harmonizes with the neutrality assumption.

I hope that the preceding pages have shown that our theory of ontological categories, which was first and foremost developed in order to give an account of ontological categories which does not suffer from the problems of the treatments usually found in the literature, has interesting philosophical implications for ontology in general, in particular in helping to correct the absolutist and essentialist conceptions of ontological categories often held. In serving as an argument against the fundamental status of the distinction between individuals and properties it also shows to have wider philosophical consequences in the way in which it influences recent and frequently discussed approaches to logic and semantics. Some of these consequences I have been able to sketch; many more will remain as subjects of further study.

[74] A rare (and interesting) exception is Seligman (1990).

Appendix

§96   Complex descriptions and type descriptions: an example

Suppose that our set A_1 consists of the following complexes: Pa, Pb, Qab, Qaa, Qbb, Qba. (For example we might imagine that a–d are names, P a monadic, and Q a dyadic predicate.) Suppose further that these are divided up to give us the basis containing the elements P, Q, a, and b. The basis is divided into three types:

$$\tau_1 \;=\; \{a, b\}$$
$$\tau_2 \;=\; \{P\}$$
$$\tau_3 \;=\; \{Q\}$$

Now let c be a choice function which selects exactly one member when applied to a type. Then the complex-forming behaviour of the elements of the basis can be described by the following complex descriptions:

1. $\mathbf{C}(c(\tau_1), c(\tau_2))$
2. $\mathbf{C}(c(\tau_1), c(\tau_1), c(\tau_3))$

Intuitively 1 means that for any string ϕ consisting of any one member of τ_1 and any one member of τ_2 and nothing else, $\mathbf{C}\phi$. Similarly, 2 says that for any string ϕ consisting of any two (not necessarily distinct) members of τ_1 and any one member of τ_3, $\mathbf{C}\phi$.

It is now easy to derive the type descriptions from these complex descriptions. They are

$$\tau_1 \;:\; (\tau_2|\mathbf{C}), (\tau_3|(\tau_1|\mathbf{C}))$$
$$\tau_2 \;:\; (\tau_1|\mathbf{C}))$$
$$\tau_3 \;:\; (\tau_1|(\tau_1|\mathbf{C})$$

A type description can consist of one or more *type descriptors* (that of τ_1 above consists of two). The type description of τ_1 says that if you add any element of τ_2 to any element of τ_1 (i.e. form a string consisting of elements of the two types) you get something which can form a complex. Also, if you add anything from τ_3 to it you get something of τ_2, i.e. something such that if you add anything from τ_1 to it you get something which can form a complex.

Intuitively, we can think of our set $\mathbf{A}_1$ as a set of wffs which can be formed in a very simple formal language consisting of two names, as well as of a monadic and a dyadic predicate of first order. The type descriptions then constitute a categorial grammar for that language.

§97   Generating a containment hierarchy: an example

Consider a set of data $\mathbf{A}$ with the basis a, b, c, d, P, Q, R, where the a–d can be understood intuitively as names, P as a monadic predicate applicable to all the names, Q as a monadic predicate applicable to a–c and R as a dyadic predicate applicable to a and b only. Dividing this basis into strong form-sets we get six types:

$$
\begin{aligned}
\tau_1 &= \{a, b\} \\
\tau_2 &= \{c\} \\
\tau_3 &= \{d\} \\
\tau_4 &= \{P\} \\
\tau_5 &= \{Q\} \\
\tau_6 &= \{R\}
\end{aligned}
$$

These have the following type descriptions:

$$
\begin{aligned}
\tau_1 &: \quad (\tau_4|\mathbf{C}), (\tau_5|\mathbf{C}), (\tau_1|(\tau_6|\mathbf{C})) \\
\tau_2 &: \quad (\tau_4|\mathbf{C}), (\tau_5|\mathbf{C}) \\
\tau_3 &: \quad (\tau_4|\mathbf{C}) \\
\tau_4 &: \quad (\tau_1|\mathbf{C}), (\tau_2|\mathbf{C}), (\tau_3|\mathbf{C}) \\
\tau_5 &: \quad (\tau_1|\mathbf{C}), (\tau_2|\mathbf{C})) \\
\tau_6 &: \quad (\tau_1|(\tau_1|\mathbf{C}))
\end{aligned}
$$

Now consider a restriction $\mathbf{A}_1^-$ of $\mathbf{A}$ which we get by deleting all the complexes containing R. Typing this there will only be four types:

$$
\begin{aligned}
\tau_1' &= \{a, b, c\} \\
\tau_2' &= \{d\} \\
\tau_3' &= \{P\} \\
\tau_4' &= \{Q\}
\end{aligned}
$$

with the following type descriptions

$$\begin{aligned}
\tau_1' &: \quad (\tau_3'|\mathbf{C}), (\tau_4'|\mathbf{C}) \\
\tau_2' &: \quad (\tau_3'|\mathbf{C}) \\
\tau_3' &: \quad (\tau_1'|\mathbf{C}), (\tau_2'|\mathbf{C}) \\
\tau_4' &: \quad (\tau_1'|\mathbf{C})
\end{aligned}$$

The objects a, b, and c now belong to one type since the R which drove them apart is missing from $\mathbf{A}_1^-$. We repeat this procedure, restricting $\mathbf{A}_1^-$ further to $\mathbf{A}_1^{--}$ by deleting all the complexes containing Q. Now there are only two types:

$$\begin{aligned}
\tau_1'' &= \quad \{a, b, c, d\} \\
\tau_2'' &= \quad \{P\}
\end{aligned}$$

and the type descriptions are just

$$\begin{aligned}
\tau_1'' &: \quad (\tau_2''|\mathbf{C}) \\
\tau_2'' &: \quad (\tau_1''|\mathbf{C})
\end{aligned}$$

If we continue deleting all the complexes containing P as well, the resulting $\mathbf{A}_1^{---}$ will be empty, and there will be nothing left to type.

The restrictions $\mathbf{A}_1^-$ and $\mathbf{A}_1^{--}$ of $\mathbf{A}$ are sufficient for constructing a containment hierarchy on the types containing a–d. In order to do the same for types containing P, Q, and R (i.e. the members of $\mathbf{A}$ we deleted in forming the restrictions), we need to consider a further restriction $\mathbf{A}_2^-$ of $\mathbf{A}$. This is obtained by deleting all the complexes containing c and d. Dividing $\mathbf{A}_2^-$ into strong form-sets gives us three types:

$$\begin{aligned}
\tau_7 &= \quad \{a, b\} \\
\tau_8 &= \quad \{P, Q\} \\
\tau_9 &= \quad \{R\}
\end{aligned}$$

These have the following type descriptions:

$$\begin{aligned}
\tau_7 &: \quad (\tau_8|\mathbf{C}), (\tau_7|(\tau_9|\mathbf{C})) \\
\tau_8 &: \quad (\tau_7|\mathbf{C}) \\
\tau_9 &: \quad (\tau_7|(\tau_7|\mathbf{C}))
\end{aligned}$$

In order to develop a containment hierarchy from the above restrictions we need some rules for identifying types across restrictions. We will formulate them in terms of type-membership, rather than in terms of type-descriptions. Here they are:

1. If τ_n is a type in a partition of the basis of some set of data $\mathbf{A}$ into types, and τ_o is a type in a restriction $\mathbf{A}^-$ which has the same members, they are identical.

2. If τ_n in $\mathbf{A}$ is a proper superset of τ_o in $\mathbf{A}^-$ they are identical.

3. If the union of some $\tau_1, \ldots \tau_n$ in $\mathbf{A}$ is the same as some τ_o in $\mathbf{A}^-$, τ_o contains the $\tau_1, \ldots \tau_n$.

Thus types which remain the same or just lose some of their members if some of the data are deleted are taken to be identical, while those which are 'merged' in a restriction are taken to be contained in the resulting type.

It is then easy to see that the restrictions $\mathbf{A}_1^-$, $\mathbf{A}_1^{--}$, and $\mathbf{A}_2^-$ of $\mathbf{A}$ generate a three-level containment hierarchy on the partition of the basis of $\mathbf{A}$ into strong form-sets. τ_1'', the most inclusive type, contains τ_3 and τ_1', which in turn contains τ_1 and τ_2, while τ_8 contains τ_4 and τ_5. Put more concisely, the containment structure generated is $((\tau_1, \tau_2), \tau_3), (\tau_4, \tau_5), (\tau_6)$.

Let us also note that once a containment hierarchy of types relative to some set of data has been constructed, it will remain a hierarchy if new data are added. In order to see this we need the equivalent of the above rules for identifying types across *expansions*. These are straightforward:

1. If τ_n in $\mathbf{A}$, and τ_o in an expansion $\mathbf{A}^+$ have the same members, they are identical.

2. If τ_n in $\mathbf{A}$ is a proper subset of τ_o in $\mathbf{A}^+$ they are identical.

3. If the union of some $\tau_1, \ldots \tau_n$ in $\mathbf{A}^+$ is the same as some τ_o in $\mathbf{A}$, τ_o contains the $\tau_1, \ldots \tau_n$.

It is easy to see on the basis of these rules that adding new data can never merge old types. New elements of the basis can be located in new types, or in old types, but they can never bring together types which were kept apart in the old typings. It is not too difficult to see why this should be the case. Assume that the objects a and b are assigned to different types in some typing. This will be because there is one object which can go together with the one but not with the other. Now if we expand the typing by an object which *can* go together with both, this will not mean that a and b belong to one type in the expansion. The old object keeping them apart is still in place, so we will instead say that the new object can go together with objects of different types, namely with objects contained in the types of a and b.

In fact there is only one case in which an expansion could lead to a merging of types (so that the number of types is reduced in the expansion), and this is excluded by the information assumption. Suppose our $\mathbf{A}$ contains Pa, Pb, Qa. We would divide this into four types, containing P, Q, a, and b, respectively. But if we extend $\mathbf{A}$ by Qb this will reduce the number of types to two, since now

P and *Q* as well as *a* and *b* are intersubstitutable. However, such an expansion would not be in accordance with the information assumption which says that we know about the joining behaviour of every member of the basis.

As new data about complexes come in (i.e. as we enlarge our set **A**) our typings will always be refined but never simplified. New types can be added; old types can be expanded (by adding new elements to them) or refined (by splitting them into different smaller types). However, it can never happen that the typing of an expansion contains fewer types than that of the set we started from, nor can it happen that the boundaries of types are changed, that is that a type in the expansion properly overlaps a type from the original set.

§98   Proof of the flexibility result

A typing of the graph according to the above conventions where some object a *is at level* n *can by successive applications of the three transformations be made into another typing which is also in accordance with the data but where* a *is located at level* m, *for any* m.

It is clear that we can move a graph arbitrarily far upwards by LIFTING. Showing that this also holds for the downwards direction is a bit more difficult. We will prove the downwards case, the full result will then be entailed. The downwards case can be formulated as follows:

Let a *(the* candidate*) be a vertex in a graph located at level* n *(the* candidate-level*). It is possible to transform that graph by repeated application of the three transformations* LIFTING, MIRRORING, *and* FOLDING *such that in the result* a *is at level* n' *(the* target-level*), where* n' < n.

We first observe that since the set of data we consider is always finite each graph in a typing will contain some *maximal* element (which is not connected to any vertex at a higher level) and some *minimal* element (which is not connected to any vertex at a lower level). If *t* is the level of the maximum, *b* that of the minimum, the length *l* of the graph will just be $(t - b)$.

We now need to establish two simple lemmas which together entail the downwards case.

L 1. *If* a *is a vertex in a graph in some typing the graph can be transformed in such a way that in the result* a *is minimal.*

Proof. If *a* is not maximal we FOLD the graph upwards at *a*. Now everything which used to be below *a* is above it, so that *a* is minimal. If *a* is maximal we simply mirror the entire graph upwards, so that the maximal element becomes the minimal element.   □

We will therefore always assume in the following that the candidate is minimal.

L 2. *If the candidate is at level* n, MIRRORING *downwards* x *times results in a graph whose minimal element is located at level* $n - xl$.

It is now possible to describe a procedure for moving the candidate to any lower target-level which will serve as a proof of the downwards case.

Proof. Let x be an even number ≥ 2. We can distinguish three cases:

1. The candidate is at level n and the target-level is $n - xl$.
2. The candidate is at level n and the target-level is lower than $n - xl$.
3. The candidate is at level n and the target-level is higher than $n - xl$.

In the first case by L2 we know that we can just apply MIRRORING downwards x times, which moves the entire graph downwards, so that the candidate is now at the target-level.

In the second case we apply MIRRORING downwards until applying it two times more would either be impossible (because there would not be 'enough space' below) or would move the candidate below the target-level. We have then reduced the second to the third case.

In the third case we know that the target-level is $n - xl + 1$ or higher. Now if we want to move the candidate to $n - xl + 1$ we first LIFT the entire graph by one level and then MIRROR downwards x times. The graph will then have been moved downwards, with the candidate now being at the target-level. If we want to move the candidate to $n - xl + 2$ we first LIFT the entire graph by two levels and then MIRROR downwards x times. Generally, if we want to move the candidate to $n - xl + y$, where $xl + y > 0$ and $y \geq 1$ we first LIFT the graph y levels and then MIRROR downwards x times. □

§99 Proof of the uniqueness of proto-typings

Given any set of ontological data D there is only one proto-typing in accordance with D.

It is sufficient to establish the following two lemmas:

L 1. *The partition T of a basis B in a proto-typing $\mathfrak{T}$ of some data D is unique.*

Proof. First of all note that T is a partition of B. This is due to the fact that the above way of constructing proto-typings results in types which are exclusive. But since the only members of types can be elements of B, the types jointly exhaust B, thus constituting a partition.

Let S, S' be two different partitions of some set $\mathbf{S}$. There must at least be two sets s_1, s_2 in S, s_1', s_2' in S' such that $s_1 \cup s_2$ and $s_1' \cup s_2'$ are not disjoint and not identical. So there will be at least one object such that it is in s_1 in

S but in s'_2 in S' or vice versa. But what this means is that according to one partition this object could always be interchanged with all the other objects in the set, while the other partition says that it cannot. But only one of the two can be right, so the two partitions cannot be alternatives.   □

L 2. *For a given D and a given T from some proto-typing $\mathfrak{T}$ there is only one choice of rules R which results in a proto-typing which is in accordance with the data.*

Proof. The rules are taken to have the form $+(\tau_i, \tau_j, \ldots)$. The intuitive reading of this is that one member of τ_i together with one member of τ_j etc. can form a state of affairs.

Let $\mathbf{C}(abc)$ be an element of the ontological data D. We want to find out whether there can be two different entries in R which produce this element from a fixed T. Clearly since only single members of B are in the t_i, the length of the entries in R is identical to the length of the elements of the ontological data they produce. Let $+(t_i, t_j, t_k)$ be such an entry in R. No longer or shorter entry would do. Now suppose there is an alternative entry $+(t_l, t_m, t_n)$ in R which also gives $\mathbf{C}(abc)$. Clearly a must be in one of the t_i, t_j, t_k, and b, c must be each in one of the other two for $+(t_i, t_j, t_k)$ to produce $\mathbf{C}(abc)$. But this also has to hold for t_l, t_m, t_n for $+(t_l, t_m, t_n)$ to produce $\mathbf{C}(abc)$. But since T is a partition of B each element of B can only be in one t_i. So t_i, t_j, t_k and t_l, t_m, t_n must be identical. This result generalizes for strings of arbitrary lengths and so it follows that given a fixed T, there is only one choice of R which can produce a particular element of the ontological data.   □

Bibliography

Kazimierz Ajdukiewicz. Syntactic connexion. In Storrs McCall, ed., *Polish Logic 1920–1939*, pp. 207–31. Clarendon Press, Oxford, 1967.

Kazimierz Ajdukiewicz. *'The Scientific World-Perspective' and other Essays. 1931–1963*. Reidel, PWN Polish Scientific Publishers, 1978.

William Alston. Ontological commitments. *Philosophical Studies*, 8: 8–17, 1957.

G. E. M. Anscombe. *An Introduction to Wittgenstein's Tractatus*. Harper, New York, 1963.

G. E. M. Anscombe. Retractation. *Analysis*, 26 (2): 33–6, 1965.

David M. Armstrong. *Nominalism & Realism*. Cambridge University Press, Cambridge, 1978.

David M. Armstrong. *Universals: An Opinionated Introduction*. Westview Press, Boulder, CO, 1989.

David M. Armstrong. *A Combinatorial Theory of Possibility*. Cambridge University Press, Cambridge, 1990.

David M. Armstrong. *A World of States of Affairs*. Cambridge University Press, Cambridge, 1997.

Mitchell G. Ash. *Gestalt Psychology in German Culture 1890–1967: Holism and the Quest for Objectivity*. Cambridge University Press, Cambridge, 1995.

John Bacon. Four modal modelings. *Journal of Philosophical Logic*, 17: 91–114, 1988.

John Bacon. *Universals and Property Instances: The Alphabet of Being*. Blackwell, Oxford, Cambridge, MA, 1995.

John Bacon. Tropes. In Edward Zalta, ed., *The Stanford Encyclopedia of Philosophy*. 2002. URL http://plato.stanford.edu/archives/fall2002/entries/tropes.

Mark C. Baker. *The Atoms of Language: The Mind's Hidden Rules of Grammar*. Oxford University Press, Oxford, 2001.

Yehoshua Bar-Hillel. Husserl's conception of a purely logical grammar. *Philosophy and Phenomenological Research*, 17: 362–9, 1956–7.

Yehoshua Bar-Hillel. *Aspects of Language: Essays and Lectures on Philosophy of Language, Linguistic Philosophy and Methodology of Linguistics*. Magnes Press, North-Holland, Jerusalem, Amsterdam, 1970.

Jon Barwise and John Perry. *Situations and Attitudes*. Bradford, MIT Press, London; Cambridge, MA, 1983.

George Bealer. *Quality and Concept*. Clarendon Press, Oxford, 1982.

David Bell. The formation of concepts and the structure of thoughts. *Philosophy and Phenomenological Research*, 61 (3): 583–96, 1996.

John Bigelow and Robert Pargetter. *Science and Necessity*. Cambridge University Press, Cambridge, 1990.

Max Black. Russell's philosophy of language. In Paul Arthur Schilpp, ed., *The Philosophy of Bertrand Russell*, pp. 229–55. Northwestern University Press, Evanston, 1944.

Max Black. *A Companion to Wittgenstein's 'Tractatus'*. Cornell University Press, Ithaca, NY, 1966.

Wayne D. Blizard. Multiset theory. *Notre Dame Journal of Formal Logic*, 30 (1): 33–66, 1989.

E. J. Borowski. Sentence meaning and word meaning II. *Philosophical Quarterly*, 29: 111–24, 1979.

Andrew Bradford. *Transformational Grammar: A First Course*. Cambridge University Press, Cambridge, 1988.

Ross T. Brady. Significance range theory. *Notre Dame Journal of Formal Logic*, 21 (2): 319–45, 1980.

Klaus Brockhaus. *Untersuchungen zu Carnaps Logischem Aufbau der Welt*. PhD thesis, Mathematisch-Naturwissenschaftliche Fakultät der Westfälischen Wilhelms-Universität zu Münster, 1963.

Robert W. Burch. *A Peircean Reduction Thesis: The Foundations of Topological Logic*. Texas Tech University Press, Lubbock, Texas, 1991.

Rudolf Carnap. *Der logische Aufbau der Welt*. Weltkreis-Verlag, Berlin, 1928.

Rudolf Carnap. *The Logical Syntax of Language*. Kegan Paul, Trench, Trubner & Co, London, 1937.

Rudolf Carnap. The elimination of metaphysics through the logical analysis of language. In A. J. Ayer, ed., *Logical Positivism*, pp. 60–81. Free Press, Glencoe, 1959.

Peter Carruthers. On object and concept. *Theoria*, 49 (2): 49–86, 1983.

Charles E. Caton. Essentially arising questions and the ontology of a natural language. *Noûs*, 5 (1): 27–37, 1971.

Gregory Chaitin. *Algorithmic Information Theory*. Cambridge University Press, Cambridge, 1987a.

Gregory Chaitin. Information-theoretic computational complexity. In *Information, Randomness & Incompleteness: Papers on Algorithmic Information Theory*, pp. 23–32. World Scientific, Singapore, New Jersey, Hong Kong, 1987b.

Leo K. Cheung. The Tractarian operation *N* and expressive completeness. *Synthese*, 123: 247–61, 2000.

Roderick Chisholm. *On Metaphysics*. University of Minnesota Press, Minneapolis, 1989.

Roderick Chisholm. *A Realistic Theory of Categories*. Cambridge University Press, Cambridge, 1996.

Arkadiusz Chrudzimski. Two concepts of trope. *Grazer Philosophische Studien*, 64: 137–55, 2002.

Richard F. Clarke. *Logic*. Manuals of Catholic Philosophy. Longmans, Green & Co, London, 1889.

Jack Copeland. *Artificial Intelligence: A Philosophical Introduction*. Blackwell, Oxford, Cambridge, MA, 1993.

I. M. Copi. Objects, properties, and relations in the *Tractatus*. *Mind*, 67: 157–8, 1958.

Edward Craig, ed. *Routledge Encyclopedia of Philosophy*. Routledge, London, 1998.

D. A. Cruse. *Lexical Semantics*. Cambridge University Press, Cambridge, 1986.

Donald Davidson. Reality without reference. In *Inquiries into Truth and Interpretation*, pp. 215–25. Clarendon Press, Oxford, 1984.

Nicholas Denyer. Pure second-order logic. *Journal of Symbolic Logic*, 33 (2): 220–4, 1992.

Nicholas Denyer. Names, verbs and quantification. *Philosophy*, 73: 619–23, 1998.

Randall Dipert. The mathematical structure of the world: the world as a graph. *Journal of Philosophy*, 94 (7): 329–58, 1997.

Robert William Ditchburn. Visual information rate. In Richard L. Gregory, ed., *The Oxford Companion to the Mind*, pp. 795–6. Oxford University Press, Oxford, New York, 1987.

David R. Dowty, Robert E. Wall, and Stanley Peters. *Introduction to Montague Semantics*. Reidel, Dordrecht, 1981.

Theodore Drange. *Type Crossings: Sentential Meaninglessness in the Border Area of Linguistics and Philosophy*. Mouton & Co., The Hague, Paris, 1966.

Eli Dresner. Wittgenstein's builders and Perry's objection to sentence priority. *Dialectica*, 56 (1): 49–63, 2002.

Michael Dummett. *Frege: Philosophy of Language*. Duckworth, London, 1981. 2nd edn.

George Englebretsen. A reintroduction to Sommers' tree theory. In George Englebretsen, ed., *Essays on the Philosophy of Fred Sommers*, pp. 1–31. Edwin Mellen Press, Lewiston, Queenston, Lampeter, 1990.

Charles Everitt. Chemistry. In *Encyclopaedia Britannica*, vol. 6, pp. 33–76. Encyclopaedia Britannica Company, New York, 11th edn., 1910.

Robert Fahrnkopf. *Wittgenstein on Universals*. Peter Lang, New York, Bern, 1988.

Robert Fahrnkopf. Wittgensteinian realism. *International Journal of Philosophy*, 26 (2): 91–5, 1994.

Kit Fine. The logic of essence. *Journal of Philosophical Logic*, 24: 241–73, 1995a.

Kit Fine. Ontological dependence. *Proceedings of the Aristotelian Society*, 95: 267–90, 1995b.

Kit Fine. Neutral relations. *Philosophical Review*, 109 (1): 1–33, 2000.

Gottlob Frege. Über Begriff und Gegenstand. In Günther Patzig, ed., *Funktion, Begriff, Bedeutung: Fünf logische Studien*, pp. 64–78. Vandenhoeck & Ruprecht, Göttingen, 1962a.

Gottlob Frege. Über Funktion und Begriff. In Günther Patzig, ed., *Funktion, Begriff, Bedeutung: Fünf logische Studien*, pp. 16–37. Vandenhoeck & Ruprecht, Göttingen, 1962b.

Gottlob Frege. Die Verneinung. In Günther Patzig, ed., *Logische Untersuchungen*, pp. 54–71. Vandenhoeck & Ruprecht, Göttingen, 1966a.

Gottlob Frege. Gedankengefüge. In Günther Patzig, ed., *Logische Untersuchungen*, pp. 72–91. Vandenhoeck & Ruprecht, Göttingen, 1966b.

Gottlob Frege. Über die Grundlagen der Geometrie. In Ignacio Angelelli, ed., *Kleine Schriften*, pp. 267–72. Olms, Hildesheim, 1967.

Gottlob Frege. Aufzeichnungen für Ludwig Darmstaedter. In Hans Hermes, F. Kambartel, and F. Kaulbach, eds., *Nachgelassene Schriften*, pp. 273–7. Meiner, Hamburg, 1969a.

Gottlob Frege. Ausführungen über Sinn und Bedeutung. In Hans Hermes, F. Kambartel, and F. Kaulbach, eds., *Nachgelassene Schriften*, pp. 128–36. Meiner, Hamburg, 1969b.

Gottlob Frege. Booles rechnende Logik und die Begriffsschrift. In Hans Hermes, F. Kambartel, and F. Kaulbach, eds., *Nachgelassene Schriften*, pp. 9–52. Meiner, Hamburg, 1969c.

Gottlob Frege. Logik in der Mathematik. In Hans Hermes, F. Kambartel, and F. Kaulbach, eds., *Nachgelassene Schriften*, pp. 219–70. Meiner, Hamburg, 1969d.

Gottlob Frege. *Wissenschaftlicher Briefwechsel*. Meiner, Hamburg, 1976. Edited by Gottfried Gabriel, Hans Hermes, F. Kambartel, and Christian Thiel.

Gottlob Frege. *Die Grundlagen der Arithmetik: Eine logisch-mathematische Untersuchung über den Begriff der Zahl*. Felix Meiner, Hamburg, 1986. Critical edition with supplementary material by Christian Thiel.

Gottlob Frege. *Begriffsschrift und andere Aufsätze*. Olms, Hildesheim, 2nd edn., 1993. Edited by Ignacio Angelelli.

Peter Gärdenfors. *Knowledge in Flux*. MIT Press, Cambridge, MA, 1988.

Jean-Louis Gardies. *Rational Grammar*. Philosophia, München, Wien, 1985.

Richard Gaskin. The unity of the declarative sentence. *Philosophy*, 73: 21–45, 1998.

Peter Geach. *Reference and Generality*. Cornell University Press, Ithaca, 1968.

Peter Geach and Max Black, eds. *Translations from the Philosophical Writings of Gottlob Frege*. Blackwell, Oxford, 1980. 2nd edn.

Nelson Goodman. *The Structure of Appearance*. Harvard University Press, Cambridge, MA, 2nd edn., 1951.

Nelson Goodman. A world of individuals. In Charles Landesman, ed., *The Problem of Universals*, ch. 17, pp. 293–305. Basic Books, New York, London, 1971.

Dale Gottlieb. Ontological reduction. *Journal of Philosophy*, 73 (3): 57–76, 1976.

James Griffin. *Wittgenstein's Logical Atomism*. Clarendon Press, Oxford, 1964.

Reinhardt Grossmann. *The Categorial Structure of the World*. Indiana University Press, Bloomington, 1983.

Reinhardt Grossmann. *The Existence of the World: An Introduction to Ontology*. Routledge, London, New York, 1992.

Sören Halldén. *The Logic of Nonsense*. Lundequistska, Harrassowitz, Uppsala, Leipzig, 1949.

William Hamilton. *Lectures on Metaphysics*. Blackwood, Edinburgh, 1959–60. Edited by H. L. Mansel and John Veitch.

Nicolai Hartmann. *Der Aufbau der realen Welt: Grundriß der allgemeinen Kategorienlehre*. Anton Hain, Meisenheim, 2nd edn., 1949.

C. Hartshorne, P. Weiss, and A. Burks, eds. *Collected Papers of Charles Sanders Peirce*. Harvard University Press, Cambridge, MA, 1958.

Jane Heal. Sentence meaning and word meaning I. *Philosophical Quarterly*, 29: 97–110, 1979.

Mary Henle. Some new Gestalt psychologies. *Psychological Research*, 51: 81–5, 1989.

H. Hiż. The intuitions of grammatical categories. *Methodos*, 12 (48): 311–20, 1960.

Jack Hoeksema. The semantics of the non-boolean 'and'. *Journal of Semantics*, 6: 19–40, 1988.

Donald D. Hoffman. *Visual Intelligence: How we Create What we See*. W. W. Norton & Company, New York, 1998.

Joshua Hoffman and Gary S. Rosenkrantz. *Substance Among other Categories*. Cambridge University Press, Cambridge, 1994.

Joshua Hoffman and Gary S. Rosenkrantz. *Substance. Its Nature and Existence*. Routledge, London, New York, 1997.

David Hume. *A Treatise of Human Nature*. Oxford University Press, Oxford, 2000.

James Hurford. The neural basis of predicate-argument structure. *Behavioral and Brain Sciences*, 26: 261–83, 2003.

Edmund Husserl. *Logische Untersuchungen*. Niemeyer, Halle a. d. S., 3rd edn., 1922.

Peter Hylton. The nature of the proposition and the revolt against idealism. In Richard Rorty, J. B. Schneewind, and Quentin Skinner, eds., *Philosophy and History*. Cambridge University Press, Cambridge, 1984.

Frank Jackson. Ontological commitment and paraphrase. *Philosophy*, 55: 303–15, 1980.

Immanuel Kant. *Kants Werke: Akademie-Textausgabe*. de Gruyter, Berlin, 1968.

David Katz. *Gestalt Psychology: Its Nature and Significance*. Methuen & Co., London, 1951.

Jerrold J. Katz. *The Philosophy of Language*. Harper & Row, New York, London, 1966.

Jerrold J. Katz. *Semantic Theory*. Harper & Row, New York, Evanston, San Francisco, London, 1972.

Frank C. Keil. *Semantic and Conceptual Development: An Ontological Perspective*. Harvard University Press, Cambridge, MA, London, 1979.

W. E. Kennick. Review of 'Wittgenstein on universals'. *International Studies in Philosophy*, 23 (1): 114–15, 1991.

Jaegwon Kim. Events as property exemplifications. In Myles Brand and Douglas Walton, eds., *Action Theory*, pp. 159–77. Reidel, Dordrecht, 1976.

Ulrike Kleemeier. *Gottlob Frege: Kontext-Prinzip und Ontologie*. Alber, Freiburg, München, 1990.

Reinhard Kleinknecht. Quasianalyse und Qualitätsklassen. *Grazer Philosophische Studien*, 20: 23–43, 1969.

Arnold Koslow. *A Structuralist Theory of Logic*. Cambridge University Press, Cambridge, 1992.

Arnold Koslow. The implicational nature of logic: A structuralist account. In Achille Varzi, ed., *The Nature of Logic*, pp. 111–55. CSLI Publications, Stanford, CA, 1999.

George Lakoff. *Women, Fire, and Dangerous Things: What Categories Reveal about the Mind*. University of Chicago Press, Chicago, London, 1987.

Desmond Lee, ed. *Wittgenstein's Lectures: Cambridge 1930–32*. Blackwell, Oxford, 1980.

John Lehrberger. *Functor Analysis of Natural Language*. Mouton & Co., The Hague, Paris, 1974.

Douglas B. Lenat and R. V. Guha. *Building Large Knowledge-Based Systems: Representation and Inference in the CYC Project*. Addison-Wesley, Reading, MA, 1990.

David K. Lewis. Policing the *Aufbau*. *Philosophical Studies*, 20 (1–2): 13–17, 1969.

David K. Lewis. Languages and language. In *Philosophical Papers I*, pp. 163–88. Oxford University Press, Oxford, 1983.

David K. Lewis. Against structural universals. *Australasian Journal of Philosophy*, 64 (1): 25–46, 1986a.

David K. Lewis. *On the Plurality of Worlds*. Blackwell, Oxford, 1986b.

Leonard Linsky. The unity of the proposition. *Journal of the History of Philosophy*, 30 (2): 243–73, 1992.

Gert-Jan Lokhorst. Ontology, semantics and philosophy of mind in Wittgenstein's Tractatus: A formal reconstruction. *Erkenntis*, 29: 35–75, 1988.

E. J. Lowe. Ontological categories and natural kinds. *Philosophical Studies*, 26 (1): 29–46, 1997.

E. J. Lowe. *The Possibility of Metaphysics: Substance, Identity and Time*. Clarendon Press, Oxford, 2001.

Fraser MacBride. Where are particulars and universals? *Dialectica*, 52 (3): 203–27, 1998.

Fraser MacBride. Could Armstrong have been a universal? *Mind*, 108: 471–501, 1999.

Van McGee. Logical operations. *Journal of Philosophical Logic*, 25: 567–80, 1996.

Brian McGuinness, ed. *Gottlob Frege: Collected Papers on Mathematics, Logic and Philosophy*. Blackwell, Oxford, 1984.

Ulrich Majer. Ist die Sprache der Chemie eine Begriffsschrift in Freges Sinne? In Peter Janich and Nikolaos Psarros, eds., *Die Sprache der Chemie*, pp. 91–100. Königshausen & Neumann, Würzburg, 1996.

Edwin Martin. Fregean incompleteness. *Philosophia (Israel)*, 13: 247–53, 1983.

Norman M. Martin and Stephen Pollard. Closed bases and closure logic. *The Monist*, 79: 117–27, 1996a.

Norman M. Martin and Stephen Pollard. *Closure Spaces and Logic*. Kluwer, Dordrecht, 1996b.

Uwe Meixner. *Axiomatic Formal Ontology*. Kluwer, Dordrecht, Boston, London, 1997.

Uwe Meixner. *Einführung in die Ontologie*. Wissenschaftliche Buchgesellschaft, Darmstadt, 2004.

D. H. Mellor, ed. *F. P. Ramsey. Philosophical Papers*. Cambridge University Press, Cambridge, 1990.

D. W. Mertz. *Moderate Realism and its Logic*. Yale University Press, New Haven, 1996.

George A. Miller. *Language and Communication*. McGraw-Hill, New York, 1951.

C. Ulises Moulines. Making sense of Carnap's 'Aufbau'. *Erkenntnis*, 35: 263–86, 1991.

Bryan G. Norton. On defining 'ontology'. *Metaphilosophy*, 7 (2): 102–15, 1976.

Bryan G. Norton. *Linguistic Frameworks and Ontology: A Re-examination of Carnap's Metaphilosophy.* Mouton, The Hague, New York, Paris, 1977.

L. Oeing-Hanhoff. Axiom. In Joachim Ritter, ed., *Historisches Wörterbuch der Philosophie*, vol. 1, pp. 737–48. Wissenschaftliche Buchgesellschaft, Darmstadt, 1971.

Charles Kay Ogden. *Basic English: A General Introduction with Rules and Grammar.* Kegan Paul, Trench, Trübner, London, 1930.

Alex Oliver. Could there be conjunctive universals? *Analysis*, 52: 88–97, 1992.

Alex Oliver. A few more remarks on logical form. *Proceedings of the Aristotelian Society*, 159: 247–72, 1999.

Alex Oliver and Timothy Smiley. Strategies for a logic of plurals. *Philosophical Quarterly*, 51 (204): 289–306, 2001.

Kenneth Russell Olson. *An Essay on Facts.* CSLI Publications, Stanford, CA, 1987.

W. G. Palmer. *Valency, Classical and Modern.* Cambridge University Press, Cambridge, 2nd edn., 1959.

W. G. Palmer. *A History of the Concept of Valency to 1930.* Cambridge University Press, Cambridge, 1965.

L. E. Palmieri. Bare particulars, names, and elementary propositions. *Synthese*, 12 (1): 71–8, 1960.

Alvin Plantinga. De essentia. *Grazer Philosophische Studien*, 7/8: 101–21, 1979.

Michael Potter. *Reason's Nearest Kin: Philosophies of Arithmetic from Kant to Carnap.* Oxford University Press, Oxford, 2000.

Willard Van Orman Quine. *Word and Object.* MIT Press, Cambridge, MA, 1960.

Willard Van Orman Quine. Ontological reduction and the world of numbers. In *The Ways of Paradox*, pp. 212–20. Harvard University Press, Cambridge, MA, London, 1976.

Willard Van Orman Quine. *Philosophy of Logic.* Harvard University Press, Cambridge, MA, London, 1986.

Frank P. Ramsey. Universals. In D. H. Mellor, ed., *Philosophical Papers*, pp. 8–33. Cambridge University Press, Cambridge, 1990.

Alan W. Richardson. *Carnap's Construction of the World: The Aufbau and the Emergence of Logical Empiricism.* Cambridge University Press, Cambridge, 1998.

Eleanor Rosch. Prototype classificaton and logical classification: The two systems. In E. Scholnick, ed., *New Trends in Cognitive Representation*, pp. 73–86. Lawrence Erlbaum Associates, Hillsdale, 1981.

Gary Rosenkrantz and Joshua Hoffman. The independence criterion of substance. *Philosophy and Phenomenological Research*, 51 (4): 835–53, 1991.

Richard Routley and Valerie Routley. Categories—expressions or things? *Theoria*, 35: 215–38, 1969.

Edmund Runggaldier and Christian Kanzian. *Grundprobleme der analytischen Ontologie*. Schöningh, Paderborn, 1998.

Bertrand Russell. *The Principles of Mathematics*. Allen & Unwin, London, 1903.

Bertrand Russell. Logical atomism. In J. H. Muirhead, ed., *Contemporary British Philosophy*, pp. 359–83. Allen & Unwin, London, 1924.

Betrand Russell. *Russell's Logical Atomism*. Fontana/Collins, London, 1972.

Gilbert Ryle. Categories. *Proceedings of the Aristotelian Society*, 38: 189–206, 1938.

Gilbert Ryle. *The Concept of Mind*. Hutchinson's University Library, London, 1949.

Nils-Eric Sahlin. *The Philosophy of F. P. Ramsey*. Cambridge University Press, Cambridge, 1990.

Charles Sayward and Stephen Voss. Absurdity and spanning. *Philosophia (Israel)*, 2 (3): 227–38, 1972.

Jerry Seligman. Perspectives in situation theory. In Robin Cooper, Kuniaki Mukai, and John Perry, eds., *Situation Theory and its Applications*, vol. 1, pp. 145–91. CSLI Publications, Stanford, 1990.

Stewart Shapiro. *Foundations without Foundationalism: The Case for Second-Order Logic*. Oxford University Press, Oxford, 1991.

Peter Simons. Unsaturatedness. *Grazer Philosophische Studien*, 14: 73–95, 1981.

Peter Simons. *Parts. A Study in Ontology*. Clarendon Press, Oxford, 1987.

Peter Simons. Linearity and structure. Notes on the discrepancy between speaking and thinking. In Axel Burri, ed., *Language and Thought*, pp. 30–41. de Gruyter, Berlin, New York, 1997.

Brian Skyrms. Tractarian nominalism. *Philosophical Studies*, 40: 199–206, 1981.

J. J. C. Smart. A note on categories. *British Journal for the Philosophy of Science*, 4: 227–8, 1954.

Barry Smith and Roberto Casati. Naive physics: an essay in ontology. *Philosophical Psychology*, 7 (2): 225–44, 1994.

Robin Smith. Logic. In Jonathan Barnes, ed., *The Cambridge Companion to Aristotle*, ch. 4, pp. 27–65. Cambridge University Press, Cambridge, 1995.

Fred Sommers. The ordinary language tree. *Mind*, 68: 160–85, 1959.

Fred Sommers. Types and ontology. *Philosophical Review*, 72: 327–63, 1963.

Fred Sommers. Structural ontology. *Philosophia (Israel)*, 1: 21–42, 1971.

Lothar Spillmann. Colour in larger perspective: the rebirth of Gestalt psychology. *Perception*, 26 (11): 1342–52, 1997.

Erik Stenius. *Wittgenstein's Tractatus: A Critical Exposition of its Main Lines of Thought*. Basil Blackwell, Oxford, 1960.

Leslie Stevenson. A formal theory of sortal quantification. *Notre Dame Journal of Formal Logic*, 16 (2): 185–207, 1975.

Leslie Stevenson. On what sorts of things there are. *Mind*, 85: 503–21, 1976.

Leslie Stevenson. Extensional and intensional logic for criteria of identity. *Logique & Analyse*, 20: 268–85, 1977.

Albert Stöckl. *Lehrbuch der Philosophie*. Franz Kirchheim, Mainz, 7th edn., 1892.

Peter F. Strawson. *Individuals: An Essay in Descriptive Metaphysics*. Methuen & Co, London, 1964.

Peter F. Strawson. The asymmetry of subjects and predicates. In Howard F. Kiefer and Milton K. Munitz, eds., *Language, Belief and Metaphysics*, pp. 69–86. State University of New York Press, Albany, 1970.

Peter F. Strawson. *Subject and Predicate in Logic and Grammar*. Methuen & Co., London, 1974.

Frank Stubbings. *Bedders, Bulldogs and Bedells: A Cambridge ABC*. Cambridge University Press, Cambridge, 1991.

Peter Sullivan. The functional model of semantic complexity. *Journal of Philosophical Logic*, 21: 91–108, 1992.

Alfred Tarski. What are logical notions? *History and Philosophy of Logic*, 7: 143–54, 1986. Edited by John Corcoran.

Barry Taylor and A. P. Hazen. Flexibly structured predication. *Logique & Analyse*, 139–40: 375–93, 1992.

Erwin Tegtmeier. *Grundzüge einer kategorialen Ontologie: Dinge, Eigenschaften, Beziehungen, Sachverhalte*. Alber, Freiburg, München, 1992.

Athanasios Tzouvaras. Worlds of homogeneous artifacts. *Notre Dame Journal of Formal Logic*, 36 (3): 454–74, 1995.

Johan van Benthem. *Essays in Logical Semantics*. D. Reidel, Dordrecht, Boston, 1986.

Johan van Benthem. Logical constants across varying types. *Notre Dame Journal of Formal Logic*, 30 (3): 315–42, 1989.

C. van Leeuwen. PDP and Gestalt. An integration? *Psychological Research*, 50: 199–201, 1989.

Christian von Ehrenfels. Über 'Gestaltqualitäten'. *Vierteljahresschrift für wissenschaftliche Philosophie*, 14: 242–92, 1890.

Jan Westerhoff. A taxonomy of composition operations. *Logique et Analyse*, 47 (187–8), 2004.

Alfred North Whitehead and Bertrand Russell. *Principia Mathematica*. Cambridge University Press, Cambridge, 1925.

David Wiggins. *Identity and Spatio-Temporal Continuity.* Blackwell, Oxford, 1971.

D. C. Williams. The elements of being. *Review of Metaphysics*, 7: 3–18, 171–92, 1953.

Ludwig Wittgenstein. *Notebooks 1914–1916.* Blackwell, Oxford, 1961. Edited by G. H. von Wright and G. E. M. Anscombe.

Ludwig Wittgenstein. *Logisch-Philosophische Abhandlung: Tractatus logico-philosophicus. Kritische Edition.* Suhrkamp, Frankfurt am Main, 1989. Critical edn. by Brian McGuinness and Joachim Schulte.

Wilhem Wundt. *Grundzüge der physiologischen Psychologie.* Wilhelm Engelmann, Leipzig, 1902–3.

Eddy M. Zemach. Names and predicates. *Philosophia (Israel)*, 10: 217–23, 1981.

Index